PSYCHOLINGUI

ONE

Routledge English Language Introductions cover core areas of language study and are one-stop resources for students.

Assuming no prior knowledge, books in the series offer an accessible overview of the subject, with activities, study questions, commentaries and key readings – all in the same volume. The innovative and flexible 'two-dimensional' structure is built around four sections – introduction, development, exploration and extension – which offer self-contained stages for study. Each topic can also be read across these sections, enabling the reader to build gradually on the knowledge gained.

Psycholinguistics:

❑ is a comprehensive introduction to psycholinguistic theory
❑ covers the core areas of psycholinguistics: language as a human attribute, language and the brain, vocabulary storage and use, language and memory, the four skills (writing, reading, listening, speaking), comprehension, language impairment and deprivation
❑ draws on a range of real texts, data and examples, including a Radio Four interview, an essay written by a deaf writer, and the transcript of a therapy session addressing stuttering
❑ provides classic readings by key names in the discipline, including Aitchison, Deacon, Logie, Levelt and Bishop.

The accompanying website providing weblinks and extra resources for lecturers, teachers and students can be found at **http://www.routledge.com/textbooks/ psycholinguistics**

Written by an experienced teacher, this accessible textbook is an essential resource for all students of English language, linguistics and psychology.

John Field lectures and writes on psycholinguistics, with special reference to language processing. His research interests lie in first and second language listening. He has worked in many parts of the world and currently teaches at Kings College London. He is the author of *Psycholinguistics: The Key Concepts* (Routledge, forthcoming) and a range of skills based language teaching materials.

Series Editor: Peter Stockwell
Series Consultant: Ronald Carter

ROUTLEDGE ENGLISH LANGUAGE INTRODUCTIONS

SERIES EDITOR: PETER STOCKWELL

Peter Stockwell is Senior Lecturer in the School of English Studies at the University of Nottingham, UK, where his interests include sociolinguistics, stylistics and cognitive poetics. His recent publications include *Cognitive Poetics: An Introduction* (Routledge, 2002), *The Poetics of Science Fiction, Investigating English Language* (with Howard Jackson), and *Contextualized Stylistics* (edited with Tony Bex and Michael Burke).

SERIES CONSULTANT: RONALD CARTER

Ronald Carter is Professor of Modern English Language in the School of English Studies at the University of Nottingham, UK. He is the co-series editor of the forthcoming *Routledge Applied Linguistics* series, series editor of *Interface*, and was co-founder of the Routledge *Intertext* series.

OTHER TITLES IN THE SERIES:

Sociolinguistics
Peter Stockwell

Pragmatics and Discourse
Joan Cutting

Grammar and Vocabulary
Howard Jackson

FORTHCOMING:

World Englishes
Jennifer Jenkins

Phonetics and Phonology
Beverley Collins & Inger Mees

Child Language
Jean Stilwell Peccei

Stylistics
Paul Simpson

PSYCHOLINGUISTICS

A resource book for students

JOHN FIELD

A
B
C
D

Routledge
Taylor & Francis Group

LONDON AND NEW YORK

First published 2003 by Routledge
2 Park Square, Milton Park, Abingdon, Oxon, OX14 4RN

Simultaneously published in the USA and Canada
by Routledge
270 Madison Ave, New York, NY 10016
Reprinted with corrections 2004

Reprinted 2006 (twice)

Routledge is an imprint of the Taylor & Francis Group, an informa business

© 2003 John Field

Typeset in 10/12.5pt Minion by Graphicraft Limited, Hong Kong
Printed and bound in Great Britain by TJ International, Padstow, Cornwall

British Library Cataloguing in Publication Data
A catalogue record for this book is available from the British Library

Library of Congress Cataloging in Publication Data

ISBN10: 0–415–27599–7 (hbk)
ISBN10: 0–415–27600–4 (pbk)

ISBN13: 978–0–415–27599–6 (hbk)
ISBN13: 978–0–415–27600–9 (pbk)

HOW TO USE THIS BOOK

The Routledge English Language Introductions are 'flexi-texts' that you can use to suit your own style of study. The books are divided into four sections:

A Introduction – sets out the key concepts for the area of study. The units of this section take you step-by-step through the foundational terms and ideas, providing you with an initial toolkit for your own study. By the end of the section, you will have a good overview of the whole field.

B Development – adds to your knowledge and extends the key ideas already introduced. Units in this section provide data illustrating an area of interest within the main topic, and use it to expand your understanding of the topic as a whole. By the end of the section, you will have a more in-depth grasp of the topic and will be ready to undertake your own exploration and thinking.

C Exploration – provides further data and issues for reflection, and leads you into your own exploration of the field. The units in this section are more open-ended and exploratory, and you will be encouraged to try out your ideas and to think like a psycholinguist.

D Extension – offers you the chance to extend your knowledge with key readings in the area. These are taken from the work of important writers in the field and have been chosen because they are accessible to a reader who is new to the study of Psycholinguistics.

You can read this book like a traditional textbook 'vertically' straight through from beginning to end. This will take you through a range of topics on a cyclical basis. However, the Routledge English Language Introductions have been carefully designed so that you can read them in another dimension, 'horizontally' across the numbered units. Unit A1 corresponds in topic to Units B1, C1 and D1, Unit A2 to Units B2, C2 and D2. Reading, for example, Units A4, B4, C4 and D45 will take you rapidly from basic concepts of how words are stored mentally to a level of extensive knowledge. If you have a particular interest in any of the topics covered, you may wish to study it in this way. Or you may wish to use the whole book like this, aiming for in-depth coverage on a topic-by-topic basis. As a subject, Psycholinguistics falls into distinct, clearly demarcated areas, so a 'horizontal' approach is certainly an option.

The glossary at the end, together with suggestions for further reading in each Section D unit, will help to keep you oriented. Each textbook in this series has a supporting website with extra commentary, suggestions, additional materials and support for teachers and students.

PSYCHOLINGUISTICS

Psycholinguistics has not historically been an easy area to study. It has its 'linguistic psychology' branch, where discussion is often closely linked to details of Chomskyan theory. And it has its 'psychology of language' branch which sometimes demands a background in cognitive psychology. Then there are the highly technical contributions of those who work in Artificial Intelligence and in neurolinguistics. Small wonder that aspiring students sometimes find themselves overwhelmed by jargon and deterred by the kind of densely-written prose, rich in cross-references, which scientists and social scientists favour when they are writing in specialist journals.

The aim of this volume is to make psycholinguistic theory accessible to the general student. A background in basic linguistics is an advantage but is not a necessity; no prior knowledge of psychology is assumed. Terminology is introduced gradually and explained with care. Background principles are embodied in concrete examples and many essential concepts are presented in a 'hands-on' way, with readers invited to reflect on what happens in their own language performance.

The material featured here is drawn from the psychological branch of the field. It sheds light on many everyday language processes that we all engage in but tend to take for granted. What precisely goes on when we pick up a book and begin to read it? Or when we listen to the radio? Or write a letter or speak to a friend? How do we store words in our minds? How do we manage to build those words into ideas? The following topics are introduced in Section A and subsequently developed in Sections B, C and D:

1	Introduction to Psycholinguistics	2	Is language specific to humans?
3	Language and the brain	4	Vocabulary storage
5	Using vocabulary	6	Language processing
7	Writing processes	8	Reading processes
9	Listening processes	10	Speaking processes
11	Comprehension	12	Language deprivation and disability

The topics have been arranged according to the relative difficulty of the ideas involved. They are also to some extent progressive: for example, you need the framework provided by 'Language processing' in order to understand the models of writing, reading, listening and speaking which are introduced subsequently.

Section A introduces basic concepts for each subject area in a non-technical way. Important terms are highlighted in **bold type** and explained; and pointers are given to issues that are explored in other sections.

Sections B and C then focus on more specific aspects of the topic. They do so by asking you to analyse data, to engage in discovery tasks, to reflect on the findings of researchers and to evaluate ideas. Very importantly, you are also asked to reflect upon your own experience; after all, you yourself regularly employ most of the processes which are featured. Section C extends the learning experience by proposing a number of experimental tasks which you can carry out for yourself, thus putting to the test some of the effects which have been described. There are suggestions for essay topics, one based on reading which enables you to an explore a particular aspect on your own.

Finally, Section D offers readings from specialist writers. Most are drawn from books; a few are papers from psychology journals. The passages have been abridged, but should give you a flavour of how theory and research are presented in psycholinguistics. A glossary provides guidance on any complex terminology or dense argumentation which may arise.

At the end of the book, there are suggestions for further reading which may be useful to those who want to undertake an in-depth study of any of the twelve core topics covered. An asterisk marks the titles which are likely to afford a good point of departure. There is then a bibliography which gives references to all sources quoted in the book, whether in sections A to C or in the readings of section D. Finally, there is a glossary of all the technical terms used. References are given to the section where each term is first introduced and explained.

CONTENTS

CONTENTS **CROSS-REFERENCED**

CONTENTS **CROSS-REFERENCED**

C EXPLORATION	**D** EXTENSION	Topic

Material for
activities

Further
reading

References

Glossary

LIST OF FIGURES

LIST OF TABLES

ACKNOWLEDGEMENTS

I acknowledge a great debt to John Williams of the Research Centre for English and Applied Linguistics, University of Cambridge, who first introduced me to much of the material that features here. My gratitude comes with the usual proviso that any inaccuracies are entirely my own. Special thanks are also due to Joyce Fraser for allowing me to reproduce data used in her MA dissertation.

The book is dedicated to two groups of people. Firstly, to the many students who responded so positively to this material in the days when I taught it as part of an Applied Linguistics and ELT course at Kings College London. Secondly, to all those who for any reason are unable to exercise that command of language which most of us take for granted. They it is who are the greatest beneficiaries from the insights which psycholinguists work so painstakingly to achieve.

The publishers would like to thank the following for permission to reproduce material:

Jean Aitchison for the extract from *Words in the Mind*, London: Blackwell, 2nd edn., 1994

Carl Bereiter and Marlene Scardamalia for the extract from *The Psychology of Written Composition*, Hillsdale, NJ: Erlbaum, 1987

The BBC for permission to publish a transcript of an interview from the Today programme, 6th November 2001

Dorothy Bishop for two extracts from *Uncommon Understanding*, Hove: Psychology Press, 1997

Anne Cutler and Sally Butterfield for 'Rhythmic cues to speech segmentation' from *Journal of Memory and Language* 31 (1992). Copyright Elsevier Science

Terrence Deacon for two extracts from *The Symbolic Species: The Co-evolution of Language and the Human Brain*, London: Penguin, 1997. Copyright Terrence W. Deacon and W. W. Norton Inc, New York

Kenneth I. Forster for the extract from 'Lexical processing' from D. N. Oscherson and H. Lasnik (eds): *An Invitation to Cognitive Science: Volume 1, Language*, Cambridge, MA: MIT, 1990

Philip B. Gough and Sebastian Wren for 'Constructing meaning: the role of decoding' from J. Oakhill & R. Beard (eds): *Reading Development and the Teaching of Reading*, Oxford: Blackwell, 1999

Willem Levelt for the extract from *Speaking: From Intention to Articulation*, Cambridge, Mass: MIT, 1997

Robert H. Logie for 'Working Memory' from *The Psychologist*, 13/4 (1999), reprinted by permission of the British Psychological Society

George A. Miller for 'The Psycholinguists' from *The Psychology of Communication: Seven Essays*, Harmondsworth, Penguin, 1968. Copyright: Beacon Press, Boston

Ib Ulbaek for 'The origin of language and cognition' from J. R. Hurford, M. Studdert-Kennedy & C. Knight (eds): *Approaches to the Evolution of Language*, Cambridge: Cambridge University Press, 1998

Nicola Yuill and Jane Oakhill for the extract from *Children's Problems in Text Comprehension*, Cambridge: Cambridge University Press, 1992

Psychology Press for Figure B3.1

W. J. M. Levelt for Figures A4.1 and C10.1 from *Speaking: From Intention to Articulation*, Cambridge MA, 1997

Andrew Ellis & Geoffrey Beattie for Figure A10.1 from *The Psychology of Language and Communication*, Hove: Erlbaum, 1986

Terrence Deacon for Figure B3.2 adapted from *The Symbolic Species: The Co-evolution of Language and the Human Brain*, London: Penguin, 1997. Copyright Terrence W. Deacon and W. W. Norton Inc, New York

J. L. McClelland, D. E. Rumelhardt and the PDP Research Group for Figure B6.3 from Rumelhardt, D. E. & McClelland, J. L. (eds): *Parallel Distributed Processing, Vol. 1*, Cambridge, Mass: MIT Press, 1986)

Keith Rayner and Alexander Pollatsek for permission to adapt data from *The Psychology of Reading*, Englewood Cliffs, NJ: Prenctice Hall, 1989

Macel Just and Patricia Carpenter for Figure B8.2 from *The Psychology of Reading and Language Comprehension*, Newton, Mass: Allyn & Bacon, 1987

Charles Perfetti for Figures C8.1 and C8.2 from *Reading Ability*, New York: Oxford University Press, 1985

Every effort has been made to obtain permission to reproduce copyright material. If any proper acknowledgement has not been made, we would invite copyright holders to inform us of the oversight.

A KEY TO ENGLISH PHONEMIC SYMBOLS

Consonants

Voiceless				Voiced	
		stops/plosives			
p	pin			b	bin
t	ton			d	done
k	cap			g	gap
		fricatives			
f	fan			v	van
θ	thing			ð	this
s	said			z	zed
ʃ	ship			ʒ	measure
				h	hit
		affricates			
tʃ	chip			ʤ	gym
		nasals			
				m	met
				n	net
				ŋ	sing
		approximants			
				w	wet
				r	red
				j	yet
		laterals			
				l	let

Vowels

	Short			*Long*	
ɪ	hit		i:	heat
e	head			
æ	hat			
ʌ	hut		ɑ:	heart
ɒ	hot		ɔ:	hoard
ʊ	foot		u:	hoot
ə	ahead		ɜ:	hurt

Diphthongs

eɪ	hate		əʊ	boat		ɪə	here
aɪ	height		aʊ	bout		eə	there
ɔɪ	boil					ʊə	cure

Triphthongs

aɪə	fire		aʊə	flower

The values illustrated are those of British RP. In addition, the symbol /a/ is used to represent the General American realisation of the vowel in *heart, pot*.

Section A

INTRODUCTION:
KEY CONCEPTS IN PSYCHOLINGUISTICS

A1 **PSYCHOLINGUISTICS: WHAT IS IT?**

Psycholinguistics explores the relationship between the human mind and language. It treats the language user as an individual rather than a representative of a society – but an individual whose linguistic performance is determined by the strengths and limitations of the mental apparatus which we all share. Its agenda is to trace similar patterns of linguistic behaviour across large groups of individual speakers of a particular language or of all languages. In this way, we hope to gain insights into the way in which the configuration of the human mind shapes communication – even though the processes involved may be so well established that we are no longer aware of them.

In fact, the notion that language is a product of the human mind gives rise to two interconnected goals, both the concern of Psycholinguistics:

a   to establish an understanding of the processes which underlie the system we call language.
b   to examine language as a product of the human mind and thus as evidence of the way in which human beings organise their thoughts and impose patterns upon their experiences.

Psycholinguistic research falls into six major areas, some of which overlap:

Language processing
What precisely goes on when we are listening, speaking, reading and writing? What stages do we go through when engaging in these skills? How do we manage to turn a grammatical structure into a piece of information?

Language storage and access
How is vocabulary stored in our mind? How do we manage to find it when we need it? What form do grammar rules take?

Comprehension theory
How do we manage to bring world knowledge to bear upon new information that is presented to us? How do we manage to construct a global meaning representation from words that we hear or read?

Language and the brain
What neurological activity corresponds to reading or listening? Where does the brain store linguistic knowledge and semantic concepts? What neurological and muscular activity is involved in speech? Can differences in the human brain account for the fact that our species has developed language?

Language in exceptional circumstances
Why do some infants grow up with language impairments such as dyslexia or stuttering? How does brain damage or age affect language? What is the effect of profound deafness upon language acquisition?

First language acquisition

How do infants come to acquire their first language? What stages do they go through in developing syntax, vocabulary and phonology? What evidence is there that we possess an innate faculty for language which enables us to acquire our first language, despite the supposedly poor quality of the input we receive?

Some commentators include second language acquisition in the study of psycholinguistics. However, SLA is best regarded as a different discipline. Its content ranges widely over topics drawn from sociolinguistics, from social psychology and from educational psychology. By contrast, mainstream Psycholinguistics bases itself heavily upon a body of theory provided by cognitive psychology. Furthermore, whereas mainstream Psycholinguistics uses a limited range of established experimental techniques, studies in second language acquisition tend to be more eclectic in the methods they employ.

All of the six areas identified above are explored in this book, with the exception of the last. This is not because it is unimportant. Far from it: it is such a major area of psycholinguistic research that it merits a separate volume to itself.

A glance at the contents page will show you that the book begins with two topics which fall under the fourth heading above: one examines animal language and the other examines how language is organised in the brain. These are followed by two explorations of the nature of vocabulary: examining how it is stored in the mind and how it is retrieved. Language processing forms a major part of the book, with five different areas explored. There is special emphasis on the four language skills (reading, writing, listening and speaking). The last two topics covered are comprehension theory and exceptional circumstances.

You will discover that Psycholinguistics spreads its net wide. It draws on ideas and knowledge from a number of associated areas, such as phonetics, semantics and pure linguistics. There is a constant exchange of information between psycholinguists and those working in neurolinguistics, who study how language is represented in the brain. There are also close links with research in artificial intelligence. Indeed, much of the early interest in language processing derived from the AI goals of designing computer programs that can turn speech into writing and programs that can recognise the human voice. Here, there has been a two-way traffic. AI researchers have drawn upon psychological accounts of how speech is processed; and psycholinguists have used the operations of the computer as a model of how the mind works. Some of the early insights into lexical access (A5), information processing (A8) and the representation of long-term knowledge (A11) were achieved by drawing analogies with computational processes.

The discipline of Psycholinguistics as described here potentially sheds light on a number of associated fields. Can you suggest the ways in which it might assist our knowledge of the following?

❑ first language education
❑ medical and physiological problems which affect language
❑ syntactic structure

❑   phonology and phonetics
❑   lexicography
❑   language learning

LANGUAGE, SPEECH AND COMMUNICATION

Is speech special? This question, frequently asked in Psycholinguistics, can be interpreted in two ways:

❑   Is language **species-specific**? Is it the human race alone that has developed a system of communication which resembles language?
❑   To what extent is the language faculty separate from other mental operations? To use a more precise term, is the language faculty part of **general cognition** or not? The first of these issues is considered in this section; the second will be referred to in Sections A3 and A12.

In considering whether language is a skill peculiar to the human race, three approaches are possible:

1   We can specify what we mean by 'language' and then attempt to establish if the communication system of any other species fits our criteria (Section B2).
2   We can establish whether other species are capable of acquiring speech or language (Section C2).
3   We can try to establish how language evolved and how long it has been a property of the human race and its ancestors (Section D2).

At the outset, we need to distinguish between **communication**, **language** and **speech**. The first includes the second and the second includes the third.

Communication

The term covers any means by which two individuals exchange information. While language is one type of communication, it is not the only one. Consider, for example, the function of a set of traffic lights. They communicate an instruction in symbolic form without relying upon language. All that is necessary is that everybody who uses the traffic lights should have a knowledge of the system and be aware that red = 'stop' while green = 'go'.

Human beings can convey ideas and feelings by means of many devices, among them hand signals, facial expressions, body language, nods, smiles and winks. These **paralinguistic** techniques do not involve vocalisation. However, there are other non-linguistic means of communication which do: for example, grunts, groans, snorts, sighs and whimpers. Bear in mind that we can only classify such sounds as communication if the producer intends by using them to express some kind of message. Thus, snoring, though based upon sound, is not a form of communication. The examples just given are voluntary: they are under the control of the user. Contrast laughter and sobbing which are usually triggered automatically and therefore cannot be regarded as 'intentional' in the same way. This is an important distinction when we come to consider animal communication.

Consider ways in which the following might or might not represent communication:

a belch – a scream – a cough

Language

In Section B2 we will look in some detail at what distinguishes language from other forms of communication. For the moment, it is worth taking note of four important characteristics:

- ❏ Language is voluntary. It is under our individual control.
- ❏ Language is symbolic. It represents something other than itself. The connection between the word ROSE and a multi-petalled flower with a thorny stem is a purely arbitrary one. If all English speakers agreed to change the word to DWORP or SMIDGE, it would not in any way change the nature of the object that it represents. The critical factor is that the entire speech community agrees on the label that is attached to a particular entity – thus enabling a speaker to transmit meaning to a listener who shares the system. To this extent, language has something in common with the earlier example of traffic lights: that system too is symbolic, with its arbitrary connection between red and stopping.
- ❏ Language is systematic. In terms of vocabulary, this means that words operate in sets, dividing up an area of meaning between them. To give an example, in English we do not use the word AFRAID for the whole range of types of fear because we have alternatives in TIMID or TERRIFIED or SCARED. In terms of grammar, language is **structure-dependent**, with words combining into phrases and phrases combining into sentences. We cannot regard a sentence as simply a string of words like beads in a necklace, because words cluster together to form higher-level patterns.
- ❏ Language operates in two different **modalities**: speech and writing. Of the two, speech is regarded as primary. This is partly because it preceded writing historically; writing is a by-product of speech. It is also because, in the life of an individual, reading and writing are learnt as a consequence of having acquired speaking and listening skills.

Consider the following phenomena in the light of these criteria:

laughter – snoring – doodling – nods – winks – traffic lights

How can we say that they are not part of language?

Speech

Speech may be characterised by the fact that it involves **vocalisation** (though, as we have seen, so do other non-linguistic forms of communication such as grunts and sighs). Two factors determine the ability of the language user to produce speech-like sounds:

a   The shape, size and position of the **articulators** that we use. Speech demands a complex interrelationship between our tongue, teeth, soft palate, jaw and nasal cavity as well as the ability to flex our vocal cords at will.

b   The ability to breathe and utter sounds at the same time. Human beings are able to exercise much greater control over their breathing than most other species. This enables us to produce a flow of air from the lungs upon which the articulators can operate freely without impeding the process of breathing out.

Speech usually involves the communication of a message. However, there are two types of speech which we might regard as less 'meaningful' than others:

–   **expletives** such as *Oh!* to express surprise or *Ow!* to express pain. To what extent can we regard these as 'words'? To what extent are they involuntary rather than intentional?

–   **phatic utterances** such as *Nice day!* or *All right?* where we may not intend to communicate a specific meaning and may not anticipate any response. This form of speech is said by some to be a survival of the mutual grooming which many animal groups engage in as part of a bonding process. It thus plays an important part in discussions of how human language evolved.

Having broadly distinguished communication, language and speech, we have laid down a few pointers for later.

❑   We can characterise the ways animals exchange information as 'communication'. But is there anything in the methods they use which can be said to resemble 'language'?

❑   Is there anything special about the human mind which accounts for the fact that we have developed the particular form of communication that we refer to as language?

❑   Is there anything special about the human vocal apparatus that accounts for the fact that we have developed speech and other species have not?

LANGUAGE AND THE BRAIN

Three important issues emerge in relation to language and the brain.

Comparison

In what way do our brains differ from those of other primates which do not possess language?

Nativists argue that a human infant must have some kind of genetically transmitted language faculty in order to acquire language as rapidly and successfully as it does. If that is the case, then we can expect the human brain to be different in structure from those of primates not capable of language. Of course, evidence of differences between human brains and those of other species does not necessarily prove the nativist case. We might approach the issue from the opposite (**cognitivist**) angle and suggest that differences in the operation of the human brain are what enabled us to evolve language when other species could not.

Localisation

Where is language located in the brain?

Attempts to locate language in the brain have a long history. Added impetus was given to the issue when Noam Chomsky (1965) and others drew attention to the fact that every normal child successfully acquires a first language, no matter what its intelligence or learning style. This suggested to some commentators that language must be an independent faculty and not part of our general powers of thought and reason. Evidence supporting this hypothesis comes from accounts of individuals who have serious learning difficulties but in whom the language faculty appears to be spared. It is therefore of interest to find how language relates to the other operations performed by the brain.

Lateralisation

Is there a difference in the way the right side and left side of the brain contribute to language? At what age does that difference become established?

Early evidence suggested that damage to the left side of the brain impaired language in a way that damage to the right did not. Where the damage occurred before the age of about five, the sufferer would sometimes fully recover their powers of speech. Hence a theory (Lenneberg 1967) that, in infancy, the relationship between the two parts of the brain is flexible enough for language to relocate itself on the right when necessary. This led to much discussion as to whether the period of flexibility constitutes a **Critical Period** for learning a first language, after which a child is not be able to achieve full competence.

We consider the characteristics of the brain in this section, localisation in section B3 and lateralisation in section C3.

A quick geography of the brain

1 Upper vs lower

The upper surface of the brain consists of 'grey matter' (that is its colour when exposed to air) known as the **cortex** (or **cortical** area). It deals with many of the more complex operations, including making connections with stored information, analysing input and controlling sophisticated muscular movements. Below it is the **sub-cortex** of 'white matter', which is mainly nerve cell fibres. In general, the lower parts of the brain are responsible for reflex actions, controlling functions such as breathing and heart beats. The **cerebellum** at the base of the brain has a delicate role in co-ordinating a range of muscular movements which have become highly automatic.

2 Left vs right

The brain divides into two **hemispheres**, one on the left (from the perspective of the owner of the brain) and one on the right. They are joined by a complex web of nerve connections known as the **corpus callosum**. The left hemisphere controls movement and sensation on the right side of the body while the right hemisphere is linked to the left side. Generalising enormously, the left hemisphere in most individuals is associated with analytic processing and symbolisation, while the right is associated with perceptual and spatial representation.

3 Front vs back

The outer surface of the brain is marked by mounds (**gyri**) and valleys (**sulci**). These serve to mark out four major regions in each hemisphere, known as lobes. They are the **frontal lobe** at the front, the **temporal lobe** running from front to back and the **occipital** and **parietal lobes** at the back.

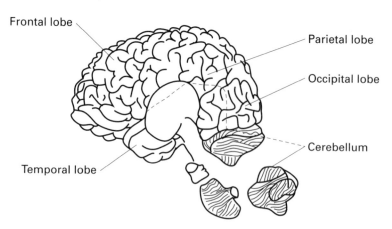

Figure A3.1   The lobes of the brain
Source: Based on 'The parts of the central nervous system' (Kandel & Schwartz, 1981)

Especially important are the **pre-frontal** areas, which appear to be responsible for recognising similarities between objects and grouping them into categories. Damage in these areas may reduce the ability to choose between alternatives and to suppress old routines when new information tells us to modify them. It may also limit the sufferer's ability to perform tasks that involve seeing things from the perspective of others.

A narrow area controlling **motor operations** (i.e. muscular movements) runs about midway down the side of each hemisphere.

Comparisons

Here are some comparisons between the brains of human beings and those of other primates:

❏ The cortex is much more extensive in human beings.
❏ Human pre-frontal areas are up to six times bigger than those of chimpanzees (in relation to body size).
❏ The brains of other species are divided into two hemispheres. Like human beings, a number of species (birds, rodents and other primates) have a left hemisphere which is more developed. In monkeys, the left hemisphere dominates in the processing of rapid auditory stimuli.
❏ In human beings, a greater proportion of the motor area is given over to the control of mouth, tongue and jaw.
❏ The human cerebellum is very much larger, relative to brain size, than in other species.
❏ The motor areas in the human cortex appear to exercise a high degree of control over the larynx, which regulates the passage of air in breathing and speech. In other species, the operation of the larynx is mainly or entirely controlled by the lower parts of the brain.

Consider speech from three angles. In what ways do you think the brain is engaged in each one? Which would you describe as 'motor' processes   ★ **Activity**

❏ the control of reflex processes such as breathing
❏ articulation (making the sounds of speech)
❏ cognitive processes (producing and understanding speech)

Now try to relate these processes to the functions mentioned above under 'A quick geography of the brain' for:

– the cortex   – the pre-frontal areas
– the left hemisphere   – the cerebellum   – the motor cortex

Examine again the comparisons made above between the human brain and those of other species. Can you suggest ways in which these differences might equip human beings for speech?

'KNOWING' A WORD

This section and the next explore the nature of vocabulary. They ask what information we need to carry in our minds and what processes we need to apply in order
to locate any word that we need. Note that much of the discussion will necessarily
be tentative. Psycholinguists have come to certain conclusions by reflecting on what
we know of words and how they operate. From these, they have constructed **models**
(diagrammatic representations) of our lexical competence. Although the models are
tested experimentally, the results are sometimes contradictory or difficult to interpret.
So be warned that this section and the next pose questions to which we may not yet
have single or clear answers. You will be encouraged to form your own views.

First, a note of caution about the term 'word'. We think we know what a word
is because we are so used to seeing words separated by pauses on the printed page.
But this does not serve to characterise a word when it occurs in connected speech.
The best way of conceiving of a word is as a moveable unit of meaning which cannot
be broken into smaller free-standing pieces.

Furthermore, we should not lose sight of the fact that some units of meaning
(e.g. 'in front of', 'bus stop', 'by and large') consist of more than one word. So it is
often more precise when discussing vocabulary to refer to **lexical items** rather than
to words.

Psycholinguistic studies of vocabulary and how we use it fall into three areas:

❑ Lexical entries: What information do we need to store in our mind about a
lexical item?
❑ Lexical storage: how are lexical items stored in relation to each other?
❑ Lexical access: What is the process that enables us to retrieve lexical items when
we need them?

Sections A4, B4 and C4 focus mainly on the first question. The present section reviews
the information that a lexical entry has to contain. Section B4 examines more closely
what we need to know about the forms of words, while Section C4 focuses upon how
we attach meanings to them.

We start by assuming that each language user has a personal vocabulary store,
or **lexicon**, from which they select words for use and to which they refer the words
they encounter in the utterances of others. We envisage each person's lexicon as consisting of a large set of **lexical entries**, one for each lexical item. The question to be
considered is: what does a lexical entry of this kind need to contain?

Content vs function words

An important distinction needs to be made between two types of item in the mental store:

❑ CONTENT words (nouns, verbs, adjectives and adverbs) which carry the kind of
meaning that we can look up in a dictionary. They are also referred to as **lexical
words**.
❑ FUNCTION words (or **functors**): words which do not have a clear meaning but
which contribute to the syntactic structure of the text. Examples might be: *the, of,*

the auxiliary *do* (as in *Do you like . . . ?*). These are also termed **grammatical words**.

Prepositions of position and movement have a demonstrable meaning but a function that is mainly grammatical. (In some languages, the same function might be performed by a prefix or a suffix.) Generally, these prepositions are classed as function words.

Function words form a **closed set**: we rarely add to their number. By contrast, the set of content words is open, with language users very prone to coin new lexical items to express new concepts. In English, function words usually carry weak stress:

the BUNCH *of* FLOWERS *that he* BOUGHT *for* JANE.

This gives the listener some help in distinguishing them auditorily from content words.

Evidence from brain imaging suggests that function words may be stored and processed separately from lexical ones. Why might this be an advantage? Compare the different processes that a listener goes through:

❑ On encountering a function word, a listener only needs to match the word to a phonological sequence which is stored in the mind.
❑ On encountering a content word, a listener not only has to find a match in the phonological store but also has to access the meaning of the word.

Contents of a lexical entry

What information do we need in order to be able to recognise and understand an item of vocabulary when we encounter it in speech or writing? As we have just seen, a lexical entry for a content word must provide information of two different types – it must tell us about **form** and about **meaning**.

One model (Levelt 1989) suggests that a lexical entry is composed as shown below. Let us consider each of the components in turn.

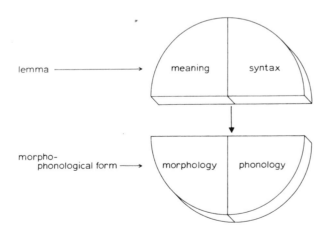

Figure A4.1 A lexical entry
Source: Levelt (1997: 188)

Form (See also Section B3)

❑   **Phonological/orthographic information.** We need some kind of mental representation of a word against which we can match any example of the word that we encounter. This stored information will obviously vary according to modality. If we are dealing with speech, we need a phonological model of the word; if we are dealing with reading, we will need an orthographic one. We can assume that the two are closely related, and are connected to the same unit of meaning. So forms of the word GIVE might be linked in this way:

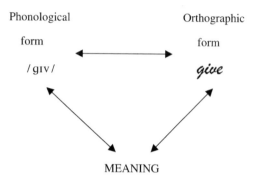

Figure A4.2   Form and meaning

In fact, the situation is not quite as simple as this account suggests. Both phonological and orthographic representations have to allow for **variation**. They have to take account of the fact that a speaker may have any one of a number of regional accents or that a written text may appear in any one of a number of different typefaces.

In addition, there is the issue of **homonymy**. There is a single phonological and orthographic representation of the word LIKE, but it must be connected to two entirely different entries, as in:

I LIKE ice-cream.   She looks LIKE my sister.

❑   **Morphological information.** In order to use a word, we need to know how to modify it when, for example, we want to refer to more than one item or to place an event in the past. So we need to store information on the entire range of **inflections** associated with the word. For GIVE, we would need:

Besides inflectional morphology, we also need to store information on the **derivational morphology** of a word. Part of the lexical entry for the word HAPPY must be an indication that we form the opposite by adding UN- and not IN- or DIS-:

HAPPY ─────────▶ UN- (or UNHAPPY)

This, as we will see, is a controversial area. Some commentators argue that the whole word UNHAPPY is stored; others that there is simply a link between HAPPY and the prefix UN-.

Meaning

The meaning component of a lexical entry is sometimes referred to as its **lemma**.

❑ **Syntax**. It might seem strange that the lemma includes syntactic information about a word. However, this reflects current approaches to grammar which see vocabulary and grammar as closely linked. Using the example of GIVE, the lexical entry would need to contain information on word class (GIVE = a verb) to enable the word to be used in generating sentences. It would also need to include information on the types of syntactic structure that are associated with the word:

GIVE (_ NP, NP)   GIVE (_ NP, *to* + NP)
[Where NP is a noun phrase such as *Mary* or *a present*]

This tells us that, once we choose to construct a sentence around the verb GIVE, we commit ourselves to using one of the two sentence patterns shown: *give (Mary) (a present)* or *give (a present) to (Mary)*.
   The entry can contain further semantic information about what we could appropriately fit into each of the NP slots. It might tell us that, in the 'NP, NP' pattern, the first NP has to be a recipient (probably animate) while the second NP is a gift (probably inanimate).

❑ **Range of senses**. The lemma attaches meaning to the word. This is not as simple as it sounds, and it might be better to think of the lemma as containing a range of meanings. Consider the fact that:
   – One word may have several linked senses. Compare different meanings of TURN in:

I turned the corner.
Turn over the page.
The room turned cold.

   Our interpretation of a particular word may also vary according to context. Compare the meaning of the word SURGERY as used in relation to a doctor and to a surgeon.
   – The issue of word meaning is complicated further by the fact that most words do not refer to single objects in the real world, but represent a whole class of objects or actions. It is not too difficult to explain how meaning can be attached to the expression *the moon* because what is involved is a one-to-one relationship The expression refers to a single entity which forms part of our knowledge of our environment. It is much less easy to explain how in everyday speech we manage to use **categories** such as DOG or JUMP. Where does a DOG end and a WOLF begin? What is the difference between JUMPING and LEAPING?

There are two extremely important issues here, so far as lexical storage is concerned:

a   The area of meaning covered by any given word is heavily influenced by the existence of other words alongside it. We can only fully understand how to use the word HAPPY if we recognise the existence of alternatives such as CONTENT or PLEASED or DELIGHTED which limit the semantic boundaries within which HAPPY operates. The conclusion to be drawn is that there are very close links between lexical entries which fall within a particular area of meaning. Only in this way would we be able to select exactly the item we needed and rule out others. To put it simply, 'No word is an island': the meaning of word X is very much determined by its relationship to Word Y and Word Z.

b   The area of meaning that we associate with a word is heavily dependent upon the way in which we categorise the world around us. To give an example, English uses one verb *to be*, but Spanish has two (temporary being vs permanent being) and Portuguese has three. A major area of research in psycholinguistics attempts to establish the nature of the categories that we form, and how they become established in the process of acquiring our first language.

The description above should have given you some idea of what a complete lexical entry needs to contain. The entry for the word GIVE might include the following:

GIVE

Form: Phonological: /gɪv/   Orthographic: *give*
            Morphological: gives – gave – given

Syntax: Word class: verb
            Phrase structure: (_NP$_1$, NP$_2$)   (_NP$_2$ *to* + NP$_1$)
              NP$_1$: a recipient, usually animate
              NP$_2$: a gift, usually inanimate

Core meaning: transfer an entity from one person to another.

Activity ✪   Now suggest what you would expect to find in a lexical entry for the following items:

TELL   AFRAID   ACCUSE   END (noun)

LEXICAL STORAGE AND LEXICAL ACCESS

The psychology of words and word meaning makes an important distinction between:

Lexical storage: how words are stored in our minds in relation to each other.
Lexical access (or lexical retrieval): how we reach a word when we need it.

This section introduces some basic concepts. Section B5 examines evidence of how words are stored; Section C5 examines models of how we manage to retrieve them.

Storage assists access

Words are not stored in the mind independently. On the contrary, every content word appears to have close links to others. Let us consider why this is necessary.

Assume a speaker is seeking a word for a fruit. Using the meaning as a point of departure, the speaker might retrieve the whole set of fruit, which includes:

APPLE – PLUM – PEAR – GRAPE – BANANA – ORANGE – PEACH – CHERRY

The fruit is yellowish, which restricts the search to the first five. It is roundish and of medium size, which limits us to the first three.

So far, our speaker has only tried to access the word through meaning. But the word can also be found through its form. It is possible that, **in parallel** (i.e. at the same time as exploring the lexicon through meaning sets), the speaker has associated the sound /eə/ with the word that is being sought. This would provide a different a set of words:

BEAR – CARE – DARE – FARE – PEAR – RARE – SHARE – TEAR – WEAR etc.

There is only one word which fits both criteria – PEAR.

This is an extremely simplified version of what happens. But it illustrates the way in which form and meaning can interact in helping us to retrieve a word that we need.

Now consider the process in reverse – from the point of view of a listener who hears the word CARROT.

- in form, the initial sounds link in to the whole set of words beginning with /kæ/
- in meaning, the context might (or might not – a controversial issue) indicate that the current topic was vegetables and lead the listener to open up the set of vegetables.

The result might be a tie between CABBAGE and CARROT, which would be resolved when the speaker heard the next sound /r/.

The notion of words as linked by a network of forms and meanings is an important one when considering how an infant or a foreign-language learner acquires their vocabulary. Learning a new lexical item is not just a question of mastering the form of the item and associating it with a sense or range of senses. It is also a question of linking the item to the whole network of previously learnt words. If a child learns the word TERRIFIED, it has to

a   form a connection with HORRIFIED and TERRIER which are similar in form.
b   form a connection with AFRAID and SCARED which are similar (but distinct) in meaning.

Weak links and strong links

Within the mental lexicon, some words are clearly more closely linked than others. Recent accounts of these links have been strongly influenced by a **connectionist** view of language processing (McClelland *et al.* 1986). Connectionism models itself upon the way in which the brain operates by transferring signals across multiple neural (nerve) connections. Simplifying greatly, it suggests that, when a connection is used a great deal, it gets proportionately stronger; when a connection is little used, it gets weaker. Thus, the link between the words FISH and CHIPS is a strong one because the two often occur together; similarly the link between AFRAID and SCARED is a strong one because the two often compete when we need a word to express fear. A link exists between FISH and RIVER or AFRAID and CALM but it is not of the same strength.

The notion of connection strength is useful because it accounts for

frequency: the words we use most are the ones that are easiest for us to retrieve. This is because the connections to them are more often used.

collocation: we retrieve certain words together because they are so closely connected: we talk about a *heavy smoker*, never a **large smoker* or a **compulsive smoker*.

Spreading activation

Part of the evidence for associative links between words comes from a phenomenon called **spreading activation**. If you have just recently seen the word DOCTOR, you will recognise words such as *patient, hospital* or *medicine* more quickly as a result.

The idea is that activation (think of it as a kind of electrical impulse) runs along the connections which link the words in our minds. When we see or hear the word DOCTOR, it triggers off a reaction which 'lights up' words which have close connections to DOCTOR. This means that the words are more readily available to us in case we need them. Of course, activation does not last for long; it quite quickly **decays**.

Note that the activation effect is automatic. We cannot turn it on or off. It is not the same as a **context effect**. Consider what might happen if you read a text with the title CAMELS. Your reading would benefit from two distinct processes:

❏ **Spreading activation**. Seeing the word CAMEL would trigger automatic associations with closely connected words in your lexicon such as *hump, desert, sand* and help you to recognise those words more quickly if they occur.
❏ **World knowledge**. Knowing that the text is about camels might lead you to create certain expectations at a rather more conscious level: there may be something in the text about storing water in the hump, something about the two types of camel, something about survival in a hot climate.

Spreading activation is believed to be the explanation for an effect known as **priming**. In the example above, CAMEL is said to **prime** *hump, desert* and *sand*. A researcher might show a subject a sentence containing the world CAMEL and then test how quickly the subject responds to words that are or are not associated with it. This type of experiment often takes the form of a word/non-word task (known as a **lexical decision** task) where a button has to be pressed every time a group of letters on a screen is an actual English word.

Experimenter: You'll see/hear a sentence and afterwards you'll see/hear a word or a non-word. Press the button if you recognise the word.
[We saw a camel at the zoo . . . fosk – bank – lidge – hump]

The time taken to press the button is measured in milliseconds. This **Reaction Time** will be quicker to *hump* than to *bank*, because *hump* has been activated by prior exposure to CAMEL.

Priming can be used to discover important facts about spreading activation such as:

❏   How closely associated do words have to be for activation to occur?
❏   How long does the activation of associated words last?

AN INFORMATION PROCESSING APPROACH   A6

During the first half of the twentieth century, work in psychology was heavily influenced by a movement known as **behaviourism**. Behaviourists argued that the human mind was unknowable. They insisted that the only scientific source of data for psychology was human behaviour, which was observable in a way that mental processes were not. Human behaviour came to be seen as the product of **habit**, represented in the relationship between an external situation or **stimulus** and a standardised **response** to it.

In the 1950s, cognitive psychologists reacted against behaviourism by proposing an approach which charts the flow of information through the brain while a particular mental task is performed. The basic idea is that raw data is acted upon stage by stage by the mind and is progressively reshaped. Here is the kind of **information processing** which occurs when somebody asks you the way to the station. You have to:

identify the words in the question
⇓
organise the words into a syntactic pattern
⇓
turn the question into a **proposition** (an abstract idea)
⇓
search your memory for information
⇓
retrieve the information
⇓
turn the information into words
⇓
utter the words

This approach to analysing cognitive operations has influenced psychological descriptions of the language skills, and lies behind the flowchart graphics that often appear in Psycholinguistics books. Directly or indirectly, the information processing approach has provided us with several new ways of looking at how language is processed by the user. We review five of them here.

Perception and pattern recognition

For the reader or listener, there are two important stages in processing a stimulus:

sensation: the unanalysed experience of sound meeting one's ear or light meeting one's eye.

perception: the mental operation involved in analysing what the signal contains. The term 'perception' is applied to **lower-level processes**, where the language user is decoding information that is physically there.

An important part of the perceptual process is **pattern recognition**, where the form of a word is matched to a stored representation in our mind (see Section B4). Many studies in cognitive psychology have investigated how we recognise patterns of all kinds. The process is said to involve

a   breaking the input into different characteristics (colour, shape, size, relationship of the parts)
b   matching the whole to a representation which is based upon previous experiences and is stored permanently in Long Term Memory.
c   allocating an identity or a category to the sensation

Activity   How might these stages of pattern matching apply in the case of:

–   a reader who sees the letters *t-a-b-l-e* on the page?
–   a writer who starts from the concept TABLE and needs to find a word for it?

The storage of data

Early information processing theory (Atkinson and Shiffrin 1968) suggested that there were three types of memory store, with data transformed as it passed between them:

sensory storage   an exact trace of the current stimulus
short term storage   of information currently being processed
long term storage   of knowledge

The sensory store held a trace of a stimulus while the stimulus was being matched to a pattern. In terms of language, the trace might be visual, in the form of an impression of the word on the page. Or it might be auditory, in the form of an 'echo' of the voice of a speaker. It was suggested that we have two separate sensory stores – a visual one referred to as **iconic memory** and an auditory one called **echoic memory**. In both, the trace of the stimulus appeared to fade quickly. It was suggested that iconic traces lasted for only about 0.5 seconds; but that echoic traces lasted longer, with a first phase of about 0.25 seconds for pattern recognition and a second phase of at least 3 seconds as a back-up against which an interpretation could be checked.

Activity

Think about the differences between the reading signal and the listening one. Can you suggest why we might not need iconic memory in order to retain the visual form of words in reading? Why does it seem logical for echoic traces to last longer than iconic ones?

The listening and reading processes were represented as follows:

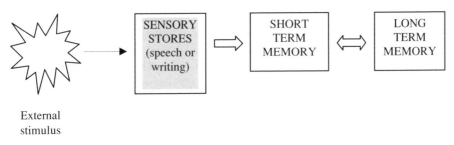

External
stimulus

Figure A6.1 A three-store model of human memory

Let us follow this path in terms of a reader reading a single word. The reader briefly retains an image in their sensory store of the actual word as it appears on the page. The form of the word is passed to **Short Term Memory**, which stores current information. In order to identify the word, the reader needs to make a lexical search. However, the STM only holds temporary information needed for immediate purposes. So it has to extract lexical information from **Long Term Memory**. This means that the STM is more than just a store: it is also responsible for language operations. (For this reason, the title **Working Memory** is now usually preferred.) Later, after processing a complete clause or sentence, the reader may want to store the piece of meaning they have acquired. In that case, they transfer it into Long Term Memory.

We will look at a more recent theory of memory and language in Section C6.

Processing as subject to limitations

Working Memory is believed to have a very **limited capacity** for information. This has important consequences for the way in which we process language:

- Some language tasks (e.g. listening and speaking simultaneously) make impossibly heavy demands on Working Memory.
- We need to rapidly transform the language we hear and read into pieces of abstract information. It is easier to retain a few pieces of information than many words.
- We constantly need to transfer useful information into Long Term Memory to avoid congestion in Working Memory.

Processing as a constructive operation

Listening and reading were once considered 'passive' skills. They were seen as part of a simple process of transmitting information: the speaker/writer encoded a message which was then decoded by the listener/reader. In fact, it is an enormous simplification to think of a message changing hands in this way.

– We now recognise that listening and reading are active processes. The minds of listeners and readers are actively engaged in constructing a **meaning representation** on the basis of the evidence they receive. Once they have built such a representation for the current sentence, they then have to attach it to what they have heard or read so far. So the receptive skills involve not just **constructing** meaning but also **integrating** it into what has already been understood.

– Listeners and readers may have to guess the intentions of the speaker/writer. So they do not simply receive a message; they have to remake it.

– Listeners and readers are independent individuals. They select what they want from a piece of speech or writing. They make judgements about which parts appear most relevant to them, or which parts constitute major pieces of information and which are minor. These may be different from the intentions of the speaker/writer.

Levels of representation

The process of producing or understanding language involves taking linguistic information through a series of stages (**levels of representation**) and changing it at each step. The listener, for example, might need to build acoustic features into phonemes, phonemes into syllables, syllables into words, words into syntactic patterns, syntactic patterns into propositional (abstract) meaning. The process of listening, it seems, involves assembling larger units from smaller ones. This is often referred to as **bottom-up processing**.

Which features in reading are different from those in listening? Which are similar? What 'bottom-up' stages do you think the reading process goes through?

However, information can, of course, flow in the other direction. We potentially receive important cues from:

❑ **Context**. The next word in the following sentences is highly predictable:

Later, heavy clouds will come in from the West, bringing a chance of . . . The weather is likely to be cool for the time of . . .

No prizes for inserting the words RAIN and YEAR. Some commentators believe that we are able to recognise predictable words like these more quickly thanks to the evidence provided by the preceding context.

❑ **Known words**. Suppose I hear the following sentence:

A lot of our VELATIVES were there.

The only candidate that remotely fits the fifth word is RELATIVE. Because the word is well-established in my lexicon, it is possible that I might fail to notice the irregular pronunciation.

Both of the above are referred to as **top-down processing** because they involve using higher-level information (context and whole words) to support lower-level processes (respectively, word and phoneme recognition).

The terms 'bottom-up' and 'top-down' have come into Psycholinguistics from computer science. There, a bottom-up process is one that is **data-driven** – it relies upon evidence that is physically present. A top-down one is **knowledge-driven** and relies upon external information. You can see parallels in the way in which the terms are used in Psycholinguistics. We will examine bottom-up and top-down processing more closely in Section B6.

WRITING SYSTEMS

In comparing writing across languages, we need to distinguish between:

 A7

– a **writing system**: a method of writing such as the alphabet
– a **script**: a form of writing (Arabic script, Greek script)
– an **orthography**: the writing conventions of a particular language.

 ✪ **Activity**

Below are examples of various orthographies (sources: Garman 1990; Coulmas 1989; Harris and Coltheart 1986). Describe the differences between them. Then put yourself in the position of somebody using each of these types of writing. Describe the process of mapping from an idea in your mind to a word on the page.

Chinese

木	mù	tree
木木	lín	woods

Japanese

車	kuruma	car
車 で	kuruma + de	car + *de* (= in the car)
水 で	mizu + de	water + *de* (= in the water)

Arabic

كَتُب	(letters **ktb**)	kutub	books
كَتَب	(letters **ktb**)	katab	he wrote

Spanish

teléfono	tay-lay-foh-noh	telephone
supermercado	soo-per-mer-cah-doh	supermarket

English

telephone	tel-ə-fohn	telephone
supermarket	soo-pə-mah-kit	supermarket

(Except for ə, transcriptions are approximate English orthographic equivalents, to avoid using unfamiliar IPA characters.)

Three different types of writing system are used by the world's languages. No language's orthography provides an exact example of one of these systems. But, in 'idealised' terms, they are:

a **alphabets**: with a symbol for each phoneme of the language
b **syllabaries**: with a symbol for each syllable of the language
c **logographic systems**: with a symbol for each word of the language.

In principle, the first two are based upon the phonology of the language, while the third is based upon the language's lexical system. In practice, the situation is more complex. But two important questions immediately arise. Is the mental process of writing logographs different from the process of writing in alphabetic form? And does phonology play a part in the process of alphabetic writing or do we draw written words from a separate store for visual forms?

Logographic systems

Chinese writing is usually characterised as logographic on the basis that Chinese characters represent whole words, and sometimes represent semantic relationships between words. For example,

子 means *child* and 孖 means *twins*;

However, about 90 per cent of Chinese characters consist of two parts: a radical followed by a phonetic element. Thus (Coulmas 1989: 101) the character for 'sugar' is composed of a symbol for 'cereal' plus a symbol which represents the proper name Tang. This is because the Mandarin word for sugar is *táng*. The same word *táng* can also mean 'embankment', 'to block' and 'pond', and the symbol is part of the character for each of these words. The point here is that Chinese orthography does not rely solely upon a link between a character and a meaning. It also has features in its writing system which represent how words are said and thus makes an association between **homophones** (words which are pronounced the same way).

It is possible that the mark of a skilled writer of Chinese is the ability to map instantly from a concept to a detailed whole-word character. However, there are around six times as many pronunciation markers as radicals. So the pronunciation marker is more informative than the radical. It seems likely that, when recalling a character, a Mandarin speaker is influenced in part at least by the phonology of the word. Furthermore, any Mainland Chinese writer educated from 1958 onwards has some phonological awareness through having done their first writing in Pinyin, a phonemic representation of Mandarin based upon the Roman alphabet.

The fact that phonology plays a part in Chinese writing is tellingly illustrated by the following sequence of characters (Harris and Coltheart 1986):

可 口 可 樂

They represent the words *ke* (be able), *kou* (mouth), *ke* (be able) and *le* (laugh) – and together constitute the Chinese word for *Coca Cola*.

This still leaves open the issue of whether the process of employing a logographic system is different in psychological terms from the process of employing an alphabetic one. Here, there has been much interest in the writing of Japanese. Japanese orthography is mixed. Its lexical items are represented by **kanji** characters derived from Chinese; but its inflections and function words are represented by seventy-one much simpler **kana** characters which correspond to the entire set of syllables in Japanese. The system is thus a mixture of a logographic and a syllabic one.

Evidence suggests that the two systems do involve two different types of processing. Thus, when Japanese brain-damaged patients suffer from **agraphia** (the loss of writing ability), kana and kanji are affected to different degrees. In cases of senile dementia, the ability to produce kanji characters is usually lost well before the ability to produce kana. This evidence suggests that the phonologically based kana is the more robust; but it may simply reflect the fact that Japanese children acquire kana characters first. In dementia, early acquired skills and information are often the last to go.

Alphabetic systems

A logographic system has to be learnt and stored character by character. With a phono-logically based system, a writer can guess spellings from a knowledge of how words are pronounced. For children, learning can take place through analogy with words that have already been mastered. But we should not take it for granted that children find alphabetic systems easy to acquire because they already speak the language before they learn to write it. Having access to an extensive spoken vocabulary is not the same thing as being able to identify the individual sounds which make up the words. Evidence from adult Portuguese illiterates (Morais *et al.* 1979) suggests that we learn to recognise the individual phonemes of our language *as a result of* learning an alphabet and not the other way round. Evidence also suggests that children acquiring syllabaries make fewer mistakes than those acquiring alphabets.

Alphabetic systems vary considerably. Some, such as Arabic, represent consonants but do not need to distinguish vowels. Orthographies can also be characterised according to how close the match is between **graphemes** (units of writing) and phonemes. Spanish, for example, provides an example of a **transparent orthography**, with a one-to-one relationship between written forms and sounds. All its words can be interpreted using consistent **grapheme-phoneme correspondence** (GPC) rules. English provides an example of an **opaque orthography**, because it contains a mixture of:

- words that can be spelt using GPC rules (e.g. *canteen, hospitality*).
- words where the weak phoneme /ə/ is represented by any one of the five vowels
- words that can be spelt by **analogy** with other words (e.g. *light, rough*)

– words that are unique in their spellings (e.g. *yacht, buoy*) and thus demand the kind of whole-word processing by an English writer that we find in a logographic system like Chinese.

Is one system easier?

Is one system easier to process or faster to produce than another? Clearly a logographic system makes great demands on the writer's memory store – though apparently Chinese writers can manage with about 2000 characters. A writer of Spanish can rely upon a set of internalised fail-safe GPC rules, but, if the writer employs them, the writing process has to be mediated through the pronunciation of the word. The situation with a mixed alphabetic system like English is less clear. It must rely partly upon stored whole-word forms, partly upon GPC rules and partly upon analogy. The last might involve a system that stores word forms by their **rime** (final vowel + consonant(s)): *light, fight, might*, etc.

As for Arabic, part of the representation in the writer's mind must be based upon semantic links between words, since the same letter string *ktb* represents: 'books', 'he wrote' and 'clerk'. Note the resemblance to similar links in the lexicon of the logographic writer (see the *tree* and *woods* example above). A consonantal system of this kind is clearly fast in execution, since not all sounds are represented; but it is a system that throws up ambiguities which the reader has to resolve by reference to context.

Interestingly, writing systems seem to have evolved to fit the characteristics of the language they represent – and thus, by extension, the experience of generations who have attempted to produce the language in written form. Chinese possesses many homophones, which the logographic system serves to differentiate. Languages such as Japanese and Devanagari possess a simple and limited range of syllable types which are well represented in a syllabary. In Arabic, inflections to mark (for example) plural or past tense take the form of **infixes** which involve changing vowels within words but retaining the consonants. Hence the appropriacy of a consonantal system. Even the English system, with its lack of consistent GPC rules, has benefits. It enables writers to reflect etymological relationships between words which are no longer phonologically similar (e.g. *relative* /ˈrelətɪv/ and *relation* /rɪleɪʃn/) and to mark, for example, all plurals with *-s*, whereas some are pronounced /s/ (books) and some /z/ (pens).

So much for the systems. Later sections will explore the process of writing. Section B4 considers low-level processes (how we write and spell words) while Section C4 considers how we plan writing and execute our plans.

DECODING IN READING

Lower and higher level processing

In reading, as in writing, it is useful to distinguish between lower level and higher level processes.

❑ **Lower level processes** include **decoding** (recognising words in the text) and accessing lexical entries. They are highly automatic in a skilled reader. This means that they make few demands upon Working Memory, leaving capacity spare for higher level processes such as building overall meaning.

Here is an example which shows how automatised your word recognition skills have become. Look at the words on page 208. As quickly as you can, name not the words but the shapes within which they appear.

You will almost certainly have experienced interference from the sight of familiar words. This is because the process of recognising the words is so highly automatised that you find it difficult to suppress it in order to perform the task. The experience demonstrates that automatic responses are rapid and not normally subject to our control – and that they are difficult to overrule once they have become established.

(The task you did was adapted from the **Stroop colour test**, where subjects are shown, for example, the word RED written in blue ink and asked to report not the word but the colour that it is written in.)

❑ **Higher level processes** include applying background knowledge to the text, inferring meaning which is not explicitly stated in the text, interpreting the writer's intentions and constructing a global meaning representation of the text. They are much more under the conscious control of the reader, who is sometimes able to report on them. Because of this, they make considerable demands upon Working Memory.

In this section, we consider the part that phonology plays in reading. In Section B8, we consider evidence of lower level processing from studies of readers' eye movements. In C8, we consider the way in which lower level and higher level processes interrelate.

Decoding

A major issue in studying reading is: To what extent does the spoken word contribute to the process? Obviously it does so in the early stages of reading when we learn to recognise written forms by reference to spoken ones. But is this just a stage – leading to the development of an entirely separate visual vocabulary store? Or does reading continue to be mediated through the spoken word, even for an adult reader? Does the role of the spoken word vary from language to language, given that some languages such as English have orthographies which do not depend upon simple one-to-one links between letters and sounds?

Look at the non-words below and say each one aloud. If possible, write your interpretation alongside each one in phonemic script.

GEAD	DOISE
PIVE	NEAN
TOOD	PIGHT
FOWN	MARD
KEAR	SOAT
LORK	GAIR
VOME	BICE
SCERE	RAWN
HEAF	LIDGE
VINT	WIRT
SOVE	GOPE

Check your answers with other students. To what extent did you agree?
Ask yourself how you allocated spoken forms to these non-words.
Did some of the decisions seem easier than others?

Several conclusions can be drawn from this exercise:

a A sub-lexical route

The English spelling system is relatively opaque; this might suggest that a reader uses a whole word as a visual symbol and does not bother about the letter-sound relationships within it. They might, for example, map straight from the letter sequence READ to the concept behind it, in a process not unlike that performed by a Chinese reader.

However, if this were the only process available, English readers would not be able to attribute pronunciations to non-words as you have just done. A widely accepted **dual route** account of the reading process sees it as using both a **lexical route** based on the whole word and a sub-lexical route based upon phonology in the form of GPC rules.

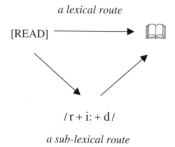

a sub-lexical route

The two may be seen as being in competition to produce the fastest reading of a word. The lexical route is usually the faster because it is the more automatic; but we need the sub-lexical route when we have to match unfamiliar words with their spoken forms.

b Analogy

It was suggested (Section A7) that English readers and writers do not simply make use of the GPC rules that link graphemes and phonemes but also rely upon analogy between new words and those that we already know.

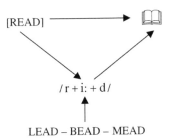

Especially important may be the rime of a word (its vowel plus final consonant), but a preferred pronunciation may also be based upon embedded words. For example, the non-word PIND above resembles BIND but many people interpret it as /pɪnd/ because the first three letters form the word *pin*.

c Neighbourhood effects

There is a further problem that you may have spotted. The rime -EAD in READ actually has two possible phonological interpretations. You could have pronounced the non-word GEAD as /giːd/ by analogy with BEAD, LEAD (verb) and READ or as /ged/ by analogy with HEAD, DEAD, LEAD (noun) and READ (past form). Lexical decision experiments ('Press a button when you see an actual word rather than a non-word') show slower reaction times to words like READ whose rime is phonologically ambiguous than to words like HOPE whose rime is not. The significance of this should not be overlooked. It shows that phonological criteria play a part not just when we have to assign pronunciations to unknown words but in the processing of *known* written words.

The ease with which a word is identified is said to reflect the composition of its **neighbourhood** (i.e. the number of words that share its rime). Consider READ. Among its neighbours are four 'friends' with similar pronunciations and at least eight 'enemies' with different pronunciations. Some of the enemies are very frequent words.

	Friends	*Enemies*
READ	BEAD LEAD (vb) PLEAD MEAD	HEAD DEAD READ (past) BREAD LEAD (n) DREAD TREAD THREAD

This means that the written word READ is less easy to process than we might expect from its high frequency.

 Activity

Review your experience of doing the non-word task above. Did you find the items in the second column easier to interpret? They were words whose rimes have only one possible interpretation.

Choose four or five of the items in the first column and work out how many monosyllabic words they have in their neighbourhood. When you did the non-word task, was the pronunciation you chose that of the larger and more frequent group or not?

It is possible that at times it was not. For example, many of you may have chosen /giːd/ rather than /ged/ as your preferred interpretation of GEAD. These mixed results create some uncertainty about how readers assign pronunciations in these circumstances. One possibility is that we take account of multiple factors. In assigning a pronunciation to GEAD we might take account of sequences which begin with GEA (GEAR, conGEAL) as well as the fact that overall the grapheme EA represents /iː/ in far more words than it represents /e/.

Some further thoughts on the dual-route model

❑ **Phonology and learning to read**. There has been much controversy about the best way of teaching children to master English orthography. The pendulum has swung between:

- the **whole word** approach based upon what we have called the 'lexical route'
- the **phonics** approach based upon mastering GPC rules
- an **analogy** approach, teaching new words by reference to known ones.

It would seem from the discussion so far that what is needed for competent reading skills is a combination of all three. Past dogmatism has certainly disadvantaged children in relation to the diverse ways in which English readers seem to decode.

❑ **Other languages**. What of readers of languages with a transparent orthography? Do they use a single sub-lexical route based upon GPC rules and ignore the lexical route? Current evidence is unclear. But it seems likely that speakers of, say, Spanish do indeed employ a dual-route process. Remember that a lexical route is generally more rapid than a sub-lexical one.

Inner speech

Phonology contributes to reading in another way.

 Activity

Study the following sentence; you have eight seconds to try to commit it to memory.

It was when he was parking his car that he noticed a long horizontal scratch on the left side of the windscreen.

Close your book and try to write it from memory.

Now ask yourself: In what form did I try to store that sentence in my mind? You will almost certainly report that you rehearsed the sentence in something like a spoken form – an 'inner voice' in your head. You did not try to store it in a visual form.

Although the learning-by-heart task was an artificial one, 'inner speech' appears to be present when we read in normal circumstances. We only become aware of it when we accord it more attention than usual because we are reading a piece of text that is difficult or because we are tired and having difficulty in concentrating. But you will almost certainly recall at some time reading a letter from a friend and hearing their voice in your head as you read.

Why is this a spoken form rather than a visual? Two explanations often given are:

a   Spoken information in memory is more durable than visual.
b   If we store words in spoken form, they are less likely to interfere with the visual process of decoding words on the page.

There is one confusing aspect of this phenomenon, however. We can read with our eyes much faster than we read with our voices. Silent reading (average: around 300 words a minute) is much faster than reading aloud (average: around 150–200 w.p.m.). However, the 'voice in the head' appears to follow very closely behind the reader's eye. So inner speech cannot be an exact replica of spoken language. It appears that some kind of phonological encoding of the reading text takes place, but that it must be in a reduced form. It might feature key words only, or parts of words or content words without functors. The precise nature of inner speech has yet to be established. When readers attempt to analyse what the inner voice says, they receive the impression that it encodes in full everything they have read. However, in focusing full attention upon inner speech, they may have resorted to a slower, more controlled and less efficient process than is involved in normal silent reading.

What we do know is that inner speech seems to play an important part in supporting comprehension processes. It enables us to hold a string of words in memory while we impose a syntactic pattern upon them.

ISSUES IN LISTENING

At the higher levels of processing (constructing a meaning representation and applying background knowledge), there are strong parallels between listening and reading. Indeed the same processing route may be used by the two skills. But at lower levels, they are not comparable. The reason is that the raw material of listening – connected speech – is very different in form from the word on the page. Here are a few issues which pose challenges to the listening researcher.

❑ The **linearity** issue. The spoken signal does not consist of a string of phonemes in the way that written language consists of a string of letters. Take the word /kæt/. There is no precise point at which the sound /k/ can be said to end; it blends into the succeeding /æ/, just as the /æ/ blends into /t/. We are not dealing with beads on a necklace, it has been said, but something more like the result of dropping a box of eggs.
Question arising: do listeners actually analyse a speech signal into phonemes?

❑ The **non-invariance** issue. Because of this blending effect (known as **co-articulation**), there is no such thing as an unvarying 'pure' example of /k/ or /æ/ in connected speech. Researchers have studied the cues that are physically present in the speech stream, but so far have failed to find any combination of features that is peculiar to one phoneme alone. Try saying *kill* and *cool* and compare the position of the initial /k/ sound in your mouth. The sounds we hear are unavoidably shaped by the sounds that come before and after them.
Question arising: what kind of mental phonological representation of the sound /k/ enables us to recognise it in all its forms?

❑ The **normalisation** issue. Every speaker has a distinctive voice:
  – Our articulators (mouths, jaws, tongues, teeth) vary greatly in size, shape and position.
  – Many of us have regional accents.
  – There are important differences in pitch between the voices of men and the voices of women.
  – We all speak at different rates; and a speaker's speech rate may vary on different occasions.
Question arising: how do we manage to normalise (adjust) to the voice and speech rate and accent of a wide range of individuals?

❑ The **accommodation** issue. A speaker is sometimes faced with a difficult move from one articulatory setting to another (consider, for example, the complicated consonant sequence /ndm/ in the middle of *tinned meat*). The speaker often adopts a short cut and adjusts the first sound to the second. This accommodation suits the convenience of the speaker, but what of the listener? It means that some words in connected speech differ markedly from their **citation forms**. There may be **assimilation**, when the last sound of a word adjusts to the position of the first sound of the word that follows: *green paint* → [gri:m peɪnt]. There may be **elision**, especially where there are complicated sequences of consonants: *next spring* → [nek sprɪŋ].
Question arising: how do we succeed in recognising spoken words when they are subject to such variation?

- ❏ The **lexical segmentation** issue. There are no consistent gaps between words in connected speech as there are in written language.
  Question arising: how do we manage to work out where one word ends and the next begins?
- ❏ The **storage** issue. Readers have a permanent record on the page of the words they have encountered and can refer back to them if they lose the thread of the argument. Listening is not recursive in the same way: the speech signal is transitory and listeners are entirely reliant upon their own mental representation of the utterance so far.
  Questions arising: in what form do we store the products of listening? Verbatim text or propositions? Does listening depend to some extent upon the listener's ability to store information i.e. upon the extent of their Working Memory?

Here, we consider some possible solutions to the first four issues – those that concern the high degree of variation in the speech signal. There has been much interest in this area by researchers in **Artificial Intelligence** (AI) because the phenomenon has been a major obstacle to developing equipment which can interpret the human voice. Broadly, the solutions fall into two types:

- – those which focus on how we process the signal.
- – those which focus on how phonological information is represented in our mental store.

Process solutions

An early attempt to deal with the non-invariance problem was proposed (1967) by Liberman and his colleagues at the Haskins Laboratories in the USA. **Motor Theory** suggested that we are able to interpret the sounds we hear in connected speech by relating them to the muscular movements that we make when producing them. The possibility was raised that listening might be associated with a degree of **sub-vocalisation**, with the listener forming silent articulatory settings to match the sounds that they heard. There is evidence that limited sub-vocalisation sometimes accompanies reading.

Do you see any loopholes in the theory? Consider (a) what we know about phonology in the parallel skill of reading; (b) the situation of a learner of a second language.

A second line of attack was to discuss whether the phoneme is indeed a **unit of perceptual processing**. There is much evidence from the teaching of reading that pre-literate children find it very difficult to break a spoken word into its component sounds; there is similar evidence from studies of illiterate adults. Is the concept of a phoneme therefore something that we acquire only when we learn an alphabet?

One theory is that there is no 'phonological' level at all, but that we use phonetic features such as 'plosive', 'voiced', 'labial' when making matches with words in our lexicon. Other proposals retain the notion that listeners 'package' the speech signal into units before submitting it to the lexicon – but suggest a unit larger than the extremely variable phoneme. Among those suggested are the syllable and the **half-syllable** (the latter might analyse the sequence /kæt/ as a combination of initial /kæ/ and final /æt/)

Activity

1   Why do you think the syllable might be a better unit of processing than the phoneme?

2   Now consider storage. Would a listener need to store more syllable forms or more demi-syllable forms?

3   There is some evidence that the syllable may operate as a unit of processing in French. But how appropriate would it be for English? Compare the syllables of the French word BALANCE /ba – lās/ and the English word BALANCE /bæləns/.

Say the English word aloud several times. Comment on the sharpness of the syllable boundary – the duration of the syllables – the vowel quality of the syllables.

A more radical solution to the 'unit of perception' discussion is that we do not package the signal into linguistic units at all but divide it up into equal sections determined by **time**. This approach is adopted by the best-known computer simulation of listening. **TRACE**, a connectionist model, was designed by Elman and McClelland in 1986, and makes a virtue of the fact that listening takes place in real time. It processes the signal in small **time-slices** which are independent of phoneme, syllable and word boundaries. Each time-slice is connected to those that immediately precede it, so the processor can combine evidence from current input with evidence from what has immediately gone before.

TRACE's time-slice basis and its interconnections enable it to deal with the way in which phonemes overlap; and accounts for how we manage to adjust to differences of speech rate across different speakers. However, as its critics point out, the solution is bought at the cost of a cumbersome process in which a massive system of lexical connections has to be re-engaged after every third time-slice.

Some limited assistance in identifying phonemes is provided by lip movements; hence what is known, after one of its discoverers, as the **McGurk effect**.

Massaro & Cohen (1983) used a computer to produce a synthesised set of sounds which ranged in small steps between [ba] and [da]. They played these in conjunction with two silent video recordings: in the first, the speaker was saying [ba] and in the second he was saying [da]. The experimenters demonstrated that what subjects reported hearing was influenced by the lip movements on the video: when presented with a marginal example of [da], they were more likely to interpret it as [ba] when that is what the lips of the speaker were signalling. It thus seems that listeners use lip movements to some extent to disambiguate phonemes.

Activity Which phonemes would be more easily identified thanks to the McGurk effect?

Storage solutions

A different approach suggests that our minds contain representations of the phonemes of our language which allow for a degree of variability in the signal.

Let us say that we have a representation in our minds of a **prototype**, an idealised version of the sound /æ/ against which to match evidence in the speech signal. It might be that we are able to identify occurrences of /æ/ not on the basis of an exact match but probabilistically on the basis of a partial match (or **goodness of fit**).

This, of course, is still really a 'process' solution; but we could alternatively suggest that our representation of /æ/ is **under-specified**. In other words, certain characteristics of /æ/ are tagged as being important to identifying an example of it, and others are tagged as being incidental.

Recently there has been interest in a theory which suggests that, instead of storing a single idealised representation of a phoneme, we may store a whole range of exemplars. We might, in fact, retain traces of many different versions of /æ/, said in a variety of voices and a variety of phonological contexts (before /t/, after /k/ and so on). From all these traces, we might be able to recognise certain core values which mark out most instances of /æ/, and others which are present in some circumstances but not all.

Consider these two storage solutions: ✪ **Activity**

– one with a single under-specified representation for a phoneme
– one with multiple traces which produce a core value.

Which seems to you the more plausible?

Section B9 gives further thought to lower level listening – specifically, how we are able to recognise and distinguish the sounds of our native language. Section C9 examines the higher level process of turning a spoken text into a representation in the mind.

CHARACTERISTICS OF SPEECH   A10

A speaker with a normal speech rate produces some 150 words per minute . . . – on the average, one every 400 milliseconds. Under time pressure the rate can easily be doubled to one every 200 milliseconds. A normal, educated adult speaker has an active vocabulary . . . of about 30,000 words. A speaker makes the right choice from among these 30,000 or so alternatives not once but, in fluent speech, continuously two to five times per second – a rate that can be maintained without any clear temporal limit. There is probably no other cognitive process shared by all normal adults whose decision rate is so high. Still, the error rate is very low. Garnham [*et al.* 1982] found . . . 191 slips of the tongue in a text corpus of 200,000 words – about one slip per 1000 words.

(Levelt 1989: 199)

This section introduces some of the features of connected speech. Section B10 examines evidence for the various stages involved in assembling an utterance; and Section C10 takes you through the stages.

The discussion below comes from the BBC news programme *Today*. The programme aspires to a casual style, with interviews allowed to take their own course; so it provides interesting samples of relatively informal speech.

 Activity ⭐   Study the extract and decide what are the important differences it illustrates between spoken and written language.

PRESENTER: we were speaking a-a little earlier in the programme you may have heard us just before half-past seven about the problem + of DUMPED + CARS + THOUSands of them + they're EVerywhere they're becoming a terrible problem for some local authorities in particular + so much so that the Transport Secretary had to come up with a PLAN for dealing with them + he's going to give us some details today he's in our Westminster studio ++ now er Secretary of State good MORning + [21]

POLITICIAN: good MORning [1]

PRESENTER: What you going to say in BROAD terms [3]

POLITICIAN: well I think there are two things we need to do + first of all is in the SHORT term to provide powers + to actually get these cars off our STREETS at the moment you can wait up to thirty-five DAYS before any action can be TAKen + and [ænd] we're proposing that you could reDUCE that to act(ua)lly twenty-four HOURS + where the car has no real VALUE but in the longer term what we HAVE to do is to make car registration far more efFECTive there are prob- [19]

PRESENTER: How do you DO that + [2]

POLITICIAN: well there are probably about a million CARS unregistered at the moment + we need to have + far better enFORCEment + we need to take unlicensed cars + SERious because the rest of us er + who pay our licence are basically SUBsidising + people who are not complying with the legal reQUIREments + and [ænd] we effectively need to have a rolling REGister so we have a registered KEEPer + of each car on the road + and they have to take responsiBILity + for that car [24]

PRESENTER: does that mean that + a car with a missing TAX disc is going to be treated + as a more SERious matter by + strolling poLICEmen + + and [ænd] that + erm as they do checks as they drive along + police + you know p- er + just keying in a car NUMber + they will chase up anything with it they can't find regisTRAtion for + [18]

POLITICIAN: I don't think + it's not just poLICE + I think it's traffic wardens and people who have responsibility for PARking I think can usefully identify CARS + which are not LIcensed and the reason why this is imPORtant is that + inCREASingly quality of life ISSues + + are [ɑː] matters of great concern to the PEOple you know the the street in which they LIVE is imPORtant ++ and abandoned CARS + graFFIti dereLICtion + are all issues which we DO have to tackle and we have to take seriously + [23]

PRESENTER: and of course it's it's not just (the) people are getting more concerned
              about the STREETS + it IS that more cars are being DUMPed and that's
              the REAL problem because + er apparently + scrap metal + costs + a- a- profits
              + mean that it's not worth taking a car away so people just DUMP them
              they throw them aWAY + [16]

POLITICIAN: that's right + five years ago you probably would have got thirty or forty
              pounds for your your vehicle + er toDAY er the scrap has got no real VALue
              you have to PAY for the car to be taken aWAY + we're seeing about a
              THOUsand cars a day being DUMPED + er at the present time + so we
              need to upDATE our proCEDures to deal with the new situation + and that's
              what we're proPOSing to do + [19]

PRESENTER: well let's be clear what this means + you talk about a twenty-four HOUR
              + + period for example + if a car doesn't have a TAX disc + and it's left for
              twenty-four HOURS does that mean it's taken away and PULPED + [9]

POLITICIAN: no + because there will obviously need to be discretion in relation
              to the VALue of the car what will HAPPen is if the car has no VALue +
              then a notice will be placed on it and then within twenty-four hours it can
              be taken aWAY + + if the car has SOME value + then we're saying per-
              haps SEVEN days is the appropriate TIME [14]

PRESENTER: but if there's an old + car that's that's all but burnt out with you know one
              WHEEL missing and all the rest of it [5]

POLITICIAN: yes if it's an old BANGer that you know w- + when you see it you know
              what it is + + if it's an old banger you can put a notice on it and [. . .] [5]

PRESENTER: who's going to bear the COST of that + [2]

POLITICIAN: + well at the moment it's local authorities they've got a legal DUty the
              problem they've got the real cost for THEM + is that when they take it
              off the STREET + they've then got to KEEP it for up to thirty-five days +
              in case someone wants to claim it BACK ++ and that's where the real costs
              comes IN [11]

The symbol + indicates a short silence (more than 200 milliseconds) and ++ a
longer one (more than 600 milliseconds). There is also another type of pause, known
as a **filled pause**. This is marked by **hesitation markers** such as *erm* or *er* or by **fillers**
such as *you know, I mean to say, do you know what I mean?* or some instances of *well*.

Examine the empty and filled pauses of both presenter and interviewee to establish if
there is a particular part of the sentence where pauses occur quite regularly. Why do
you think the pauses occur there? Now examine the location of the more irregularly
placed pauses. Look at the words that come after them. Do you reach any conclusions
about why these pauses might have occurred?

Activity

Although speech appears to be effortless, it actually requires **planning** and the
components (clauses, words, phonemes) have to be assembled. Many of the pauses
in informal speech reflect this planning operation. They tend to come at or near clause
boundaries, when the speaker has delivered one clause and is preparing the next one.
There is a great deal of evidence that the clause is the major unit of planning in speech.

For example, the vast majority of speech errors occur within a clause. An exchange of words within a clause ('a catful of houses') is much more likely than one which crosses clause boundaries ('I don't know that I'd hear one if I knew it.')

At the end of a clause, we need to remove what is in our speech buffer (i.e. the group of words we have just produced) and to replace it with a new chunk of speech for the next stage of the utterance. Pausing seems to be vital to this process. When experimenters have forced speakers to suppress pausing, it has resulted in confused and sometimes incoherent discourse.

A second reason for pausing is because the speaker finds difficulty in retrieving an item from the lexicon. This may be because of the item itself: it might be an infrequent word or a word that is quite complex in form. Or it may be because of the circumstances of the speaker: they might be tired or ill or simply not concentrating very well. One can identify this kind of hesitation pause because it occurs irregularly and is often just before an infrequent lexical item. (But be careful: speakers also sometimes pause before unusual words in order to draw attention to them.) The situation can be explained in terms of demands upon Working Memory. Retrieving a difficult word makes demands that are heavier than usual, requiring that the speaker focus attention on the task. Or tiredness may restrict the capacity of Working Memory and the speaker's powers of attention, making the retrieval task more challenging than usual.

Pauses serve two other important purposes. At the end of an utterance, they may indicate that the speaker is prepared to hand over the **turn** to the listener. They can also be used rhetorically to indicate that what comes next is of importance.

Activity Figures in square brackets after each turn in the interview show how long it lasted to the nearest second. Count the number of syllables for several turns and work out the speaking rate in syllables per second. Does the rate strike you as being fast or not? Is there a difference in **speaking rate** between presenter and interviewee?

It is important to keep in mind the distinction between speaking rate (reflecting the overall quantity of speech produced) and articulation rate (reflecting how rapidly the speaker formed the syllables). Average articulation rate varies between languages because it partly reflects the types of syllable that a language contains. A typical rate for English is 4.4 to 5.9 syllables a second. The absolute maximum that the human articulators are capable of is probably about eight syllables per second.

People listening to speech in a foreign language often comment that it is 'too fast' to understand. In fact, it is often normal in terms of articulation. What gives the impression of speed may be a lack of pausing. You can understand why this might be problematic. Remember that there are no regular gaps between words in connected speech. A speaker who hesitates and inserts a lot of pauses assists the non-native listener because they mark proportionately more word beginnings and endings.

Activity Now, for each turn, deduct the time taken up by pausing. Allow 250 milliseconds for a filled pause and a + pause; allow 750 milliseconds for a ++ pause. The resulting figures show the approximate amount of time when actual vocalisation was occurring. Calculate the **articulation rate** for each turn in syllables per second. How much faster is it than the speaking rate? Does the amount of pausing time vary between turns?

Now study the length of the **runs** between the pauses. Calculate the number of syllables in some of the shorter ones and some of the longer ones. Do they vary very much? Researchers have sometimes felt that they are able to make a distinction between **hesitant speech** with short runs and **fluent speech** with longer runs. Do you notice any pattern in the interview in terms of switches from hesitancy to fluency and vice versa?

John Laver in his major study of phonetics (1994) suggests that there are three main types of speech. He defines them in relation to the **phonological phrase**, a small chunk of speech, consisting of words which seem to cluster together.

❏   In **continuous fluent speech**, a speaking turn of several phonological phrases is produced without pauses.
❏   In **non-continuous fluent speech**, a speaking turn of several phonological phrases has pauses between the phrases but they coincide with clause boundaries
❏   In **non-continuous hesitant speech**, there are **hesitation pauses** which fall within phonological phrases

Research (e.g. by Beattie 1983) has suggested that speech proceeds in phases: a hesitant phase of about nine clauses is followed by a fluent one of about nine clauses. The pattern is shown in Figure 10.1 below. If this is the case, it suggests that speech planning may take place on two levels. There may be short term planning, marked by relatively regular planning pauses and longer-term planning marked by a period of hesitant speech.

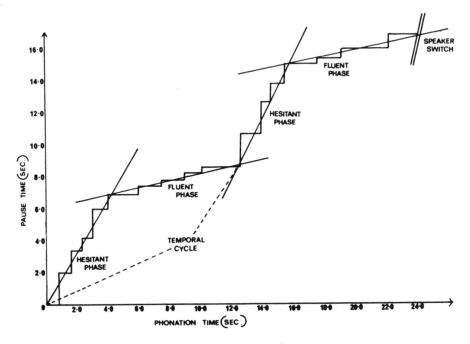

Figure A10.1   Hesitant and fluent phases in speech
Source: Ellis and Beatie, 1986

Activity   Study this figure. It plots time spent pausing against time spent articulating (phonation time = articulation time).

1   What is the significance of lines that are vertical?
2   What is the significance of lines that are horizontal?
3   What does the figure as a whole tell us about hesitant and fluent phases in speech?

A11 **LONG TERM MEMORY AND SCHEMA THEORY**

Theories of memory distinguish between

- **Working** (or Short Term) **Memory** in which currently relevant information is stored temporarily and current processing operations are undertaken (see Section C6).
- Long Term Memory in which permanent information is stored.

This section discusses the nature of Long Term Memory. Section B11 then considers how we construct meaning representations in the mind; and Section C11 examines the part that inference plays in that process.

Long Term Memory (LTM)

Some transfer of information into LTM is intentional and even conscious (as part of a planned piece of learning). Much occurs automatically. Language competence is stored in LTM – including the lexicon and knowledge of the syntactic system.

LTM would appear to involve multiple memory systems, each with different functions. A distinction is made between:

declarative memory (for facts and concepts): knowing *that*
procedural memory (for skills and processes): knowing *how*

John R. Anderson of Carnegie-Mellon University used this as the basis for an influential model of skills acquisition (**ACT***), which shows how certain kinds of declarative knowledge gradually become **proceduralised**. The example often given is learning to drive. The learner driver begins with declarative information, and has to work through a series of steps in a very controlled (= attention-demanding) way. Gradually, as the driver becomes more experienced, two things happen:

- the steps become compressed so that short cuts can be taken
- the procedure becomes more and more automatic.

There are strong advantages to proceduralisation. As the skill becomes more auto-matic, it makes fewer demands on Working Memory. This then makes Working Memory resources available for other activities: in the case of the driver, for observing the road and talking to passengers.

Can you apply this theory to the acquisition of a very different skill – the learning of a second language?

Within declarative memory, a distinction (Tulving 1972) is often made between

episodic memory – memory for specific events and experiences
semantic memory – memory for facts and concepts relating to the world.

1   Consider an infant learning the word DOG. It first associates the word with the family pet. It then gradually realises that DOG represents a whole class of entities. Can you relate this to the two types of declarative memory?
2   Consider a second language learner who acquires the sequence *Have you been waiting long?* by learning a grammar rule for the Present Perfect Progressive. Now consider the 'naturalistic' language learner who picks up the sequence as a com-plete chunk during a conversation with somebody at a bus stop. Can you relate these types of learning to the two types of declarative memory?

Schema Theory

Background knowledge is often essential to an understanding of a text. Our know-ledge of the world is said to be stored in the form of schemas (or, using the original Greek plural, 'schemata'). **Schema Theory** was first proposed in 1932 by the Cambridge memory researcher Sir Frederic Bartlett, and has been considerably expanded since. A schema is a set of interrelated features which we associate with an entity or concept. Here, for example, is a rough idea of the kind of schema that we might hold for the notion TABLE.

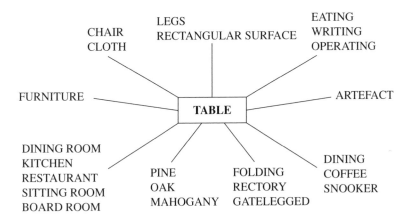

Figure A11.1   A schema for the concept TABLE

When considering how listeners and readers process language information, it is useful to think in terms of three types of schema:

a   'World knowledge': including encyclopedic knowledge and previous knowledge of the speaker or writer. This helps us to construct a **content schema** for a text.

b   Knowledge built up from the text so far: a current meaning representation.

c   Previous experience of this type of text (a **text schema**). This can be extended to include: previous experience of the type of task that the listener/reader has to perform.

Consider how this might apply in practice. You are going to a talk on *the camel*. The speaker is a zoologist who has just returned from doing some research in the Sahara.

Activity   How might you use schematic information to set up expectations before you hear the talk?

The talk begins by considering why the camel is so well suited to life in the desert. It tells you that a camel's hump is not a water store but a food store made of fatty tissue. Because the food store is on the camel's back rather than spread all over its body, the animal is able to keep cool in very hot temperatures. The camel has a double row of eyelashes which prevent sand from getting into its eyes.

Activity   In what way has your content schema been confirmed and in what way has it been adjusted as a result of the talk so far?

The speech event was in the form of a lecture. It was not (say) a discussion in a bar or an interview. Your text schema would lead you to expect the speaker to construct their information in a particular way. Can you suggest how? Your previous experience of this kind of speech event tells you something about how you are expected to perform in relation to the speaker. Can you suggest what?

In brief:

❑   World knowledge serves to
   –   provide a framework for understanding
   –   enable predictions about the text, against which the actual contents are matched
   –   support recall.
❑   Processing a text involves:
   –   setting up a representation of the text so far into which new information is constantly integrated
   –   determining what is / is not important in the text.
❑   Previous experience of a text type helps us to
   –   recognise how information is likely to be distributed
   –   recognise how we should engage with the speaker or writer.

A schema framework

Constructing a content schema may be critical to the understanding of a text.

You have 15 seconds to read the untitled passage that follows.

> You wander around, looking high and low, and fill up a metallic container. Some people know in advance what to put in; others just make things up as they go along. Two important tips. Make sure that you know what today's date is, as it can prove helpful. And don't put hard things on soft. Take the container and unload it on to a rubber surface. The contents travel a short distance Each of the objects, round and square, big and small, has to be put on to a piece of glass. Sometimes weight will be an issue, and money will certainly have to change hands.

Close your book. Try to recall as much as you can of the passage.

You may have found the recall task quite difficult because you lacked the schematic background that a title would have provided. The omitted title was: 'In the super-market'. Read the text again, and see how this information assists understanding.

The exercise you have just done is admittedly a rather artificial one – based on a famous experiment (Bransford and Johnson 1973) which involved a similarly obscure text on using a washing machine. However, it serves to underline the importance of having a pre-established framework when you read a text.

Shared knowledge

A special type of schema relates to our knowledge of familiar events. Schank and Abelson (1977) termed it a **script**. A script creates a set of expectations which enable us to deal with everyday encounters such as, for example, going into a restaurant.

Describe, step by step, your script for eating in a restaurant. You want a table for three, but you have not made a reservation. What happens when you walk through the door? To what extent does your script shape the form of the communication you have with the manager/owner of the restaurant and with the waiter who serves you?

One of the most important effects of a script is the way it enables writers and speakers to adopt a kind of shorthand. Consider the opening line from a chapter of Dashiell Hammett's *Maltese Falcon* (Cassell, 1930): 'A telephone bell rang in darkness'. What Hammett does not need to spell out is that somebody somewhere looked up Sam Spade's number, picked up a telephone receiver, put their finger in the dial and dialled the number – and that this had the effect of making Sam's phone ring. All of this is part of a script for making a phone call which both author and reader are assumed to share.

A few sentences later, Hammett writes: 'A switch clicked and a white bowl hung on three gilded chains from the ceiling's centre filled the room with light'. Here, the writer relies again upon the assumption that certain knowledge is shared with the reader. What is shared this time is not a script but a more general schema. In order to under-stand the sentence, we must be capable of making an association between switches and electric lights, and must possess the knowledge that light fittings are often suspended from the middle of the ceiling.

Here is a final example, illustrating the importance of having a schematic framework in order to achieve understanding:

Heard on the radio: *He has a good chin.*

What do you make of it? Would it help to know that it was during a boxing commentary?

EXCEPTIONAL CIRCUMSTANCES

This section offers a brief look at the way in which psycholinguistics can provide insights into the processing problems of those with language difficulties – supporting the work of general practitioners, psychiatrists and speech therapists.

The term 'exceptional circumstances' can be taken to include:

– studies of the effects of deafness or blindness upon language
– studies of **language disorders** where some aspect of linguistic processing is impaired
– studies of individuals with cognitive difficulties where at least part of the language faculty is spared.

An important consideration is whether the circumstances affect language in terms of

❏ **delay** in acquisition – where, for example, a child of a physical age of five shows the language competence of a child of three; or
❏ **deviance** from standard forms – where a child acquires language in an order that is different from most others; or where a child or adult produces language that diverges markedly from that of most native speakers.

Sensory impairment

Deafness
Modern approaches to deaf education prioritise the teaching of sign language. This means that many profoundly deaf people are regarded as possessing a language in which they are fluent – namely Sign. For them, spoken and written English are effectively a late-acquired second language, mediated through **Sign**. A research project exploring this perspective on deafness will be described in Section C12.

A major issue has been the extent to which prelinguistic deafness affects language acquisition. There is evidence that it leads to delayed acquisition – infants may reach the fifty-word threshold around ten months later than their hearing peers.

But experts are unsure whether the route taken in acquisition deviates from that of a hearing infant.

Blindness

Does visual impairment lead to delays in language acquisition, given that the child receives no support from adult facial expressions, gestures or the sight of objects in the environment? Blind infants certainly appear to acquire a phonological system a little more slowly than is normal. They sometimes confuse phonemes which are similar in manner of articulation but visually distinct: for example, /n/ and /m/. Their first words emerge at about the same time as those of sighted infants. However, there may be some differences in the content of the early vocabulary. Blind children generally engage less in sorting activities; this suggests that blindness may limit the capacity to form categories, with consequences for vocabulary acquisition.

Language disorders

Language disorders can be **developmental** (i.e. present from early childhood) or they can be **acquired** as the result of surgery, a stroke, an accident or old age. Section B3 looks briefly at acquired impairment in relation to studies of the brain; here, our concern is with developmental impairment. The areas of research can be divided into those which deal with linguistic impairment alone (this section) and those which raise questions about the relationship between language and cognition (p. 44).

❏ **Problems of fluency**. For some speakers, the problems are largely psychological, as in the case of stuttering, examined in Section B12. Other speakers have difficulty because of physiological problems involving malformation or misoperation of the articulators (mouth, tongue, jaws, palate, etc.). Cases such as these might appear to lie outside the scope of psycholinguistics. However, they raise interesting questions about the nature of language and of language acquisition.
   – What is the precise relationship between perception and production? Is a child's ability to discriminate sounds affected when it cannot produce them accurately?
   – Does a child achieve full competence in its language when it is mainly restricted to listening to it rather than producing it?
   – Does inability to produce spoken sounds affect **inner speech**, the 'voice in the head' reported by many readers and writers? Does it limit the ability to acquire grapheme-phoneme correspondences (Section A8) – connections between written letters and the way they are pronounced?
   Current evidence suggests that that, so long as hearing and intelligence are not impaired, the inability to articulate the sounds of speech does not prevent a child from developing language understanding or inner speech.
❏ **Problems of written language**. A distinction is made between **dyslexia** (reading difficulty) and **dysgraphia** (writing difficulty), though many 'dyslexics' manifest both. The degree of impairment varies greatly between individuals; as do specific symptoms. Some dyslexics appear to suffer from a phonological deficit – they have problems in guessing the spellings of non-words. Others show signs of a 'whole word' deficit and cannot recall the spellings of unusual words.

Activity Can you relate this to the 'dual-route' model of reading (Section A8)?

Dyslexia shows up as a mismatch between low achievement in reading and an average or high level of intelligence. However, it is often accompanied by difficulty in specific cognitive areas – including spatial relationships (left vs right, east vs west), temporal relationships (times, dates and months of the year) and mathematical operations. There is evidence that dyslexia may be genetically transmitted. T. R. Miles, who spent his career studying dyslexia, comments (1993: 190–1):

> . . . there may be an anomaly of development which sometimes gives rise to an unusual balance of skills. This anomaly is sometimes, but not always, the result of hereditary factors. Reasoning is unaffected, and in some areas such as art or engineering there may be exceptional talent. There are weaknesses, however, which may show themselves as early as age 3 in spoken language and thereafter when the child is required to deal with written language.

We will examine an example of dyslexic writing in Section B12.

The relationship between language and cognition

It is a remarkable fact that nearly all human beings grow up to achieve full competence in their native tongue, regardless of wide variations in their intelligence and environment. This has suggested to some commentators that language may develop independently of general cognition. Confusingly, some of the evidence of language acquired in 'exceptional circumstances' appears to contradict this hypothesis, while some appears to support it.

❏ Studies of **Down's Syndrome** suggest a connection between cognitive impairment and failure to acquire full linguistic competence. Down's sufferers show limitations of attention, short-term memory and perceptual discrimination; they also have difficulty with symbolic representation of any kind. All of this appears to affect language performance, though there is great variation between individuals. Phonological development is slow. Only a limited vocabulary is acquired, and utterances usually remain short and **telegraphic** (lacking function words and inflections). There has been much discussion as to whether language development in Down's sufferers is different in kind from that of unaffected children or simply delayed. The issue is hard to resolve because of the wide differences in individual performance, and because a delay in one area of language (say, a limited vocabulary) might well affect the course of another (say, length of utterance).

❏ **Autism** represents a combination of cognitive and social impairment. Child sufferers may be mute until the age of five, or may do little more than echo the words that adults say to them. Underlying the condition appears to be a failure to relate to others, and thus to appreciate the value of communication. One theory suggests that autistic children lack a **theory of mind** – the ability to see the world from the point of view of another person. All aspects of communication seem to suffer in autistic individuals, with the possible exception of phonology. The development of language skills is not just delayed but is deviant as well.

Down's Syndrome and autism appear to demonstrate links between cognitive development and language. However, the reverse is suggested by three other situations: one where language is impaired but cognition is not, and two where cognition is impaired but language is not.

❑ **Specific Language Impairment**: on rare occasions, a child who appears otherwise normal fails to acquire language like its peers. These children achieve a linguistic competence that is less than complete: they sometimes have restricted vocabularies or make relatively basic errors of grammar. They may show problems of comprehension as well as problems of production: finding it difficult to follow the utterances of others or to put thoughts into words. In particular, they seem to have difficulty in sustaining a contextual framework for a conversation. What is striking is that this linguistic deficit cannot be clearly linked to low intelligence or cognitive impairment. It is known as Specific Language Impairment (**SLI**) because it appears to affect language but not other faculties.

Some commentators have suggested that SLI may result from a deficit in the child's ability to recognise recurring patterns such as inflections in the language it encounters. Such a deficit could be specifically linguistic (a gap in the child's innate Universal Grammar) but it might also be perceptual or cognitive (a lack of auditory pattern-matching skill). Two different accounts of SLI are contrasted in Section D12. Dorothy Bishop, who has researched comprehension in SLI for many years, raises a third possibility (1997: 37): that SLI may not be a unitary disorder but the result of a combination of several different language impairments.

❑ Sufferers from **Williams Syndrome** present symptoms which are the reverse of those of SLI sufferers. They show signs of cognitive impairment, including low IQs, yet their language competence appears to be relatively unaffected. This may be due to imbalances in brain structure, with a reduction of some areas but a sparing of the cerebellum and frontal lobes. The neurologist Terrence Deacon comments (1997: 268):

> [Williams Syndrome] is characterised by highly verbal individuals who seem adept at storytelling and recitation of verbal information, but who also exhibit major cognitive deficits in analysing thematic-level language processes, very poor problem-solving abilities and very impaired spatial reasoning. Though they may have IQ scores in the range of 50, their vocabulary and speaking skills test above normal at early ages. . . . they are also intensely social and gregarious . . .

❑ A similar mystery attends **savants**. These are individuals who are severely mentally impaired, but show exceptional gifts, usually in relation to painting and music. Recently, a savant has been discovered who possesses such gifts for language. Christopher was diagnosed as brain-damaged early in life and has to live in care. Yet he is able to translate from, and communicate in, some sixteen languages.

Modularity

There are those who believe that language and cognition are interconnected and that the acquisition of language goes hand in hand with the development of cognition. There are others who believe that language is **modular**: a separate faculty, supported by cognitive processes but not dependent upon them. The evidence from SLI, Williams Syndrome and Christopher is often cited in support of the second position. As Neil Smith and Ianthi Tsimpli put it (1995: 3):

> The existence of these varied conditions provides a classical example of double dissociation: language can be impaired in someone of otherwise normal intelligence, and – more surprisingly – someone with intelligence impaired by brain damage may none the less have normal, or even enhanced, linguistic ability. It is worth emphasising that this latter possibility constitutes a refutation of any position that insists on 'cognitive prerequisites' for the development of language.

Terrence Deacon takes a different view (1997: 269):

> Intelligence isn't a unitary brain function, and language isn't walled off from other cognitive functions. Nevertheless, in Williams syndrome we see a deficit in which cognitive functions are splintered in a manner that selectively spares certain processes most critical to language development . . . [This suggests that] the type of learning biases that favour [the] symbolic learning [involved in language acquisition] may be quite different . . . to those useful in the majority of other learning contexts.

Section B

DEVELOPMENT:
DATA

DATA IN PSYCHOLINGUISTICS

Activity 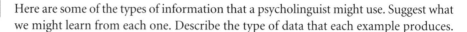 Here are some of the types of information that a psycholinguist might use. Suggest what we might learn from each one. Describe the type of data that each example produces.

Example 1:

A: Tell me about this marble.

B: Well, it's about half and half. It's a marble and it's half and half. Uhm, that uhm, I'm trying to think what the and ya know and I've been doing all this colour work and uhm, I'm trying to think. There's a white and there's a black and there's a, uhm, uhm, I'm trying to think, uh, it's, like uhm, oh, what that called? Ym, more of a, oh damn, in the colours that I have in my book is uhm more vivid, and this is a little darker, and I'm trying to think, what's it called purple, more on the purple order this is.

(Source: Dingwall 1998)

Example 2:

An experimenter shows subjects groups of four letters on a computer screen. They have to press a button every time the group of letters represents an actual word.

Example: PLIT – BRON – GIVE – ADGE – LIMP – MISH – DASE – READ – GALF – BARK – CLON – STIR – KNOW – GACK

The experimenter measures (in milliseconds) how much time elapses between the letters appearing on the screen and the subject pressing the button when appropriate. Reaction Time to GIVE, READ and KNOW is faster than to LIMP, BARK and STIR.

Example 3:

B: I'm tryin' to figure it out . . . it doesn't really make sense . . . live better . . . (laugh) . . . in society than French . . . I mean the French . . . it kinda means oh well, maybe let me just go on further . . . and see . . . *ils ont plus de form* . . . *de* . . . courtesy Oh. This is the harder one, right? (laughs) *Ils ont plus* . . . *de for* . . . *formules* . . . *de* . . . courts . . . they have more . . . they have more . . . of . . . oh . . . huh . . . yeah, so it must be they live better in society. That's what it says . . . ? than the French . . . controversial statement . . . uh . . . they have . . . *de* . . . they have greater, they have more . . . have more . . . I was wondering uh . . . *manière* . . . for . . . have courtesy, courtesy . . .

(Gerloff 1987)

Example 4:

Subjects hear a word and are asked to write down the first word that comes into their mind. Example: Subjects hear BUTTER; and their responses (Jenkins 1970) include *bread, yellow, soft, fat, knife, eggs, cream, milk, cheese.* The researcher calculates how many people gave each response. *Bread* turns out to be the most frequent.

Activity Examples 5 and 6 represent two contrasting approaches to psycholinguistic research. How do they differ?

Example 5:

A researcher wants to discover which words are most easily recalled from a list. Subjects are asked to read a list and then tested on their recall of it. Their answers are checked to see whether they remember best:

- words from the beginning, middle or end
- longer words or short words
- words which are connected semantically to the words before them or words which are unconnected.

Example 6:

Chomskyan theory maintained that there was a clause boundary after *Kate* in sentence (a) below but after *expected* in sentences (b) and (c). Other grammarians disagreed.

a   John expected Kate at the party.
b   John expected Kate to be at the party.
c   John expected Kate would be at the party.

A researcher (Cooper 1976) recorded people reading aloud the three sentences, and found that in sentences (b) and (c), they lengthened the word *expected* in a way that often marks the ends of clauses. This suggested that Chomsky's account was correct.

The techniques used by psycholinguists can be:

- ❏   **observational**: derived from recording linguistic behaviour (Example 1)
- ❏   **experimental**: derived from setting linguistic tests (Examples 2, 4)
- ❏   based upon **self-report**: where a subject describes a linguistic process as they are experiencing it or shortly afterwards (Example 3).

The results they derive can be:

- ❏   **qualitative**: featuring examples of the kinds of language used (Examples 1, 3)
- ❏   **quantitative**: with aspects of language behaviour represented numerically

Quantitative data can be the result of:

- ❏   **counting**. How many times did a word occur? How many people responded in a particular way? How many errors were made? (Example 4)
- ❏   **measuring**. How fast was the subject's reaction? How did subjects rate the truth or grammaticality of a sentence? (Example 2)

Psycholinguistic research can operate in two directions:

- ❏   **theory-driven**: it can take a well-established theory and attempt to provide evidence of the theory in terms of how people behave (Example 6). The theory might be a linguistic one (telling us about the structure of a particular language); the psycholinguistic experiment might then attempt to show that the theory was **psychologically real** – i.e. that it really represented the way in which the human mind processes speech.

❑   **data-driven**: it can examine evidence obtained through observation or experiment, and go on to suggest the best way of accounting for it (Example 5).

In many cases, a psycholinguist will start out with a hypothesis based upon observation and will put it to the test by designing an experiment. The problem with data drawn from observation is that real-life activities sometimes involve not one but several processes used in combination. They may also feature a large number of **variables**. For example:

–   The people observed might be of widely different ages or educational backgrounds.
–   More contextual information might be available in some cases than in others.
–   Some situations might cause more anxiety than others.

The advantage of using experimental conditions is that the study can focus upon a single task type. The variables can be **controlled**, so far as possible, ensuring that the subjects all fit one type or that they cover a representative range. Steps can be taken to ensure that the conditions under which the subjects operate are as similar as possible.

However, it is clearly important make sure that the experimental conditions reproduce, so far as is possible, those of real-life language processing.

ANIMAL COMMUNICATION

Design features
In order to decide if animals do or not possess language, we need to specify more precisely what we mean by 'language'.

Activity   What for you are the main characteristics of language? Think in terms of

–   how a message is transmitted
–   the relationship between the word and what it refers to
–   how we acquire language
–   the forms that are typical of language
–   what distinguishes speech from writing and other forms of communication
–   how you would describe the participants in a conversation.

An early attempt to characterise language was made by the linguist Charles Hockett, who produced (1963) a list of the most important **design features** of human speech. Many can be taken as applying to language as a whole rather than just to speech. The list below is based upon the most important of Hockett's features, but they have been regrouped. Some of Hockett's terms have been modified and additions suggested by more recent commentators have been included. Look briefly at what is included under each heading.

Channel
1 **Use of a vocal-auditory channel**: speech is based on sounds.
2 **Interchangeability**: the same person is able both to transmit and to receive messages.
3 **Complete feedback**: while speaking, we can monitor what we are saying.

Semantic features
4 **Semanticity**: we use symbols to refer to a class of objects or actions in the real world.
5 **Arbitrariness**: there is no direct connection between a word and what it refers to.
6 **Discreteness**: language is based upon a vocabulary of independent, moveable units.
7 **Displacement**: we use speech to refer to things in other times or places.

Learning
8 **Cultural transmission**: one generation transmits speech to the next.
9 **Learnability**: we can learn additional languages from those who speak them.

Structure
10 **Creativity**: we can form an infinite range of utterances, many of which we have never heard or said before.
11 **Duality of patterning**: smaller units (e.g. phonemes) are combined into larger ones (words).
12 **Structure dependence**: all known languages have a hierarchical phrase structure.

Use
13 **Control**: speech is used intentionally, unlike many involuntary sounds.
14 **Specialisation**: the forms of speech (sounds, words) serve no other purpose.
15 **Spontaneous usage**: speech does not need to be premeditated.
16 **Turn taking**: we speak, then allow the other speaker to respond.
17 **Prevarication**: we can use speech to tell lies (and can use it figuratively).
18 **Reflectiveness**: we can use language to comment on language.

Animal communciation

Here are some types of animal communication which appear to resemble language. Choose three types and use Hockett's criteria to decide if they can or cannot be described as language-like.

- ❑ **Parrots** are capable of learning chunks of human speech and of repeating them with even the intonation patterns intact. Consider features 1, 4, 6, 8 and 10.
- ❑ **Dogs** learn to associate the word FOOD with eating. They might salivate on hearing the word, even before their bowl is put in front of them. Consider features 2, 4 and 7. What would happen if, on several successive occasions, the dog heard the word FOOD and no food was produced?
- ❑ **Vervet monkeys** have been found to use three different alarm calls according to the type of danger that threatens them: one that warns of a large predatory mammal such as a leopard, one for an eagle and one for a snake. The rest of the

vervet troop clearly understand these calls as they respond in an appropriate way: jumping into a tree to avoid a leopard, jumping out of a tree when an eagle is approaching, and searching the grass if a snake is signalled. Other troop members pick up the call and repeat it. Consider features 2, 4, 5, 7, 10, 13, 15 and 17.

❏ **Bird communication** takes the form of simple **calls** and more elaborate **songs**. Calls are used when flocking, nesting or warning of danger; they occasionally signal aggression. Songs resemble language in that single meaningless notes are combined to form complex patterns. However, they appear to serve only two main purposes: to mark out territory and to attract a mate. They are used almost exclusively by males, though they sometimes give rise to turn-taking duets, where two birds try to outsing each other. In some species of bird, the song is almost entirely innate; in others, it is acquired through exposure to adult song, and in others, it is partly innate and partly learnt. Consider features 2, 5, 7, 8, 10, 11, 14 and 16.

❏ **Worker bees** perform a ritual **dance** to show their fellows where to find sources of nectar. They turn round in circles to indicate that the source is close to the hive. Alternatively, they waggle their abdomens to signal that the source is some way away. The tempo of the waggle indicates how far the source is, as does the speed at which the dancer beats its wings. The angle of the bee's body indicates the direction of the nectar; but the bee can only provide forward directions and has no way of indicating 'up' and 'down'. The dance is only performed by worker bees – and appears to be innate (genetically transmitted rather than learnt). Consider features 1, 2, 5, 7, 8, 10, 13, 14 and 16.

❏ **Dolphins** communicate under water by means of a system of 'clicks': irregular bursts of sound lasting about a millisecond and inaudible by human beings. Besides transmitting information, the clicks seem to operate as a kind of radar: their echoes enabling dolphins to locate undersea objects extremely accurately. Consider features 1, 2, 4, 13, and 14.

Some conclusions

a   Much 'animal speech' is no more than mimicry. A parrot trained to speak is repeating the form of human speech with no understanding of meaning.

b   When animals are trained to respond to language, no necessary link is established between word and object. A dog might be trained to beg when it hears the word FOOD followed by a reward. But the association would be abandoned if the rewards ceased or the dog was punished for begging.

c   Some forms of animal communication show one or two of the features which characterise language. None shows all or even most of them.

d   Let us suppose that animals are capable of language and only held back by their cognitive limitations (limited powers of thought). Then we might expect to find some animals communicating in a simplified form of language. None of the examples cited remotely fits this case.

e   Though complex, language is learnt by human infants without any specific teaching. Admittedly, successful acquisition does depend upon the infant being exposed to adult forms.

Activity

Consider this: should we be trying at all to compare animal communication with our own? Or should we be looking for other criteria to judge its effectiveness? Animal needs are much simpler than ours; it may be that evolution has equipped them with as much capacity for communication as they require and no more. Neurologists have pointed out that language comes at a large cost in terms of brain connections dedicated to communication.

LOCALISING LANGUAGE IN THE BRAIN

B3

Over the years, commentators have taken two views of the place of language in the brain:

a   that language is restricted to a single location or a limited number of locations
b   that language is widely **distributed** throughout the brain.

In this section, we examine some of the evidence they have uncovered.
Evidence for (a) would support the idea that we possess a language faculty that is independent of other thought processes – though evidence for (b) would not rule it out.

Evidence from aphasia

Early attempts to localise language in the brain relied heavily upon evidence from individuals who had suffered damage to a particular part of the brain as result of an accident, a stroke or surgery. In certain cases, this had a marked effect upon their ability to communicate in speech or in writing.

In 1863, a French surgeon, Paul Broca, described the severe language impairment of some twenty patients. In nineteen cases, the problems with language appeared to have resulted from a brain lesion on the left side of the head, just in front of the ear and slightly below the top of it (technically, the lower part of the left frontal lobe). Later, in 1874, a German doctor, Carl Wernicke, demonstrated a language deficit associated with damage to a different area. This one was just behind and above the left ear (the posterior part of the temporal lobe).

The two areas identified by these researchers have become known, respectively, as **Broca's area** and **Wernicke's area**, and seem to be especially closely associated with the processing of language by the brain. Damage to either will often (but not always) lead to a condition known as **aphasia**, in which patients lose some of their powers of speech. The type of language impairment varies considerably according to which of the two areas is damaged.

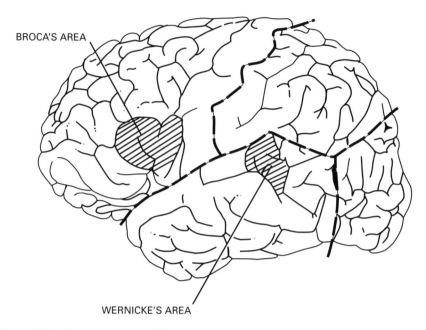

BROCA'S AREA

WERNICKE'S AREA

Figure B3.1 Broca's area and Wernicke's area
Source: Bishop (1997: 40)

Activity ✪ Below are transcripts of the speech of two patients, one suffering from Broca's aphasia and one suffering from Wernicke's aphasia (Source: Crystal and Varley 1998: 167–9).

1 Can you identify the differences between them and suggest which aspects of language may have been damaged?
2 When you have done so, consider: how reliable is it to use this kind of data as evidence for language localisation?

Broca's aphasia
A: they do all sorts of activities/ . woodwork and
B: no/ me cook/
A: you cook/ great/
B: aye/ . once a week/
A: yeah/ . that's today/ Thursday/
B: aye/ . and then/ – night-time/ seven o'clock swimming/
A: really/
B: yes / . smashing/
A: how do you manage one-handed/
B: oh it's all right/ aye/ . mate/ . mate . Jack comes and all/ but – er/ . oh dear/.Jack –
   er . old/ er – seventy/ . no . sixty-eight/ . Jack/ – but swim/ . me . me like this/ –
   swimming – er/ – I can't say it/ – but Jack/ – er – swimming on front/ . er – back
A: so he can do –
B: aye/ but one hand

Wernicke's aphasia

A: so you were at Dunkirk/

B: yes/

A: what do you remember of that/

B: [nə nə] not very far because they kicked us out/

A: do/ did you have to get a boat from the beach/

B: yes/ but then we had to come back because they were/ – [sə psə psə psə] they were sending things down/ you know/ so we came back/ . we came back/ and we came up from – / right up / then we got out/ – once/ – er er a gun/ er no/ . what do they call them/ the very little/ – the small men/ . the small –

A: the small men/

B: no/ small soldiers/ . no/ the other one/ . say . not soldier/ . not soldier– /

B: are they the Gurkhas/

B: no/ . no/ . what's the opposite to a soldier/

A: sailor

B: that's it/

Key: In both cases, A is the therapist and B the patient.
End of each unit of intonation marked by /
Pauses marked by . (short) and – (longer)

Characteristics of aphasia

Different symptoms are associated with Broca's and with Wernicke's aphasia. However, it should be stressed that the symptoms vary greatly from patient to patient.

Table B3.1 A comparison of Broca's and Wernicke's aphasia

Broca's aphasia	Wernicke's aphasia
Effortful speech; much pausing	Effortless speech – fluent, rapid
Almost no syntax	Syntactically well-structured, complex
Few function words or affixes	Function words, affixes
Mainly concrete nouns	Many general nouns (e.g. *thing, person*) and verbs (e.g. *do, go*)
Comprehension often good; but may use positional and semantic cues rather than fully understanding meaning	Comprehension often severely impaired

There are a number of problems in relying too heavily upon evidence based upon brain damage.

1 Language processing by brain-damaged patients may not provide a good model of language processing by normal users.

2 Many sufferers manifest some but not all of the symptoms listed above.

3 There are patients who have suffered damage to the areas identified by Broca and Wernicke, without showing signs of language impairment. This suggests that the location of these sensitive areas may vary somewhat from one individual to another.

Brain imaging

Research into brain and language no longer has to rely solely upon evidence of aphasia. The most recent methods make use of **brain imaging** techniques: these track the electrical impulses or changes to blood flow which result from heightened brain activity. One such technique is **PET** (positron emission tomography).

> In an ingenious experiment, researchers set subjects three tasks of increasing complexity and used PET to monitor the way in which blood flow changed in their brains. In Step 1, subjects simply listened to a rapid list of words. In Step 2, they repeated the words as they heard them; and in Step 3, they were asked to say words which were associated with those they heard.
>
> Researchers monitored the increased brain activity that occurred as the tasks became more demanding. The images below (based on Posner and Raichle 1994) indicate the areas of the brain which became newly activated at each stage.

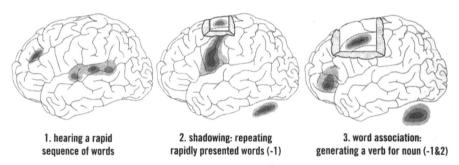

| 1. hearing a rapid sequence of words | 2. shadowing: repeating rapidly presented words (-1) | 3. word association: generating a verb for noun (-1&2) |

Figure B3.2 Increased brain activity with increased task difficulty
Source: Adapted from Deacon (1997: 296)

Activity ✪ a What is involved in each successive task? Think in terms of:

form vs meaning – articulation (pronouncing words) – matching sounds to words – thinking of other words – short-term memory.

Why does the motor strip down the centre of the hemisphere become involved in Step 2?

b Examine the areas of the brain which became active at each stage and compare them with those identified by Broca and Wernicke (Figure B3.1). Broca thought that he had discovered where in the brain language was stored. Does the imaging evidence support this view?

c Think of the operation of the brain as depending upon millions of nerve connections. If language is as distributed as the images above suggest – is there any way we can account for the extreme effects of damage to Broca's or to Wernicke's area?

Evidence from brain imaging suggests that language is widely distributed throughout the brain. There is even evidence that different lexical sets (colours, foods, tools) may be stored in different places. The brain seems to differentiate between two types of language processing – with the central parts looking after more rapid analytic operations (e.g. recognising phonemes) and other parts looking after the slower, associative operations (e.g. building meaning).

How can we square this with evidence of the loss of language when there is damage to Broca's or Wernicke's area? If language is widely distributed across the brain, then it must rely upon a massive system of nerve connections to transmit and assemble it. It seems likely that the Broca and Wernicke areas represent major junctions for these networks. So what is damaged in an aphasic patient is not a separate 'language store' but the ability to transmit language across vital neural links.

LEXICAL FORM

In this section we consider precisely what information is stored in the mental lexicon.

What constitutes a lexical entry?

Consider the following group of words:

WALK – WALKS – WALKED – WALKING

They could be represented in two ways in the lexicon:

a   with an entry for each of the four words
b   by the stem WALK plus a set of rules for adding inflections to it.

To find out how inflections are stored in the lexicon, we need to examine the way in which speakers assemble inflected words. We can do this by studying the errors that speakers make. They show what can happen when the assembly process goes wrong. Below are some examples (Aitchison 1994: 124) of **Slips of the Tongue** which involve inflections. What do they suggest about the way in which we produce the inflected forms of verbs? Do they favour (a) or (b) above?

It waits to pay.
She wash upped the dishes.
I'd forgot abouten that.
I want to get a cash checked.
All the men who fighted in it.

Now consider the word HAPPY. Do we assume that we have separate lexical entries for HAPPY – UNHAPPY – HAPPINESS – UNHAPPINESS? Or is there just a single entry for HAPPY? Here, the situation is rather different since we are dealing with **derivational morphology**. When we form UNHAPPY from HAPPY, we effectively create a new unit of meaning (or **lexeme**) – a word which might qualify for separate entry in a dictionary in a way that WALKED would not.

Another difference is that the connection between HAPPY and UNHAPPY is not fixed by a rule like the connection between WALK and WALKED. There are many ways of forming the opposite of an English adjective, including *dis-* (*dishonest*), *in-* (*insufficient*) and *non-* (*non-alcoholic*); it just happens that the appropriate prefix for HAPPY is UN-. If we assume that words like UNHAPPY are assembled rather than stored, then we need some kind of record in our lexical entry, telling us that UN- is the appropriate prefix to attach and DIS- is not.

To summarise: it seems to make sense to think of inflectional morphology as being specially assembled to fit a syntactic context. But the case for derivational forms is not so clear and indeed the evidence is contradictory. There are two general possibilities.

Solution A

Separate entries for all derived forms of a word (HAPPY – UNHAPPY – HAPPINESS – UNHAPPINESS – HAPPILY), with close links between them.

Solution B

An entry for the base form of the word (HAPPY) but not for derived forms. Separate entries for productive prefixes and suffixes. Strong links between HAPPY and UN- and HAPPY and -NESS, but none between HAPPY and DIS- or -MENT.

Those who favour this second solution suggest that a speaker assembles words such as UNHAPPY by first accessing the base form HAPPY and then adding on the prefix UN-. A listener processes the word UNHAPPY by disassembling it (a process known as **prefix-stripping**) and then accessing the meanings of HAPPY and UN- individually.

Activity   Consider:

1   Which of these solutions is the more demanding in terms of what we have to store in our minds?
2   Which seems the simpler and more rapid process?
3   Compare the two forms RECEIVE and REVISIT. Might one be a better candidate for Solution (B) than the other?

A phonological / orthographic representation

Most people assume that the identification of a word is the result of a simple matching process. We read the sequence GREEN and we match it to the stored orthographic representation GREEN in our lexicon. Or we hear the sequence /gri:n/ and we find an exact match in a stored phonological representation /gri:n/. A moment's thought will reveal that the process cannot be this straightforward. We might encounter the written form of GREEN in any one of the following shapes:

GREEN   green   ***green***   *green*   green   green

So what precise form does the orthographic representation take?

The same question can be posed of the phonological representation. We might assume that many speakers of southern British English have the word ENVELOPE stored in a phonological citation form as /'ɒnvələʊp/. But how then do they recognise the word in its alternative pronunciation /'envələʊp/? How do they recognise /'ɒnvəloːp/, the form used by many northern British speakers? Or /'ɒnvləʊp/ as it might be pronounced in more casual speech? It is evident that the spoken forms of words are subject to even greater variation than the written. Even within the speech of one individual, the pronunciation of a word varies according to where it occurs in an utterance, how rapidly the person is speaking and how much importance is placed on the word.

What kind of phonological representation can deal with all this variation? A number of solutions are possible. Here are three.

Solution A
The lexical entry includes all possible phonological variations of a word: it includes all the different versions of the word ENVELOPE that have been mentioned

Solution B
The lexical entry includes a single standard form of the word. But it is **under-specified**. In other words, when we hear the word spoken, we do not assume that all the phonological features will be present – just some. The principle is one of achieving the **best match** for the word that we hear, not a perfect match.

Solution C
The lexical entry includes a 'core value' for the word together with a range of tolerances around that value. Again, we do not expect a perfect match – but we recognise that the variations we hear may deviate from the 'core value' in relatively systematic ways.

Consider these solutions.   Activity

1   Which is the most demanding in terms of how much we have to store in our minds? Which is the most efficient in terms of storage?
2   Which enables a match to be found most rapidly?
3   Which takes most account of the ways in which words vary?
4   Do you think that any of the three is more convincing than the others?

The trade-off between storage and access
We have examined some proposals about what a lexical entry contains. They remain theoretical models because we do not have enough evidence to be sure which one is correct. But in considering them, you have achieved an important realisation about language processing. There often appears to be a trade-off between the amount of detail that we need to store in our minds and the ease of retrieving this information. Thus, a model of a simple and direct way of processing linguistic information will often involve a heavy burden in terms of how much information has to be stored in the mind. Conversely, if we try to streamline our account of what we need to store, we may find that we have to accept a more complicated process for accessing and using the information involved.

WORD ASSOCIATION

Words are stored in the lexicon with connections to other words. Words can be connected:

– by meaning
– by form (similarities in the way they are said or the way they are written).

In this section, we investigate how words are associated with each other and why.

Association by meaning

Semantic sets

Semantics offers a principled theory of the relationships between words. One of the interests of studying lexical storage is to establish if these relationships are psychologically real. Are words actually stored in our minds in sets like those suggested by semanticists? Semantics suggests three main types of association:

❑ **semantic fields**: where words are grouped according to the topic area that they fall into: *buildings, household utensils, family relationships*.

❑ **sense relations**: linking words through similarities and differences of meaning:
   a   **synonyms**: words sharing a similar meaning (though complete synonymy is rare)
   b   **opposites**: words with opposed meanings of several kinds. They might be:

   binary antonyms (*alive / dead*)
   gradable antonyms (*hot / cold*)
   converses (*buy / sell*)
   multiply incompatible words (*summer / winter*)

   c   **hyponyms**: words that are members of the same category.

   dog is a hyponym of *animal*.
   animal is a **superordinate** of *dog*
   Within the category ANIMAL, *dog* and *cat* are **co-hyponyms**.

❑ **collocates**: word which frequently appear together.

   Some collocates are **co-ordinates**: *cup and saucer, knife and fork*
   Some collocates **co-occur**: *heavy + smoker, post + letter, door + handle*

Experimental evidence

❑ **Word association experiments**: One of the earliest experiments in language psychology was the word association task. Subjects read or heard a word, then said the first word which came to mind. The results of this task provide useful insights into how words are stored in the lexicon.

Activity

Table B5.1 shows the commonest responses in order of frequency to the four stimuli BUTTERFLY, HUNGRY, RED and SALT. Look at the categories outlined above, and identify what appear to be the strongest semantic links between words.

Table B5.1 Commonest word association responses to four stimuli

	Butterfly	Hungry	Red	Salt
1	moth	food	white	pepper
2	insect	eat	blue	sugar
3	wing(s)	thirsty	black	water
4	bird	full	green	taste
4	fly	starved	colour	sea
6	yellow	stomach	blood	bitter
7	net	tired	communist	shaker
8	pretty	dog	yellow	food
9	flower(s)	pain	flag	ocean
10	bug	man	bright	lake

Source: Aitchison (1994), based on Jenkins (1970)

In word association tasks, subjects usually respond with a word associated with the stimulus in terms of meaning rather than form. This suggests that meaning associations in the lexicon are stronger than those based on similarity of pronunciation or spelling. Adults tend to choose a word in the same word class as the stimulus.

The meaning association is usually based upon semantic groupings rather than upon physical resemblance (needle associates with thread rather than with nail). The three strongest types of association appear to be: co-ordination (salt and pepper), collocation (butterfly and net, salt and water) and superordination (butterfly and insect). However, co-hyponyms (butterfly and moth, red and green), synonyms (hungry and starving) and opposites (hungry and thirsty) also feature.

❑ **Slips of the Tongue.** Much of the evidence of how words are stored and associated in the lexicon comes from Slips of the Tongue, mistakes made by speakers who produce a wrong or non-existent word instead of the one they intended to produce. By comparing the wrong word with the target one, we can often get an idea of the kind of criteria a speaker was using in their word search.

Here are several examples of slips based upon meaning. Describe the type of mistake in each of the two groups. What is the connection between the target word and the one that was said?   Activity

GROUP 1

a   he got hot under the belt (= collar)
b   I thought westerns were where people ride horses instead of cows (= cars)
c   when were you last on the west . . . east coast?

d   It's at the bottom – I mean – top of the stack of books
e   This room is too damn hot – cold
f   butterpillar and caterfly

(Examples: Fromkin 1973)

GROUP 2

a   *Father to noisy children*: Don't shell so loud!
b   I don't expose anyone will eat that
c   My data consists moanly – maistly . . .
d   the competition is a little stougher
e   didn't bother me in the sleast . . . slightest

(Examples: Hockett 1973, Fromkin 1973, Aitchison 1994,
Boomer and Laver 1968)

We have examined two types of Slip of the Tongue. In the first, a wrong word replaces the intended one. The substituted word usually belongs to the same lexical set as the target. It might be an opposite of the target word or a word that regularly co-occurs with it. The second type of slip is known as a **blend**: two words become combined to produce a non-word. The two words are usually partial synonyms or bear senses that are very close. Blends tells us a great deal about the process of **lexical retrieval** and demonstrate how closely words are linked in the lexicon by similarity of meaning.

Association by form

 Here are some more Slips of the Tongue – this time representing errors of form. What do the examples in each group have in common? Try to explain why one word was substituted for another.

GROUP 3

a   The noise sort of ENvelopes you – enVElops you
b   You're in a real adVANtag – advanTAgeous postion
c   So that we can PROgress – proGRESS

(Examples: Cutler 1980)

GROUP 4

a   white Anglo-Saxon prostitute (= Protestant)
b   a routine promotion (= proposal)
c   I've been continuously distressed (= impressed) by her
d   don't take this as an erection (= rejection) on my part

(Examples: Fromkin 1973)

Let us now look more closely at the way in which words are linked in the mind by form. Look again at Group 4 above and identify all the ways in which the substituted word resembles the target one in terms of pronunciation. Consider

– which parts of the word seem to be kept and which replaced;
– what happens to stressed and to unstressed syllables.

Examine the Slips of the Tongue below. Can you trace some of the same resemblances here?

absolute (= obsolete)   anecdote (= antidote)
anonymously (= unanimously)   average (= avarice)
compensation (= condensation)   contraceptive (= comprehensive)
convenience (= conference)   cylinders (= syllables)
detergent (= deterrent)   dismal = decimal)
legible (= eligible)

(Examples: Aitchison and Straf 1982)

Further evidence on how words are linked in the mind by form comes from **Tip of the Tongue** experiments. Here is an example. As quickly as possible, give words for the following definitions. If you feel you cannot find exactly the right word, give the one that comes to your mind. Answers appear on page 64.

Activity

1   a representation of a large black beetle, used in Ancient Egypt for decoration
2   a large hairy elephant which lived on Earth during the early stages of human development
3   to take away something owned by somebody else, often for public use and without payment
4   an extremely small piece of matter that forms the substances of which atoms are made
5   in Greek and Roman mythology, a creature that is half man and half horse
6   having leaves that fall off in autumn
                (Definitions: *Longman Dictionary of Contemporary English*)

Perhaps you had no trouble in producing some of these words. With others, you may have found yourself in a '**Tip of the Tongue**' state where you know that the word is in your vocabulary and can even get a kind of mental image of it but cannot retrieve its form. Two researchers from Harvard University, Brown and McNeil, showed (1966) that, in a TOT state, subjects often retrieve words which closely resemble the target one in form.

The TOT experience is important because it suggests that, for the speaker, lexical retrieval (finding a word in the lexicon) takes place in two stages. The meaning of the word enables us to make contact with some kind of **meaning code** (i.e. we recognise that a word exists that has the meaning we are aiming for). We then go on to determine (or sometimes fail to determine) the form of the word.

Answers: 1 scarab 2 mammoth 3 expropriate 4 quark 5 centaur 6 deciduous

Data from Slips of the Tongue (SOT) and Tip of the Tongue (TOT) experiments has shown how words are linked in the mind by form. It suggests that there are specific features of a word which guide us when we are trying to retrieve a form from our lexicon.

❑ Beginnings and endings of words are often correct in a SOT or TOT. Hence the so-called **bath-tub effect**: the important parts of the word are like somebody's head and feet sticking out of the water in a bath. The ends of long words are more robust (i.e. more likely to be correct in a SOT) than those of short ones.

❑ Stress: the stressed syllable is more likely to be correct in SOTs and TOTs, especially if the word is a short one. Stressed vowels are especially likely to be correct. In addition, the stress pattern of the target word is often retained. It seems that stress may be especially important in storing and retrieving words.

❑ Number of syllables is often correct in a SOT or TOT. When it is wrong, there seems, at least in English, to be a tendency towards a three-syllable substitute word.

To summarise . . .
Words are associated in the mental lexicon when:

a one word is a derivation of the other (HAPPY and UNHAPPY)
(Alternative view: a word may be linked to entries for the prefixes and suffixes with which it forms derivations)
b they frequently occur together (FISH and CHIPS)
c they are similar in meaning (AFRAID and SCARED)
d they are similar in form (LEGIBLE and ELIGIBLE).

BOTTOM-UP AND TOP-DOWN PROCESSING   B6

Levels of representation

You are walking through the streets of (let us say) London, when you encounter the sad sight of a homeless person in a doorway. In an accent which resembles London Cockney, the person says to you:

[ɡɒʔnɪ'ʧɑɪnʤ]

(The symbol ʔ represents a 'glottal stop' – a brief blockage of air at the back of the throat. For the other symbols, see the table on page xviii.) How from that sequence of sounds do you manage to construct words and ultimately some kind of meaning? Here are the levels of representation through which a listener might conceivably need to proceed:

Level	Form
PHONETIC	[ɡɒʔnɪ'ʧɑɪnʤ]
⇓	
PHONOLOGICAL	/ɡɒtenɪ'ʧeɪnʤ/ + rising intonation
⇓	
⇓ SEGMENTATIONAL	got # any # change
LEXICAL (lexical access)	have got = [POSSESS] change = [MONEY] [SMALL]
⇓	
SYNTACTIC	(have you) got any change? NP: you VP: [have got] [any change]
⇓	
PROPOSITIONAL (abstract meaning)	🖐 🗀 ?
⇓	
PRAGMATIC	[I want you to give me some money]

Figure B6.1 Bottom-up lexical processing

- Describe what happens at each level.
- Now describe the process in reverse. Imagine how the speaker constructs the utterance, starting with the intention: *I want you to give me some money.*

–   Are there any ways in which you feel that this analysis of the listening process might be inadequate?

It is unlikely that the process we have just examined represents what actually happens. There are a number of reasons. Among them are:

❏   Speaker and listener might have the sequence *Got any change?* stored in their lexicon as a single formulaic chunk. If so, they would not need to assemble it from its parts.
❏   It is not clear that syntactic analysis has to follow lexical access. The two might perhaps occur together.
❏   Some commentators have questioned whether there is indeed a phonological level, at which we derive a standardised form of the words we have heard.
❏   Perhaps most importantly, listening does not happen one step at a time. We do not wait until the end of an utterance before beginning to process it. We process it while the speaker is producing it.

In addition . . .

❏   This is a **bottom-up** account based entirely upon linguistic data. So far, we have taken no account of the possible effects of context (e.g. world knowledge or previous experience of homeless people).

Serial vs parallel processing

Evidence suggests that a listener begins to process an utterance about 200 milliseconds (a fifth of a second) after the speaker has begun to speak. This is about the length of a syllable. So we process an utterance while it is happening. This means that the kind of **serial** process shown in the *Got any change?* example does not happen. Instead, it seems that we process linguistic information in parallel.

Let us assume that the listener is operating at the phonological level, attributing a standard form to [ʧaɪnʤ], the last part of the utterance. By this point, they might have reached the segmentational level with GOTANY and be inserting possible word

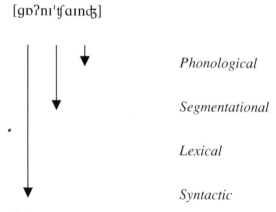

[gɒʔnɪ'ʧaɪnʤ]

Phonological

Segmentational

Lexical

Syntactic

Figure B6.2 Parallel processing

boundaries. They might have reached the syntactic level with GOT and be working out its grammatical role. So different parts of the utterance are being processed at different levels – all at the same time.

The role of context

The sequence in pp. 65–6 assumes that processing operates in one direction – bottom-up – and that it is based entirely on data in the input (on what the listener hears or the reader sees). But it is possible that our analysis of the input is influenced by external factors in a top-down way.

It may be that we recognise the sequence [gɒʔnɪ'ʧaɪndʒ] more quickly because of factors which are not essentially linguistic:

analogy: previous occasions when we have heard a homeless person utter it
world knowledge: the expectation that a homeless person may need to beg
paralinguistic evidence: an outstretched hand
an expectation based on words already uttered (*I need something to eat and I don't have any money.*)

All these factors are often loosely referred to as 'context', though it is preferable to be precise about what kind of context is involved. Outside information of this kind is clearly available to the listener at some stage. The big issue is: does it influence **on-line processing**? Is it used at the actual time we are matching the input to words?

❏   An argument for a role for context: it enables us to decide more accurately what words are present in the input, and to choose only words which are appropriate.

❏   An argument against: it enormously complicates the decisions we have to make. We not only have to match sounds to words; we also, at the same time, have to decide which words are contextually most likely – including words that do not remotely resemble the input.

> In a much-quoted experiment, a researcher (Swinney 1979) asked subjects to listen to sentences, each of which contained an ambiguous word. The sentences provided very clear contexts, indicating that one of the senses of the ambiguous word was appropriate and one was not. For example:
>
> > The man was not surprised when he found several spiders, roaches and other bugs in the corner of the room.
>
> While the sentence was being played, Swinney asked subjects to undertake a priming task, designed to test how quickly they recognised words presented to them on a screen. (You will recall that when we hear, for example, the word *doctor*, we recognise the associated words NURSE, PATIENT etc., much more quickly.) Among the words shown to subjects immediately after they had heard the word *bug* were ANT (associated with one sense of *bug*) and SPY (associated with another).
>
> Subjects showed a faster than normal recognition of both ANT and SPY.

Activity ⭐ What conclusions do you draw about whether we do or do not use context when accessing the meanings of words?

> With other subjects, the priming task was repeated a short time after the ambiguous word *bug*. Here, subjects recognised the target word faster than normal when it was associated with the appropriate sense (here ANT), but not when it was associated with the incorrect sense (SPY). This effect seems to begin about 200 milliseconds (a fifth of a second) after an ambiguous word has been heard.

What conclusions do you think the experimenters reached?

Top-down lexical processes
Read the words below. Do you notice anything about them?

Figure B6.3 Top-down processing
Source: Rumelhardt and McClelland (1986: 8)

You may have noticed that the H in THE is exactly the same shape as the A in CAT. Similarly, certain letter shapes in the degraded words are identical, but we read them differently according to the word in which they appear. For some commentators, this suggests that our recognition of letters is influenced by our knowledge of whole words. This is an example of a **top-down** effect, with knowledge at the word level shaping recognition at the letter level.

Attempts have been made to demonstrate this kind of word effect in speech.

> Ganong (1980) used a computer to produce variants of certain sounds: for example, he produced a range of sounds which went in stages from a clearly identifiable /k/ to a clearly identifiable /g/. He then added them to word stems. One of these stems was -ISS, giving a set of recorded items which changed gradually from a clear exemplar of an actual word KISS to a clear exemplar of a non-word GISS. Presented with various versions of KISS, Ganon's subjects were generally correct in identifying the /k/. But, presented with versions of GISS, they often reported the less typical variants of /g/ as /k/. This suggested that our knowledge of whole words influences the way we perceive phonemes.

Autonomous vs interactive models

The evidence we have examined appears contradictory. It suggests that there are top-down effects resulting from our knowledge of words, but none resulting from context. This may be the case. But you should note that both Swinney's and Ganon's findings have been challenged by other researchers. The area is a controversial one – and has divided psycholinguists into two camps: those who view language processing as **interactive** and those who claim that it is **autonomous**.

❑   On an **interactive** view, our minds operate in parallel, simultaneously considering a range of different types of cue to the presence of a word in the signal. Information is freely exchanged between all levels of processing, including context. When we are reading a word, parallel information is available from: letter features (curves, horizontal lines, etc.), letters, the order in which letters occur and the word as a whole. It may also be available from context.

❑   The **autonomous** view is that each level of processing operates independently. On this analysis, information from letter features feeds forward to support letter recognition; letter recognition then feeds forward to support word recognition. Contextual information does not influence perception until we have fully processed what is physically present on the page.

An interactive model might appear to have the advantage of speed. Its weakness is the complexity of the decision-making involved in considering a cocktail of cues which varies greatly from one utterance to another. An autonomous model might appear to be slower. But it has the advantage of always following the same process. As a result, it can become highly **automatic**: this means that it might in fact be faster and make fewer demands upon our mental resources.

Activity Consider the process involved in identifying a string of phonemes. Do you think that it is enhanced or complicated if at the same time we have to consider what words the phonemes might form?

B7   ## WRITING AT WORD LEVEL

An adult writing in English has to produce

- 'regular' words whose spelling conforms to their spoken form (*living, canteen*)
- 'irregular' words such as *yacht*
- words whose spellings follow a particular pattern (*light, night, tight*).

To what extent does an adult using English orthography rely upon grapheme-phoneme correspondence (GPC) rules? Or does writing in English rely mainly (like writing in Chinese) upon mapping directly from an idea to a whole word? Or do English writers store words together which have similar forms, so that they can work out spellings by **analogy**?

Slips of the pen and keyboard
One interesting source of evidence can be found in the mistakes that writers make, which offer insights into the criteria that a writer applies when retrieving the written form of a word from memory. However, we have to be careful to distinguish:

- motor errors, where there is a failure in the signal that the brain sends to the hand or in the contact between hand and keyboard
- lexical errors, where the wrong written form has been selected.

Activity Study the data below, which represents some of the author's own slips of the keyboard, collected over an extended period. To them have been added examples of slips of the pen and typewriter from a well-known set of data collected by Hotopf (1983). Try to decide the cause or causes of each group of slips.

1   Eliminate slips which you think were simple motor errors.
2   Review the other errors to see if they support a view:
    - that phonology plays a part in English writing
    - that analogy between words plays a part in English writing
    - that English writing depends mainly upon a mapping from idea to whole word.
3   Which slips seem to result from a planning process at a higher level than the word?
4   What do the slips tell us about the processing of function and lexical words?

a   the → teh   language → langauge   number → nubmer   writing → wriitng
     have → ahve   spelling → spellign   length → lenght
     discussion → disucssion   psychology → pyschology
     of the → ofthe   different fro mthe
b   paradigmatic → *paral*
c   likely → likley   details → detials   existence → existance
     mechanism → metchanism   both → bothe
d   there → their   could → good   you are → your   than → that   too → to
e   for → of   do → doe   where → were   from → for
f   inner → in a   cues → ques   H → 8   20A → 28
g   initial → intial   inhibitions → inhibtions   manager → manger
h   importan topic   these given (= give) insights
     using bothing (= both) approaches
     difference (= different) intelligence tests   neighbourshoods
i   saw the the movement   characteristics of of a language
     suggested that that they apply   it appears the (= that) the process involves
j   though these [are] not frequent   that [it] is possible   [bracketed word omitted]

Phonology does indeed seem to play a part in the processing of the written word (see
(d) and (f)), even though many English words do not accord with simple spelling
rules. Examples quite commonly occur of words being replaced by others that are phonologically identical (*there → their*); but there are rarely any of replacement by words
that are similar in form (e.g. *there → these*). Note that the *there / their* example is not
a spelling error – the writer is fully aware of the difference between the two forms;
but, under the pressure of writing, one form (often the more frequent one) is substituted for the other. Especially striking in Hotopf's data is the substitution of *28* for
20A, though this, of course, involves symbols rather than words.

But we must beware of too 'strong' a phonological interpretation. Hotopf
reported that only about 20 per cent of the slips he collected were clearly phonological in origin. Notice, too, the kind of slip shown in (g). If phonology is such a powerful criterion, then how is it that writers sometimes omit a whole spoken syllable from
a word? This kind of slip is much easier to explain in terms of the written form, where
it involves only a single letter.

You will also have noticed that some of the errors above (see (c)) reflect the writer's
awareness of common letter groups in English – in other words, the effects of analogy. Admittedly, this evidence could also reflect motor errors: it might show the
typist's familiarity with certain well-established key stroke sequences.

An important factor appears to be the difference between lexical and function words.
The latter seem very susceptible to error: they are sometimes omitted or duplicated
(see (i) and (j)), and it is quite common in rapid typing for one function word to be
substituted for another, even when they are not phonologically identical (see (e)). This
leads one to the conclusion that function words may be processed differently from
lexical ones. It seems possible that the writing process accords a higher level of attention to lexical items.

Finally, notice that some writing slips provide evidence of a planning process operating at a level higher than the word. In (h), there are several examples of a writer

anticipating material that is about to come. When writing a particular word, we already have the next few words stored in our minds, ready for production. We will look more closely at this process in Section C7.

Motor processes

Studies of typing patterns offer insights into the last (motor) stage of the writing process. Average typing speed is 7 to 8 strokes per second. The way in which the typist processes linguistic information is shown by the length and regularity of the intervals between these finger strokes. The following findings appear to be important:

❏ In terms of rhythm, the unit of typing seems to be the word rather than the phrase or sentence.
❏ Intervals between strokes are greatest at the beginnings and ends of words.
❏ Intervals between strokes are longer for letter strings which occur infrequently.
❏ Syllable boundaries appear to have some effect; the frequent sequence -*th*- is typed faster in *pathetic* than in *porthole*.
❏ Performance declines with nonsensical letter strings, but not with non-words that bear a resemblance to existing ones.

This may tell us something more about the way in which words are retrieved from the brain, or it may simply tell us something about the typing process itself. Typing is clearly an activity that demands a great deal of conscious control at the outset, but that gradually becomes proceduralised into a set of automatic keystroke sequences – particularly for very frequent words such as *the*. It may be that the keystrokes made by a typist are stored as an independent set of procedures (accounting for faster performance with more frequent letter sequences). Or it may be that they are linked to a visual representation of each word, or indeed to a phonological representation.

B8
EYE MOVEMENTS IN READING

Activity

Here are some assumptions that are sometimes made about reading as a process – especially in the 'speed reading' literature. Do you agree or disagree with them?

❏ Efficient readers do not need to read all the words in a text. They predict many words from the context in which they appear.
❏ Efficient readers make large sweeps with their eyes as they read along lines of text.
❏ Words can be identified by their overall shapes. So longer words often take the same time to read as short ones.
❏ A slow reader is one whose eyes do not move fast enough from left to right. Increases in reading speed can be achieved without loss of comprehension.

Reading involves a series of rapid eye movements (known as **saccades**) along the line of print or writing, followed by periods of fixation when the eye rests upon a point in the text. A saccade typically lasts from 20–30 milliseconds while a **fixation** can last from 150 to 500 msec and sometimes longer. At the end of a line, the reader makes a **return sweep** on to the following line.

Experimenters have learnt a great deal about lower level reading processes thanks to equipment which enables us to track the movement of the reader's eyes across the page. By comparing the eye movements of skilled and less skilled readers, we can get a clearer idea of what makes for efficient reading. We can also get an idea of what aspects of a text cause processing problems.

Figure B8.1 below is based upon eye movement data published (1989) by reading researchers Keith Rayner and Alexander Pollatsek of the University of Massachusets. The dots above the text mark the fixation points and the figures show how long in milliseconds each fixation lasted. The saccades move in a left-to-right direction except where an arrowhead indicates a **regression** (with fixations shown on a higher line).

Study the figure to find out:

★ Activity

1 How many fixations are there on average per line?
2 Where do they fall in relation to the words?
3 How many letters on average does a saccade move across?

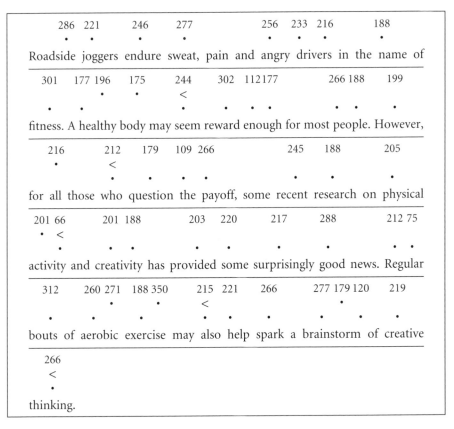

Figure B8.1 Fixation sequences and fixation durations
Source: Adapted from Rayner and Pollatsek (1989: 116)

4   Do words ever receive more than one fixation?
5   Do the words that are not fixated have anything in common?
6   What happens on a return sweep?

Fixations usually fall on the early part of a word (about a third into longer words) –
which suggests that their position may be partly determined by the spaces between
words. The reader has a **perceptual span** of about fifteen characters to either side of
the fixation point, but the words that are furthest away are processed at a lower level
of attention. Processing a long word may sometimes involve two fixations and long
words generally demand more fixation time than short ones. A return sweep typically
starts about 5–7 characters from the end of the line and the next fixation point is close
to the beginning of the next line.

Saccades cover no more than about 7–9 characters (fewer in logographic writing
systems), with the result that almost every word is fixated. In all, this means about
80 per cent of content words and 40 per cent of function words. The few words that are
skipped are short, frequent or highly predictable from the context; but the skipping
of so many function words suggests that this class of items may be recognised in a
highly automatised way and accorded less attention than content words.

| Activity | Figure B8.2 below was composed by reading researchers Marcel Just and Patricia Carpenter (1987) using early eye movement research data. It shows how the same text was read by a skilled and a less skilled reader. The saccades move from left to right unless otherwise indicated. Ovals indicate the fixation points and the figures inside |

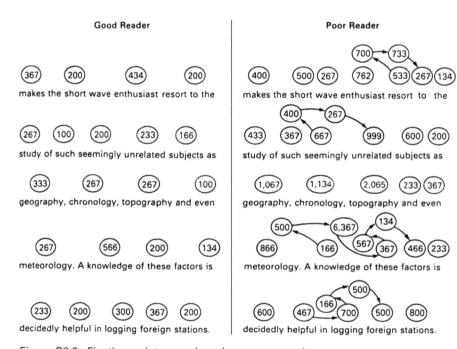

Figure B8.2   Fixation points: good reader vs poor reader
Source: Just and Carpenter (1987: 27)

them show how long the fixations lasted. What does the figure tell you about the differences in the way the two readers processed the text?

It was once believed that reading efficiency could be improved if the saccades of weak readers were made longer. However, the evidence above shows that good readers start off with about the same number of fixations as poor ones. What marks out less skilled reading (and reading in the early stages of acquiring a second language) is a much higher level of regression. Regression in an average reader only adds about 10 per cent to the fixations; in an unskilled reader, it accounts for much more. And whereas regression in skilled reading is often connected with building higher level meaning, regression in unskilled reading usually serves to check that words have been correctly decoded. Less skilled readers often have longer fixation times, especially when processing long or unusual words.

Relate these eye movement findings to the assumptions you discussed at the beginning of this section.

Activity

CATEGORICAL PERCEPTION

B9

We saw in Section A9 that the 'non-invariance' problem is a difficult one to settle. In this section, we assume that there is indeed some kind of phonological representation which enables us to discriminate between, for example, occurrences of /pa/ and occurrences of /ba/, and we look more closely at how this kind of distinction is made.

Traditional phonological accounts describe the sound /p/ as 'voiceless' and the sound /b/ as 'voiced'. In fact, the major difference lies in how quickly the voicing begins for the vowel that follows. With a sequence such as /pa/, there is a gap lasting from 30 to 80 milliseconds between /p/ and the voicing of the vowel. With a sequence such as /ba/, the onset of voicing coincides with the /b/ or occurs no longer than 25 milliseconds afterwards. It is **Voice Onset Time** (**VOT**) which enables our ears to distinguish between the two sounds.

The VOT distinction has enabled researchers to manipulate speech sounds by computer. They can produce a synthesised range of consonant-vowel sequences which proceed in regular steps from a sequence with a VOT of 0 (clearly identifiable, say, as /ba/) to one with a VOT of 80 (clearly identifiable as /pa/). Subjects are asked to (a) report what they hear; (b) discriminate (same or different?) between two exemplars within a category range (say within 0–25 milliseconds); and (c) discriminate between two exemplars on different sides of the category boundary.

Interpret the results overleaf, which illustrate what is known as **categorical perception**.

Activity

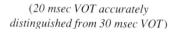

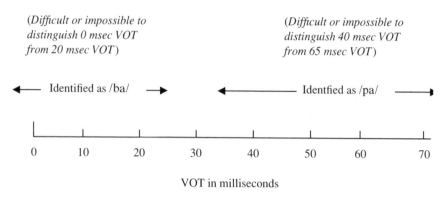

VOT in milliseconds

Figure B9.1 Typical result from a categorical perception task

It appears that our ears become so attuned to the phoneme categories of our language that we find it very hard to differentiate between sounds which fall within a single category, but can easily distinguish sounds (even acoustically similar ones) which fall into separate categories. So when do we first acquire categorical perception?

Eimas, Siqueland, Jusczyk and Vogorito (1971) devised a clever experiment to establish whether infants are capable of categorical perception. The method, known as the **High Amplitude Sucking** procedure, exploits the fact that infants tend to suck on dummies at a regular rate, which speeds up if something happens to attract their attention. The researchers gave dummies to four-month-old infants and waited until their sucking had settled into a constant rhythm. They then presented then with an auditory stimulus from the [ba–pa] continuum, which (being something novel) caused their sucking rate to increase. When the infants had heard this sequence several times, it ceased to be of interest to them, and their sucking returned to the baseline speed. The researchers now

a played a different stimulus from *within* the same perceptual category as the first one (i.e. if the first one had been in the [ba] range, so was the second) or

b played a different stimulus from the *other* perceptual category (i.e. if the first one had been in the [ba] range, the second was from the [pa]).

They found that in condition (a), the infants' sucking rate did not increase; but in condition (b) it did – indicating that they had noticed something new. This suggested that 4-month-old infants make the same kind of categorical distinctions as adults.

What conclusions do you draw from this result?

The finding raised the possibility that categorical perception might be innate. It also suggested that human speech is a separate faculty and treated differently by infants from other sounds. Could it provide conclusive evidence that speech is specific to the human race?

> Several years later, Kuhl and Miller (1978) put this to the test by trying the [ba/pa] distinction on chinchillas. Chinchillas were chosen because their auditory apparatus is believed to be very similar to that of human beings. The chinchillas were trained to respond differently to stimuli at the extreme ends of the scale – one with 0 milliseconds VOT and one with 80 milliseconds. They might, for example, continue drinking when they heard the first, but run across the cage when they heard the second. The intermediate stimuli were then played to them, to see how they reacted. Strikingly, a divide occurred (marked by a switch from one conditioned form of behaviour to the other) at almost exactly the 25 milliseconds boundary which separates [b] and [p] for the human ear.

How do you interpret this finding?

The researchers concluded that categorical perception may not after all be innate – unless one assumes that chinchillas also have a capacity for language. The finding suggests that spoken language has evolved in such as way as to take advantage of certain acoustic properties to which the human ear (and the similar ear of the chinchilla) is especially sensitive. Categorical boundaries may well coincide with **focal points** where, because of the way our hearing is constructed, we find it particularly easy to distinguish sounds. In visual processing, similar focal points are said to assist us in distinguishing between colours.

A challenge to this theory comes from the fact that certain languages (for example, Spanish and Thai) have phoneme boundaries which differ from those of English. However, there is evidence that these categories are not recognised by very young children but are acquired gradually through exposure to the language.

STAGES IN THE SPEAKING PROCESS

Adopting an information processing approach to speaking, we need to establish:

–   What are the different levels of processing involved in assembling a spoken utterance?
–   In what order do they occur?

Slips of the Tongue have provided considerable evidence in this respect. The examples given below come from Fromkin 1973, 1980 and Ellis and Beattie 1986.

Activity

TASK 1

Here are some Slips of the Tongue from the literature. What levels of processing do you think are involved?

1a	ice-cream in the fridge	→	ice cream in the oven
b	moBILity	→	mobilITy
c	drop a bomb	→	bop a dromb
d	one spoon of sugar	→	one sugar of spoon
e	He swam in the pool	→	He swimmed in the pool

It is clear that a model of speaking needs levels at which we

–   use meaning to start a lexical search
–   assign lexical stress
–   allocate form at the level of the phoneme
–   insert lexical items
–   attach inflections.

Can you suggest the order in which these operations might occur?

Activity

TASK 2

Here are some more Slips of the Tongue.

Compare the actual utterance with the target one. What makes each group distinctive?

2a	arrested and prosecuted	→	arrested and persecuted
b	such fantastic acrobats	→	such fantastic apricots
3	Can you wriggle your ankles?	→	Can you wriggle your elbows?
4a	Does it sound different?	→	Does it hear different?
b	She swore me to secrecy	→	She promised me to secrecy
c	They think they know where . . .	→	They seem they know where . . .

Groups 2 and 3 are the kinds of SOT that we have already come across in considering lexical storage. Group 2 indicates that the speaker has retrieved a wrong (but similar) form for the target word: the substituted word resembles it both in phonemes and in stress. In Group 3, a meaning-based search of the lexicon has led to a substitute that is semantically associated with the target.

It might appear that Group 4 is similar to the other two. A wrong (but semantic-ally linked) word appears to have been substituted for the target. But what makes the word inappropriate here is the syntactic structure into which it has been inserted. It looks as if the speaker had constructed the following syntactic frames (NP = Noun Phrase)

it + SOUND + Adj	semantically similar HEAR inserted in error
SWEAR + NP + *to* + NP	semantically similar PROMISE inserted in error
THINK + subordinate clause	semantically similar SEEM inserted in error

From the above data, we can derive several conclusions for our model of speaking.

❏ There is stage when a meaning-driven search of the lexicon is made.
❏ There is a stage at which words are given a phonological form. Consider the Tip of the Tongue situation where a speaker has a kind of semantic 'shape' for the word they are seeking (we will call it a **meaning code**) but cannot retrieve the exact form. This suggests that searching for a word and retrieving its form may be separate processes.
❏ There is a stage at which a syntactic structure is established. The structure may be specified by information in the lexicon. Thus, our lexical entry for one sense of SOUND would indicate the patterns *It* + SOUND + Adj. (*It sounds good*) and *It* + SOUND + *like* + NP (*It sounds like a good idea*). It would seem that word forms are inserted after this frame has been established; hence the slips with HEARS, PROMISE and SEEM. etc.

TASK 3
Now here are some slips at a very different level. Does this level come before or after those examined in Task 2? Examine the slips and see what conclusions you can draw. Pay careful attention to the relationship in Group 6 between the target phoneme and the one that has been substituted for it.

5a	You better stop for gas	→	You getter stop for bass
b	fight very hard	→	fart very hide
c	feel like playing	→	peel like flaying
d	brake fluid	→	blake fruid
e	your spine shrinks	→	your shrine spinks
6a	big and fat	→	pig and vat
b	clear blue sky	→	glear plue sky

These slips represent a late stage in the assembly of speech, at which the phonemes of a word are assembled. Or, if we take a view that the phoneme is not a unit of pro-cessing, the process entails sending a set of instructions to the articulators (jaw, tongue, mouth, vocal cords), telling them what positions to adopt. What is curious is that sometimes (as in 5c and 5d) consonant clusters appear to be assembled in parts (the /l/ in *playing* does not move) – while sometimes (as in 5e) they operate as a pre-formed chunk (both *s* and *p* move from *spine*).

In the examples in Group 6, only voicing is misapplied. So the allocation of voicing (/p/ vs /b/) may well represent a separate stage once place and manner of articulation have been settled.

Notice that for a slip such as 5a to occur, the speaker must already have a chunk of language assembled in some form. The initial sounds of *better* and *gas* could not have been exchanged unless a phrase containing both of them was already present in some kind of speech 'buffer'.

A final point: notice how robust the syllable is. Individual phonemes become dislocated, but they end up in the same syllabic position (beginning-middle-end) as in the target.

This suggests that the syllable may be an important unit of planning.

Activity TASK 4

Here is a more complex set of slips. Suggest what makes each group distinctive.

| 7a | I love to dance | → | I dance to love |
| b | I put the book on the bed | → | I put the bed on the book |

8a	you can cut trees in the rain	→	you can cut rains in the tree
b	wearing a name tag	→	naming a wear tag
c	she slants her writing	→	she writes her slanting

| 9a | I hoped he would like Chris | → | I liked he would hope Chris |
| b | I don't know that I'd know one if I heard it | → | I don't know that I'd hear one if I knew it |

10a	ministers in our church	→	church*es* in our minister
b	a watched pot never boils	→	a pott*ed* watch never boils
c	the prongs /z/ of a fork	→	the forks /s/ of a prong

| 11a | a small restaurant on the island | → | *an* island on the small restaurant |
| b | an ice cream cone | → | *a* kice ream cone |

These are examples of assembly processes involving morphology.

In Group 7, there is a simple switch of words (again, a syntactic pattern must already have been assembled, containing meaning codes for both words).

In Group 8, things are more complicated because inflectional morphemes are involved (plural and *-ing*). Notice that the inflections retain their positions; it is simply the words that are swapped. This suggests (compare the remarks after Task 2) that the speaker has already prepared a set of syntactic slots, which are tagged with morpheme information:

CUT + NP (plural) + *in* + NP (singular)
WEAR (+ *ing*) + N + N

It is into these slots that the word forms are later inserted. A similar explanation accounts for the slips in Group 9; here, it is not just a question of adding on an *-ed* inflection; the verb *know* has been transformed into its correct past tense form.

Group 10 shows some interesting phonological evidence. Look at 10c. Let us assume that the plural inflection is fixed and the content words are exchanged. Then we should expect to get:

$$prong + /z/ \textit{ of a fork} \quad \rightarrow \textit{fork} + /z/ \textit{ of a prong}$$

But this is not what happens; the plural morpheme adjusts to the word that is substituted. We get the appropriate unvoiced /s/ to match the unvoiced /k/ at the end of *fork*: /fɔːks/.

This suggests strongly that what is present before the content words are inserted is not the phonological form of the inflection (the sound /z/), but some kind of abstract indication that an inflection is needed (the kind of 'tagging' suggested above). This is given phonological shape only after the word has been inserted. So the sequence goes:

a   Assign inflection abstractly ('plural').
b   Insert phonological form of word.
c   Insert appropriate phonological form of inflection.

A footnote to this is provided by Group 11. Here, the form of the article has adjusted to the exchanged word. Instead of **an** *ice cream*, we have **a** *kice ream*. This suggests that the article too is inserted at the same late stage as the inflections. Up to this point, the sequence is presumably simply tagged as 'indefinite'.

Let us summarise what has been established so far. It seems there is:

❏   a level at which lexical access occurs. This provides us with (from the lemma)
  –   a meaning code for a word
  –   the appropriate syntactic structure for a main verb.
❏   a level at which a **syntactic frame** is built. It is tagged with abstract information about
  –   inflections (+ plural + past etc.)
  –   definiteness (+/– definite).
❏   a **buffer** in which this plan can be stored.
❏   a level at which concrete phonological information about a word is extracted from the lexicon and the word is inserted into the syntactic frame.
❏   a level at which the inflectional information and articles are put into concrete form (e.g. 'past' → /d/; 'indefinite' → *an*).
❏   a level at which the phonemes of a word (or the signals to the articulators) are prepared so that the utterance can be made.

There are three areas of processing that have not so far been mentioned – all of them phonological.

❏   The processor has to assign **intonation**. This may well happen at the same time as the building of a syntactic frame.

❏ The processor must assign **word stress**; this information can be extracted from the lexicon at the same time as the phonological form of the word.

❏ After the last stage described above, there must be a 'phonetic' stage, where the processor bunches the utterance together into an easy-to-articulate chunk. At this point, features such as assimilation and elision might alter the signals to the articulators:

green paint → greem paint   next spring → neck spring

In Section C10, we will see how all these stages have been incorporated into a model of speaking.

B11   MEANING REPRESENTATIONS

Integrating information
Readers and listeners seem to strive instinctively to construct meaning.

Activity   As an example of this 'effort after meaning', place a piece of paper over this page. Move it down the page until you come to an arrow ⇓. Read the text that follows, a line at a time, gradually moving the paper downwards. Describe your impressions.

This exercise demonstrates how strong the urge is to impose meaning upon a text. Where the information in a text is incomplete, the reader or listener will often flesh it out with their own inferences in order to construct a neat representation.

The exercise also demonstrates that a meaning representation is provisional. It is subject to revision as new information comes in. A large part of the effort of processing a text is said to lie in the need to integrate incoming information into an existing representation.

⇓_____

John was on his way to school.

He was terribly worried about the maths lesson.

Last week, he had been unable to control the class.

It was unfair of the teacher to leave him in charge.

After all, it's not usually part of a caretaker's duties.

(Text: Sanford and Garrod 1981)

> Myers, Shinjo and Duffy (1987) asked subjects to read pairs of sentences in which the second sentence of each pair was less and less closely related to the first. Examples:
>
> – *Cathy felt very dizzy and fainted at her work. She was carried unconscious to a hospital.*
> – *Cathy worked very hard and became exhausted. She was carried unconscious to a hospital.*
> – *Cathy had begun working on the new project. She was carried unconscious to a hospital*
>
> The time taken to read the second sentence became longer as its links to the first became more tenuous. This was taken to reflect the additional effort involved in integrating new information into the old.

There are those (particularly in the speed reading literature) who argue that the mark of a good reader is the ability to anticipate what is coming next so that decoding words becomes a less onerous task. The view ignores the fact that, for a skilled reader, decoding is highly automatic, whereas anticipating forthcoming text involves considerable resources of Working Memory. To many psycholinguists, it makes more sense to think of the skilled reader as using scarce WM resources for the purpose of integrating new information into old rather than for the purpose of thinking ahead to save decoding effort.

Levels of meaning representation

Look at this sentence: *Crusoe saw a footprint.*
Explain what it means literally. Then indicate if there is any additional meaning which you as a reader bring to bear on it.

✪ **Activity**

Commentators have suggested that a sentence like this is processed on three levels.

a   **Surface form**: the wording of the sentence.
b   **Propositional form**: the literal meaning of the sentence.
c   A **mental model**: this representation includes additional information from world knowledge; it also includes inferences like those you drew when reading the 'school' text above.

Crusoe: gives rise to associations of name (*Robinson . . .*)
footprint: engages our world knowledge. The footprint is likely to be in something soft: sand? snow? We infer it is human, though the text does not say so (humans have feet; animals tend to have paws, claws or hoofs). The indefinite article *a* is used; from this, we infer that the footprint is something novel. Crusoe has not seen it before.

Mental models
Research into mental models has especially focused on the way in which we form spatial representations based on what we read or hear. The big issue has been whether

we store propositional information with inferences alongside it or whether we really do construct a separate mental model, into which inferences and world knowledge have been integrated.

> Morrow *et al.* (1989) asked subjects to memorise a diagram of a building show-ing room layouts and certain objects within each room. This was regarded as factual propositional information, stored in Long Term Memory.
>
> Subjects read narratives describing somebody going through the building from one room to another.
>
> As subjects read, they were given the names of two different objects in the building. They had to say if the objects were in the same room or in different rooms. There was a quick 'same room' response when the room in question was close to the protagonist in the narrative, especially when it was a room the protagonist was approaching. Response times increased with greater distance between protagonist and objects.

What conclusion do you draw in terms of the subjects' use of **spatial representation**?

 Activity

TASK 1

Your teacher or a group member will read aloud the text on page 209. Listen care-fully. Then take 30 seconds to think about the information you have been given.

Now tick which of the following pieces of information were supplied in the text. Remember: the issue is not whether these exact words were used, but whether this was part of the evidence that the detective had to consider.

1 The sitting room was next to the library.
2 The library only had one door.
3 The key was on the inside of the library door.
4 There were people in the sitting room at the time of the murder.
5 Nobody had heard any noise from the library.
6 The library door had to be forced open.
7 There was a fireplace to the left of the body.
8 The victim was a man.
9 The victim was killed with blows to the head.
10 The fireplace was on the wall facing the door.
11 The body was face downwards.
12 The body was lying on a rug.
13 A vase had been broken.
14 There were two windows to the library.
15 The curtains in the library were drawn.
16 There was a terrace at the rear of the house.
17 It had rained on the night of the murder.

In fact, you were only specifically told five of these facts (nos. 2, 6, 7, 11 and 14). Anything else, you inferred as part of your construction of a mental model. If you do not believe this, check with the text!

This is a finding that has been repeated many times in meaning-building experiments. Subjects find it difficult to distinguish between propositional information and the inferences which they have added to that information.

One of the most-cited results features the Bransford, Barclay and Franks's 'turtles and fish' example (1972). Subjects were shown sentences such as:

Three turtles rested on a floating log and a fish swam beneath them.

After a short time delay, a significant number of subjects could not say whether they had encountered the sentence shown above or the following alternative:

Three turtles rested on a floating log and a fish swam beneath <u>it</u>.

which incorporates a reasonable inference from the original. No such difficulty was experienced by subjects who had been presented with the sentence:

Three turtles rested <u>beside</u> a floating log and a fish swam beneath them.

They confidently stated that they had not seen:

Three turtles rested beside a floating log and a fish swam beneath it.

Mental models: further points

❏   Readers and listeners are selective.
    The kind of mental model constructed often reflects the individual's own sense of what is or is not important in the information they have received. Or it might reflect the priorities of the task that they have had to perform.

TASK 2
Work in pairs. Student A reads Text A on page 209 and Student B reads Text B on page 211. You have 15 seconds only. Now each of you must write down what you remember. Compare notes.

 Activity

This material comes from an experiment by Anderson and Pichert (1978) which demonstrated that what readers remember is shaped by their reasons for using a text. Was this what happened with you?

❏   Readers and listeners are sometimes satisfied with incomplete mental models.
    a   The information we are given may not be sufficient for us to form a complete mental model. In these cases, we appear to:

–   choose one model from among several possibilities
 –   stay satisfied with a model that is less than complete but is sufficient
     for our purposes.
 b   We may make do with an incomplete mental model because of the complexity
     of the information we have to process – or because our task only requires us
     to process a text at a relatively shallow level.

Activity   As quickly as you can, give answers to the following questions:

 –   A plane crashed on the border between America and Canada. Where do you think
     the survivors were buried?
 –   How many animals of each kind did Moses lead into the ark?

                              (Erickson and Mattson 1981; Barton and Sanford 1993)

To summarise

Three important processes are involved in constructing mental models from propositional information:

 ❑ **elaboration**: adding inferences to achieve coherence
 ❑ **integration**: adding incoming information to existing information
 ❑ **selection**: reducing stored information to what is relative or important.

B12   LANGUAGE DISORDERS

In this section, we examine evidence of disordered language: one piece in the
spoken modality and one in the written. When considering how these samples
differ from normal processing, refer back to earlier sections on speech (10A) and on
writing (7A).

Stuttering

Activity   1   Compare the language of the therapist (A) and the patient (B) in the extract below.
         Take account of:
         a   pausing
         b   filled pauses (*erm*, etc.)
         c   stress patterns
         d   length of run between pauses
     2   Study the words that recur. What evidence is there that the patient has problems
         with specific words?
     3   What signs are there that the patient is aware of his own speech problems?

4   Where do you think the patient's problem arises? Is it a question of not having the right word forms stored in his mind (= phonological), of forming the wrong instructions to the articulators (= phonetic) or of the articulators not obeying those instructions (= articulatory)?

A: and do you 'have any **hob**bies/

B: **yes**/ – **one** . 'of – my . 'hob – – bies/ . is 'mus – **sic**/ . and the other – – 'one/ is erm – 'playing – – **hockey**/ – –

A: 'when you say **mu**sic/ do you 'mean do you 'like **listen**ing **to** it/ or 'do you **play** 'any-thing/

B: I – – I 'actually – – **play** in/ – – 'two erm – **bands**/ and I als . so . 'like **list** . e . ning – to 'mus.'sic/ – –

A: 'what do you **play**/

B: I – – erm – well – – my – –

A: I mean what **instru**ment/

B: **yes**/ **quite**/ – – 'my **main** 'instru – ment is the / – erm – (h h) is the – – 'bass. gui – **tar**/ – – but 'I 'also 'play – – the erm **ban** – – jo/ and **or**dinary – gui – 'tar/

(Extract (slightly modified) from: Dalton and Hardcastle 1989)

Key: A is the therapist and B the patient.
End of each unit of intonation is marked by /
Pauses are marked by: . (short) – (long) – – (very long)
bold type: shows sentence stress 'marks other stressed words

Stuttering varies considerably between sufferers. It may involve the repetition of phonemic segments, syllables or words (*c-c-computer, com-com-computer, got a-got a-got a brother* – or alternatively an extreme lengthening of segments or syllables (*af:::raid*). These features occur in the speech of any hesitant speaker, but are generally more frequent with a stutterer. The most characteristic symptom is a blocking of the airflow, which results in long pauses and effortful speech. This may be accompanied by a greater use than normal of fillers such as *erm* or *oh* to fill or anticipate a gap. The general hesitancy of speech often leads to irregularities of rhythm and intonation and words may be stressed erratically or left incomplete. Sufferers are often aware of their limitations and may paraphrase or use general terms to avoid words that they anticipate will be difficult.

Stuttering has been interpreted in terms of **demands and capacities** – the demands made by speech exceeding what the sufferer can manage to produce. The limitations may be attentional or may result from problems with signals from the brain to the articulators. Either way, the sufferer has to devote considerable Working Memory capacity to the formation of words, a process which comes automatically for others. Anxiety often increases the problem as many stutterers overestimate the severity of their symptoms. They also regard themselves as bad listeners because they feel that they have to allocate so much attention to their own productions.

A cognitive theory links stuttering to listening and to **self-monitoring**. It suggests that there may be split-second delays in the auditory feedback mechanism linking ear, brain and vocal organs, which disrupt the encoding of speech. There have also been neurological explanations suggesting that chemicals in the brain may disrupt the transmission of information across nerve connections.

Dyslexia and dysgraphia

Activity ★ Passage A was written by a 14-year-old dyslexic, Passage B by a 16-year-old dyslexic. Examine each one in terms of:

1   *Visuo-spatial awareness*: does it show one letter shape substituted for another? Does it show incorrect recall of letter order in words?

2   *Spelling*: does it reflect phonic knowledge in the form of GPC rules? Does it show recall of whole word forms? Or does it show the effects of analogy with words similar to the target ones? Are certain words misspelt in consistent ways? Are there any consistent patterns of grapheme error?

3   *Morphology*: are grammatical inflections and function words omitted or not?

4   *Content*: how selective is the writer? How coherent is the piece? (Coherence relates to the extent to which ideas are connected within a text.) How would you evaluate the writer's intelligence and powers of self-expression?

PASSAGE A

I have gust cum from whork I was ran ing rather hard I have just den lowking throw the lowchel cronicul have seen two Descos avertised. I am thinking of starting a Discho it will hcost me about 60£ dut my dad will make me the amply fiers and some things els . . . I whont to de a shef when I leve school. when I go to Dacis [dances] evry theing otside I forget my waris and proplems and the sam at Discos.

(Extract: Miles 1993: 86)

PASSAGE B

One of the most difficult thing to wright is something just of the cuff as you literat perent have not read the letter properly.

The thing which most illiterats people live perpetual feer of, is by getting into a situation were one has to read or by someone ones slipe of the tong, it get into your soshal circals. Luckerly this seldom happens becaues as one is always one your tows. You have always got to be ready to drag your frends out of the room were famerly are, when the conversation gets to deep into the suject 'o' leval.

I may be panting a very very black picker, but to be quite honest it is not as enerjetick all that becaues it become a seconed sens.

(Extract: Miles 1993: 86–7)

One view of dyslexia associates it with a delay in accomplishing one of the stages which normal reading passes through.

- ❐ In Stage 1, children engage in 'sight-reading', recognising words as if they were pictures. This stage does not appear to be critical to the development of successful reading.
- ❐ In Stage 2, children use parts of words to form matches (often inaccurate) with known written forms. There is evidence that some dyslexics may not achieve this kind of analytic processing.
- ❐ In Stage 3, when phonics begins to play a part, the child establishes a set of grapheme-phoneme correspondence rules which enable it to deconstruct written words into sounds. Some dyslexics (**phonological dyslexics**) appear to experience problems at this stage which result in delay or deviance in their reading. An important indicator is whether, at the age of about eight, the child is able to transcribe non-words.
- ❐ In Stage 4, the child develops the ability to achieve whole-word matches, and possibly the associated ability to trace analogies between word rimes (LEAD (n.) with HEAD; LEAD (v.) with BEAD). This stage is especially important for orthographies like English which are not transparent. Some dyslexics (**surface dyslexics**) experience problems at this stage – especially with spellings which permit of two interpretations (e.g. PINT/MINT) to which they attach a default interpretation, and with homophones such as SAIL/SALE.

Look again at the samples of writing above. To what extent does each of them show signs of phonological dyslexia or of surface dyslexia?

✪ **Activity**

Dyslexia varies enormously between individuals. Some dyslexics show strong signs of a phonological impairment, some of a surface impairment; but most cases represent a combination of both. Recent neurological evidence supports a view that developmental dyslexia may be partly attributable to differences in brain configuration. In non-dyslexics, an area of the brain known as the *planum temporale* tends to be larger in the left (language-associated) hemisphere than the right. However, in many dyslexics the two appear to be the same size. There have also been suggestions that some dyslexics have a larger right hemisphere, indicating a bias towards higher level language processing instead of decoding. Dyslexia appears to be more common in left-handers, suggesting a possible connection with brain **lateralisation** for language.

Section C

EXPLORATION:
ANALYSIS AND
REFLECTION

THE LANGUAGE STUDIED IN PSYCHOLINGUISTICS

Much of Psycholinguistics concerns itself with language processing, the aim being to describe how speakers manage to communicate with listeners and readers with writers. Study in this and related areas does not depend primarily upon linguistic theory – though it helps to know something of what languages are and how they are constructed. The focus is on how language is actually used. The raw material thus consists of physical realisations of speech and writing: the word as it occurs in the mouth of the speaker, the word as it appears on the page of a book.

Linguists vs psychologists

> Linguists and psychologists talk about different things . . . Grammarians are more interested in what could be said than in what people actually say, which irritates psychologists, and psychologists insist on supplementing intuition with objective evidence, which irritates linguists.
>
> (Miller 1990: 321)

Linguists concern themselves especially with the systems which underlie language. Thus, modern grammarians who follow the ideas of Noam Chomsky aspire to describe **competence** – the implicit knowledge of language rules which enables us to generate an infinite number of grammatically correct sentences, even when we have never heard them or said them before. By contrast, psycholinguists are especially interested in **performance** – in evidence of language in use.

The distinction is an important one. Linguistic theory attempts to describe the way in which language is structured. But that is not the same thing as describing the process which takes place in a user's mind when he / she actually produces or comprehends a piece of speech or writing. The hierarchical structure displayed in a Chomskyan tree diagram is a powerful way of representing the patterns which underlie language. But this does not necessarily mean that our minds store and process grammar in precisely this form. Some early psycholinguists attempted to prove that Chomskyan grammar is indeed psychologically real; but their results were generally unconvincing.

We also need to recognise a difference between an abstract account of a language system and the physical form the language takes in the ear and on the page. Psycholinguistics, especially the part of the subject that investigates language processing, is very much concerned with the latter. For the purposes of most psycholinguistic research, language must be assumed to contain all the hesitations, repetitions and false starts that theoretical linguists would wish to edit out. Similarly, the surface forms which feature in phonetic analysis are often more interesting to psycholinguists investigating speech than the phonological system which gives rise to them.

Speech vs writing

Psycholinguistics has to take account of differences in the way in which we process the two forms (or modalities) of language: the spoken and the written. You may be familiar with the major stylistic differences between the two (especially if you have studied discourse analysis). Here are three considerations which are especially important for language processing:

❏ Speech is spontaneous, whereas writing is deliberate. The result is that speech is often less precise than writing and more loosely structured syntactically. A listener takes account of this: editing out hesitations, making allowance for greater use of general nouns ('that thing in the newspaper about . . .') and coping with imprecise reference ('Fred argued with Bill, which upset *him*').

❏ Speech is connected, whereas writing uses discrete units. Where alphabetic writing has letters, speech has phonemes. But phonemes blend into each other: in a word like *cat*, we cannot say exactly where the [k] ends and the [æ] begins. Furthermore, where writing has words separated by blank spaces, pauses in speech are irregular and infrequent. So what we actually hear is a string of joined words.

❏ Speech takes place in real-time while writing can be reviewed. A reader can go back and check understanding; a listener cannot.

Compare what a listener has to do with what a reader has to do. Consider:

–   recognising sounds
–   recognising words
–   editing out unnecessary information
–   making connections (e.g. between pronouns and what they refer to)
–   carrying meaning forward from one sentence to another.

Productive vs receptive processes

Speaking and writing demand that we encode ideas into language; reading and listening that we decode language into ideas. We tend to assume that production and reception are closely linked; but this need not be so. Consider the following:

–   Are there words that you recognise in reading but that you would not normally use in everyday speech? Can you think of examples?
–   Assume that you are learning a foreign language. Your teacher introduces a set of new words for you to practise. Will you necessarily recognise them when you come across them in connected speech? Why not?

So we need to take careful account of the relationship between productive and receptive processes. Is the process of listening simply the process of speaking in reverse? Or does listening use a separate channel of its own?

Lower level vs higher level processes

Finally, we need to make a distinction between

–   processes which involve the raw data of speech or writing.
–   processes which involve shaping this data into meaning.

It is easiest to give an example from reading. Reading involves two distinct operations. A reader decodes the words on the page, and notes the sequence in which they appear. Once words have been recognised, he / she then has to build meaning at the level of the sentence and at the level of the text as a whole. These two operations would appear to involve different degrees of attention and even different parts of the brain.

TALKING APES

A number of attempts have been made to demonstrate that other primates (especially chimpanzees) can acquire language if properly taught.

The evidence

❏ The earliest attempts foundered because chimpanzees do not have an appropriate **vocal apparatus** to produce the sounds of human speech.

 Activity Does this physiological difference mean that apes cannot, by definition, acquire human language?

❏ There were then attempts to teach chimpanzees a modified form of the sign language used by the deaf. One chimp (Washoe) began learning at around one year old and mastered 130 signs in three years – a rate of acquisition much slower than that of a human infant. Washoe managed to produce sequences of two or three signs, including some original combinations; but she never developed a consistent word order. Another chimp (Nim Chimpsky) managed strings of up to four signs; and produced an impressive variety of sequences. However, Nim's productions involved much repetition of the same items and, like those of Washoe, showed great inconsistency of subject-verb-object word order. As Nim became older, he became more and more reliant on imitating his trainers. Contrast language acquisition by human infants, who employ progressively less imitation.

 Activity How would you describe what these chimps achieved? Think of: vocabulary vs syntax – phrase structure – imitation vs creativity.

❏ More recently, researchers have trained chimps to communicate by pointing to **lexigrams**, simple abstract shapes in various colours. Each shape is associated with a word such as *juice* or *banana*, but they bear no resemblance to the objects they refer to. The lexigrams appear on large keys mounted on a computer screen in the chimpanzee's cage.

One chimp, Lana, learnt over 100 symbols. She achieved quite a consistent word order, which may have been based upon habit or upon following the colour coding of the keys.

The researchers then varied the training programme with two other chimps, Austin and Sherman. They taught the chimps only a few symbols: two verbs plus four nouns for food and drink. They then rewarded them for semantically correct combinations (say, EAT + BANANA) but not incorrect ones (DRINK + BANANA). After many thousands of trials, the chimps came to recognise which combinations were appropriate. They proved quick to categorise new food and drink items when they learnt them.

What do the results with Austin and Sherman tell us about the capabilities of chimpanzees?

Compare the training process for these chimps with the process of a human child acquiring a language.

❏   One of the most successful results in language learning has been achieved with a **bonobo** (or pygmy chimpanzee) called Kanzi. Strangely, Kanzi's first exposure to language was unplanned. He was raised by a foster-mother, Matata, who proved to be a poor language learner. From a very young age, Kanzi was present at Matata's training sessions. When the researchers felt that he was old enough to begin learning, he showed that he already knew much of what they wanted to teach him. He mastered combinations of lexigrams without all the thousands of trials that Austin and Sherman had needed. In all, he learnt about 400 symbols. More importantly, he could group them in lexical sets and showed signs of using a consistent word order. He could understand some simple spoken English, even when the utterance was a novel one, and could respond appropriately to commands such as 'Put the soap on the apple'.

What explanations can you give for Kanzi's greater success?

Review the evidence given above. Do you think that chimpanzees (or bonobos) do or do not have a capacity for language? Take into account that language is OUR medium of communication, not theirs: designed by our minds to meet our needs.

The significance of chimp 'language'

Any evidence that other primates are capable of acquiring language has important implications for theories of language acquisition by humans. Those who take a **nativist** view suggest that all children are born endowed with a special language capability in the form of a **universal grammar**, which enables us to recognise characteristic patterns which occur in all of the world's languages.

Consider this in relation to the idea that chimps are capable of learning language. If chimps can be shown to recognise semantic categories like FOOD and to apply syntactic patterns (e.g. word order), then it suggests that they have access to the basic principles underlying language. But, in that case, why does some simplified form of language not emerge with chimps in the wild? This would be the logical conclusion of assuming that chimps possess a language capacity not dissimilar to that of humans. One answer would be that that chimps have a capacity for language but lack a genetically-transmitted trigger which sets it off as part of the normal process of maturation.

Experimental task

Language learning experiments are conducted on human beings as well as chimpanzees. The purpose might be to establish whether adults are capable of acquiring language implicitly (i.e. without specific attention to the material being taught). One method involves exposing subjects to an 'artificial grammar'. This is not a grammar, strictly speaking, but a set of rules which specify the order in which letters of the alphabet can appear (just as a grammar specifies the word order of an utterance).

Design a simple artificial grammar. Choose a letter (e.g. T). Choose four letters which can occur before it and four which can occur afterwards. Now compose 30 strings of four letters which obey your rules and 10 which break them. Say that N, Q, U and V are permitted before T and A, G, Y and J afterwards. Examples of correct strings might be: LNTG QTJR SVTG NTAZ ZUTY.

Divide subjects into two groups. Tell one group that they simply have to look at strings of letters; tell the second group they should look for patterns in the strings. Show 20 of the correct strings, one at a time, to subjects. The best way of doing this is by putting them on a computer, with one string per screen, and scrolling down every 2 seconds.

Immediately afterwards, give subjects a paper showing, in random order, the remaining 20 strings (half legal and half illegal). Ask subjects if they can tell which strings are correct and which are not. Compare the answers of the two groups. See if those who were not asked to look for patterns have managed to recognise regularities in the input.

Finally, evaluate this experimental method. To what extent can it really be said to resemble the process of first or second language acquisition?

Essays, further study ➤➤➤➤

1 Study the account of the bonobo Kanzi in Savage-Rumbaugh, E.S. and Lewin, R. (1994) *Kanzi: at the Brink of the Human Mind*, New York: Wiley. Do Kanzi's achievements convince you that other primates besides humans are capable of language?
2 Argue for one of the following factors as being the main reason why human beings possess language while other species do not:
   a social   b physiological   c cognitive   d genetic
3 Investigate three types of animal communication. To what extent do they fit Hockett's design features of language (page 51) and to what extent do they diverge?

LATERALISATION IN THE BRAIN

Lateralisation and language

The brain is divided into two hemispheres, joined by a mass of neural connections (the **corpus callosum**). The hemispheres have a **contralateral** relationship with the rest of the body: the right side of the brain controls movement and sensation on the left side of the body while the left hemisphere is responsible for the right side.

Very generally, the left hemisphere in most individuals is associated with analytic processing and symbolisation, while the right is associated with perceptual and spatial representation. This suggests an important role for the left hemisphere in language processing; and, indeed, the effects noted by Broca and Wernicke involved damage to the left side of the brain.

A link between the left hemisphere and language has since been confirmed by a number of different investigative techniques including:

Wada tests: where an injection into a major artery temporarily suspends the operations associated with either the left or the right hemisphere. In most (though not all) patients, language is suppressed when the left hemisphere is disabled.

dichotic listening: where different messages are fed simultaneously into two ears. The message that dominates is usually found to be the one in the right ear – i.e. the one that connects contralaterally with the left hemisphere.

commissurotomy: an operation in which the corpus callosum was severed in severe cases of epilepsy, disconnecting the two hemispheres. Patients who underwent this operation could name objects in their right field of vision (i.e. those where the image of the object connects with the left hemisphere) but not those in their left field of vision.

Factors affecting lateralisation

❐   Lateralisation and handedness: most individuals are right-handed, just as most individuals appear to be left-brain dominant for language. Recall that movement on the right side of the body is controlled chiefly by the left hemisphere. This suggests an intriguing connection between handedness and language. In evolutionary terms, could language have developed in conjunction with a right-handed advantage in using tools? There is certainly evidence that some left-handed people appear to have a right hemisphere specialised for language. But how general is this connection?

❐   Lateralisation and brain damage: many of those who suffer left hemisphere brain damage in the regions identified by Broca and Wernicke never recover their powers of speech. However, there are cases when language appears to have re-lateralised itself to the undamaged right hemisphere. These mainly involve people who have suffered brain damage at a very early age. It might be that in early life there is a period of flexibility in the brain, with neural connections yet to be fully established and language not yet lateralised. If the left part of the brain is unavailable due to an accident or surgery, then language might establish itself in the right hemisphere instead.

A major piece of research (Rasmussen and Milner 1977) used the Wada test to investigate the extent to which lateralisation is related to handedness and the extent to which re-lateralisation occurs after brain damage early in life. The results appear in the tables below (N indicates the number of people studied). What are your conclusions?

Table C3.1 Subjects with no known brain damage

Handedness	Speech representation		
	Left	Bilateral	Right
Right (N = 140)	134	0	6
	(96%)	(0%)	(4%)
Left or ambidextrous (N = 122)	86	18	18
	(70%)	(15%)	(15%)

Table C3.2 Subjects with clinical evidence of an early left-hemisphere lesion

Handedness	Speech representation		
	Left	Bilateral	Right
Right (N = 42)	34	3	5
	(81%)	(7%)	(12%)
Left or ambidextrous (N = 92)	26	17	49
	(28%)	(19%)	(53%)

Some more recent views and findings on lateralisation are discussed in the reading in Section D.

Critical period

The critical period hypothesis has it that there is a time during our early lives when we have maximum receptivity to language. If for any reason a child is not exposed to language during that period, the argument goes, it will only achieve a limited degree of competence. Lenneberg (1967) suggested a link between this theory and lateralisation: that the critical period might coincide with the time when the child's brain is flexible and before language has become fully distributed between the hemispheres.

The problem is that there is no agreement as to how long the critical period lasts and when the plasticity of the brain comes to an end. Lenneberg associated the end of the critical period with adolescence. Other researchers suggested it ended at five or at nine years of age. More recent evidence shows that some infants who undergo brain surgery do indeed suffer language impairment; and, conversely, that some aphasic adults may relocate part of their language functions in the right hemisphere.

The critical period theory has led to interest in the rare cases of children who have been deprived of language early in life. These are **wolf** (or feral) children such as Victor, the Wild Boy of Aveyron, who appears to have grown up in a forest after being abandoned; and **attic** children who have been confined by cruel or mentally incapable parents. Table 2.3 gives details of a few of the latter, including how much language they finally achieved.

Activity   1   Look at the ages at which the children were first exposed to language. Do you think the evidence supports the idea of a critical period? If so, at what age do you think it ends?

Table C3.3 Attic children as evidence of critical period

Name (country) researcher	Conditions of deprivation	Age when discovered	Amount of language achieved
Anna (USA) Davis, 1940	Tied up in storeroom Malnourished Possibly deaf	5;11	Repeated single words Tried to converse Died young at 10
Isabelle (USA) Mason, 1942	Deaf-mute mother	6;6	Vocalisation after 1 week Rapid language development After 1 year: basic reading After 18 months: 2000-word vocabulary Same language level as peers by 8;1
Twins PM, JM (Czech) Koluchova, 1972	Isolation. Confined in cellar, cupboard	7;3	Developed above-average language skills
Genie (USA) Curtiss, 1977	Confined to room; not allowed to talk	13;7	Rudimentary speech Rapid acquisition of vocabulary Failed to acquire adequate syntax Right hemisphere advantage for speech
Mary (UK) Skuse, 1984	Mentally retarded mother; children's home	3;6	Some rapid improvement Never achieved normal communication (possibly autistic)
Louise (UK) Skuse, 1984	Mentally retarded mother; children's home. Mary's sister.	2;4	Developed normal language skills
Adam (Colombia) Thompson, 1986	Reformatory school; children's home.	2;10	Normal development (at faster rate) once fostered

Source: Skuse (1994)

2   Do you think researchers should consider other factors besides age in studying delayed language acquisition? If so, what are they?

David Skuse (1993) draws the following conclusions from the language deprivation data:

a   In adverse childhood circumstances, language seems more vulnerable than other cognitive faculties.
b   In cases of deprivation, speech appears to be more retarded than comprehension. It develops more slowly after discovery.
c   Interpersonal contact makes an important contribution to the speed and success of late language development.

The concept of a Critical Period has been extended to second language learning. The hypothesis is:

–   that the plasticity of the brain permits younger learners to acquire a second language much more successfully than adult ones; or
–   that the universal grammar which permits us to acquire our first language is no longer available after a certain age.

The evidence suggests that a child who starts to acquire a language before the age of about eight is likely to end up with a native-like accent and fluency. But in areas other than pronunciation (e.g. grammar), adolescents and adults are often more successful in the early stages. There are implications here for studies of first language acquisition: the suggestion has been made that there may not be one critical period but a whole set of them, with different features of language competence being lateralised at different stages.

Experimental task

Discover the dominant hemisphere of a group of subjects by using a dichotic listening test. Record ten monosyllabic words on one cassette, with no pauses between them, and ten different monosyllabic words on a second cassette. Insert the cassettes into two different players, each with an earpiece. Attach the earpiece from one player to a subject's left ear and the earpiece from the other to the subject's right ear. Play the recordings simultaneously.

Ask subjects, immediately after listening, to write down as many words as they can recall. Check to see which recording they come from. Remember that a preference for words in the right ear indicates left hemisphere dominance and vice versa. Compare hemisphere dominance across the group. Check on handedness and see if there is any relationship between handedness and dominance.

Essays, further study ➤➤➤➤

1   Study Deacon, *The Symbolic Species*, London: Penguin, 1997, Chapter 5. Discuss the notion that human being possess language because their brains are larger than those of other species.
2   To what extent is it true that language is localised in two specific areas of the left hemisphere of the brain?

3 It has been suggested that women use the right hemisphere of their brain to a greater degree than men. If this is true, what might it tell us about their use of language?

THE MEANING OF 'MEANING'

C4

Philosophers and linguists have argued for centuries about what constitutes 'meaning'. Recently psychologists of language have joined the discussion, and brought in experimental evidence.

Central to the issue is the notion of category. As we have already noted, the word DOG does not usually refer to a single dog but to a whole class of dogs. We could define a dog in traditional terms as a household pet which barks and has four legs and a tail. But then what about a three-legged dog or a wild dog? Somehow, we still manage to recognise these as falling within the DOG category. But how? In this section, we look in depth at one theory, **Prototype Theory**, which has attempted to explain how categories operate. It is a theory to which there have been objections, and we will consider these as well. Further insight into the nature of categories will be offered by the reading in Section D4, which provides an overview of the evidence on how children form categories when acquiring their first language.

The classical view

First, let us consider the long-established view (sometimes called the **classical view**) that the meaning of a word can be broken down into a set of components. Attempts have been made to draw up a list of universal meaning components which would enable us to uniquely characterise any word in our vocabulary. Thus, we can represent the meaning of the word SQUARE by specifying that it must have (a) straight sides (b) equal sides and (c) right angles. One of the best-known attempts to argue for **componential analysis** examined the word BACHELOR; the experimenters (Katz and Fodor 1963) suggested that the main sense of the word was uniquely specified by the following:

[MALE] [HUMAN] [UNMARRIED] [ADULT]

Consider the BACHELOR example in the light of the following (* indicates a sentence that is semantically doubtful):

 Activity

*The Pope is a bachelor.

Might we have to change the term [UNMARRIED]? To what? Will the new term serve to categorise more words than [UNMARRIED] or fewer?

Now consider the word SPINSTER which can be analysed as [FEMALE] [HUMAN] [UNMARRIED] [ADULT]. Is gender the only difference between these two sentences?

Phillip is a bachelor.   Felicity is a spinster.

Prototype Theory

An alternative view of word meaning comes from the work of a researcher (Rosch 1975) who presented her subjects with a questionnaire which contained category names (bird, vegetable, fruit, clothing furniture, transport, etc.) followed by around fifty examples of each one. The task was to rate each item out of 7 as a good example of the category.

Over 200 subjects (psychology students in California) performed the task, and there was found to be a very high level of agreement between them as to which items were the most typical.

On the basis of this finding, Rosch argued that we determine a category in relation to an ideal exemplar – a prototype – of the group. We can decide which creatures belong to the category of BIRD on the basis of **goodness of fit** to the prototypical bird, which (for Rosch's subjects) was a robin. The theory also enables us to account for how we extend the category to a bird that only has one wing or cannot sing. It is simply a less typical bird.

Activity   Here is a selection based upon Rosch's items. Rate them yourself, ranging from 1 for a poor example of the category to 7 for a very good one.

Table C4.1 Categories and exemplars

Furniture	Birds	Vehicle	Fruit	Vegetable
picture	blackbird	cart	fig	pea
6 chair	penguin	bus	pear	mushroom
telephone	hawk	elevator	nut	beansprout
lamp	ostrich	ski	apple	carrot
4 piano	sparrow	car	mango	onion
vase	raven	subway	olive	lettuce
stool	bat	wheelbarrow	orange	tomato
7 table	parrot	yacht	pumpkin	potato
dresser	canary	taxi	melon	cauliflower

Source: Based upon Rosch (1975)

Activity   Compare your answers with those of other students. Now ask yourself:

1   What kind of criteria did you use in deciding whether an *ostrich* was a good example of the category BIRD?

2   What kind of criteria did you use in deciding if a *bat* was a good example of a BIRD? Or *tomato* a good example of VEGETABLE?

3   Do you think that factors other than word meaning might have affected your decision about which items were best examples of the category FRUIT?
4   Look at the items which you chose as most typical of the category VEGETABLE. What do they have in common? Is it easier or more difficult to decide how you chose a good VEGETABLE than to decide how you chose a good BIRD?
5   In choosing items for VEGETABLE, did you experience interference from any other possible category?

Your answers to the questions above should have given you some indications of the strengths and weaknesses of Prototype Theory. But now consider the theory in relation to the following:

❏   Schwanenflugel and Rey (1986) repeated the Rosch experiment with two groups in Florida: one of English-speaking monolinguals and one of Spanish-speaking monolinguals who had lived in Florida for an average of fifteen years. The table shows the most typical exemplars chosen for the category BIRD. The exemplars are ranked in order of choice, with a number in brackets showing how the other group ranked them.

Table C4.2   Prototypicality ratings for the category BIRD

English speakers		Spanish speakers	
Exemplar	Rating	Exemplar	Rating
1 eagle (3)	6.52	1 canario (canary) (16)	6.38
2 robin (24)	6.46	2 pájaro carpintero (woodpecker) (9)	6.06
3 cardinal (10)	6.40	3 águila (eagle) (1)	5.84
4 bluebird (16)	6.40	4 golondrina (swallow) (17)	5.70
5 seagull (9)	6.34	5 cotorra (parrot) (5)	5.63
6 hawk (11)	6.30	6 gorrión (sparrow) (15)	5.50
7 jay (27)	6.29	7 paloma (dove) (8)	5.46
8 dove (7)	6.18	8 perico (parakeet) (14)	5.44

Source: Based on Schwanen flugel and Rey (1986)

❏   Armstrong, Gleitman and Gleitman (1983) asked subjects to choose numbers that were good examples of the category ODD NUMBER and EVEN NUMBER. Subjects realised that it made no sense to talk of a typical even number – but went on to choose examples quite consistently. They found that 2 and 4 were 'good' examples of even numbers but that 34 and 106 were not. They also reported that *mother* and *ballerina* were prototypical exemplars of the category FEMALE, but *policewoman* and *comedienne* were not.

❏   In an early prototype experiment, Labov (1973) asked subjects to give names to drawings of vessels which resembled a cup to different degrees. He found that there was no sharp agreement on where (say) a CUP ended and a BOWL began. He went on to ask subjects to imagine the vessels full of (a) coffee, (b) flowers and (c) mashed potato. He discovered that the extent to which the vessels were identified as cups was determined not just by how closely they resembled a pro- totypical cup but also by their suggested use. Thus the switch from CUP to BOWL occurred much earlier if subjects were told to imagine the vessel full of mashed potato, as did the shift from CUP to VASE if flowers were introduced.

Some conclusions

❑ Speakers who share a particular language seem to recognise similar prototypes for at least some of the language's categories. Of course, this does not necessarily mean that we use prototypes to determine what does and does not belong in a category.

❑ The choice of a prototype is sometimes determined by a set of **attributes** which are characteristic of the category. Thus, we expect a typical bird to have wings, to sing, to have feathers, to lay eggs. We make allowances for birds which do not meet these requirements but which show at least some **family resemblances**. The trouble is that not all categories can be explained in terms of physical characteristics (What does a pea have in common with a carrot?).

❑ Category membership may sometimes be complicated by the fact that an item belongs to two categories. Thus, we might rank a lettuce as a not very typical VEGETABLE because it also falls into the smaller category SALAD.

❑ Prototypes may to some extent reflect the culture in which the individual has grown up. We should also recognise that other languages may have fewer or more categories than English. Spanish has three categories for the items that an English speaker groups together as VEGETABLES.

❑ Category membership may be more flexible than has been assumed. In classify- ing items, we may be influenced by the context in which we find them and the use to which they are being put.

❑ It has been argued that we need to make a distinction between **conceptual cores** and **identification functions**. The first tells us that an even number is any num- ber that is divisible by 2; but the second makes us aware that some even numbers are easier to recognise than others. We know that our GRANDMOTHER is the mother of one of our parents. But a grandmother with grey hair, wrinkles and twinkly eyes relates more closely to the identification function for the category than a grandmother who dyes her hair, smokes cannabis and drives a sports car. Similarly, your reasons for rejecting *bat* as a BIRD and *tomato* as a VEGETABLE may have more to do with scientific knowledge than with the way in which you conceptualise these entities.

Experimental task

Design a simple word association test and use it with a group of around 20 subjects. Choose 15 common nouns of high frequency. Read the list aloud to each subject; ask them to say the first word that comes into their head when they hear each item. Record their responses on cassette. Classify the responses in terms of the relationship between the word produced by the subject and the stimulus word (co-ordinate, co-hyponym, binary antonym, etc.). Do you notice any common patterns across subjects?

Essays, further study ➤➤➤➤

1   Read Aitchison, J., *Words in the Mind*, Oxford: Blackwell, 1994, 2003. Chapter 11. Argue for or against the idea that prefixes and suffixes are stored separately in the lexicon.
2   Present the arguments for and against Prototype Theory.
3   Suggest why it is difficult to account for the way in which the words *colour / color* and *economics* (/iːkəˈnɒmɪks/ vs /ekəˈnɒmɪks/) are represented in the lexicon. Suggest examples of your own. Which solution do you prefer?

MODELS OF LEXICAL RETRIEVAL

C5

An important distinction is often made between **lexical access** and **lexical recognition**. In most models of how listeners and readers locate words in the lexicon, access precedes recognition. The assumption is that, when we hear or see a word, we open up the entries for a number of possible matches (= access). These remain active in the mind until we are able to decide which of them is the correct one (= recognition).

Serial models vs parallel models
Let us imagine that a reader comes across the word *example* in a text. How do they match the word to a representation in their mental lexicon?

As we have already seen, the word is stored with others which share a similar form. One way of conceiving of the lexicon might be as a mammoth mental dictionary, with entries as follows:

exacerbate
exact
exaggerate
exalt
exalted
examination
examine
example
exasperate

A **search model** of lexical access would suggest that our reader looks up the EX- entries and works through them until reaching a word which forms a perfect match to the one on the page.

Activity ✪   The lexicon would not be very efficient if a reader had to go through the words in the order shown above. Look at the words and suggest why.

A more efficient search model would be one that arranged the words by form, but also took account of the fact that some words are more frequent than others, and therefore more likely to occur in our reader's text:

exact
example
examine
examination
exaggerate
exasperate
exalted
exalt
exacerbate

This is the kind of approach favoured by Forster's search model (1976). In it, words are arranged in **bins** according to similarity of form and according to modality (spoken vs written). But those that are 'higher' in the bin (and therefore reached first by the searcher) are the most frequent.

This kind of approach is **serial** – taking one word at a time. It makes few demands on the processor, but is slow in terms of time. The assumption was that the human mind worked a little like a computer (early computers were restricted to serial operations). However, another possibility is that our minds are a great deal more sophisticated and (thanks to the millions of neural connections of which they are composed) can process words **in parallel**. A search for EXAMPLE might pull out a large number of similar words and compare them simultaneously with the word on the page.

exact ↓ examine ↓ examination ↓ example ↓ exaggerate ↓ exacerbate ↓

These words are sometimes referred to as **candidates** and, in many models, are seen as competing with each other to be the one that is selected.

Activation models

This competition between words is often represented in terms of **activation**, a metaphor which was briefly introduced in Section A5. A word is activated to the extent that the perceiver regards it as likely to be present on a page or in an utterance. When we encounter a particular string of letters or sounds, we access a number of possible word matches. They are activated to different degrees – with the more likely ones (those that match most closely what is in the input) receiving more activation than the less likely. Activation level can change as the language user reads or hears more of the word – so some candidate words may have their activation boosted by late-arriving information while others may have their activation depressed. The process is a little like one of those modern fountains where various jets of water (= candidate words) spurt up to different heights at different times. Finally, one word receives enough supportive evidence for it to break through a threshold – it is recognised as the only possible match for the word that is in the input.

Two important points about activation:

❏ It is not simply a reflection of how closely a candidate matches the input. It also reflects frequency. Suppose we hear a word whose opening sounds are /ɪkˈzæ/. EXACT will receive greater activation than EXACERBATE because it is a much more common word and therefore a more likely candidate.

❏ The activation principle allows us to account for instances where we make a match that is less than 100 per cent precise. Suppose we read the word *exazerbate* or hear somebody say the word *shigarette*. The words EXACERBATE and CIGARETTE do not entirely match the signal – but they are far and away the leading candidates, with the highest amount of activation. So we settle for them as the **best fit**.

It is important to realise that creating a set of candidates involves accessing the candidates' lexical entries. This means that information about word meaning becomes available. Some commentators argue that the information boosts the activation of candidates that are semantically appropriate to the context and lowers the activation of others. Others argue that to bring in meaning at this stage adds an enormous complication, which might distract us from the task of weighing up the evidence of our eyes or ears.

The spoken word and Cohort Theory

As an example of how a set of word candidates might be generated, we consider **Cohort Theory**, an influential model of spoken word recognition (Marslen-Wilson 1987).

Unlike written texts, speech unfolds in time. At any given moment, a listener may have heard only part of a message – or indeed part of a word. Evidence suggests that a listener begins to process an utterance about 200 milliseconds (a fifth of a second) after the speaker begins to speak. 200 milliseconds is about the length of a syllable.

a So let us envisage a listener who has just heard the sequence /ɪmp/. This may be a complete monosyllabic word or it may be the first syllable of a larger word; there is no way of knowing.
   – What lexical access occurs at this stage?
   – What candidate words does the listener access?
b Now (about 200 milliseconds later), the listener has heard more. The sequence so far is /ɪmˈpɔːt/.
   – What changes have been made to the list of candidate words?
   – What has happened to words that no longer match the signal?
c Now the listener has heard more. The sequence at this stage is /ɪmpɔːtən/.
   – What will be the effect on the candidate list?
d Next, the listener hears /t/.
   – What is the situation now?

Cohort theory suggests that we open up a cohort (a set) of word candidates on the basis of the evidence provided by the beginning of a word (probably the first syllable), and gradually narrow down the candidates as more evidence becomes available.

/kæp/ opens up a cohort of
CAP – CAPITAL – CAPTAIN – CAPTIVE – CAPTION – CAPSULE, etc.
When we then hear /t/, it reduces the cohort to
CAPTAIN – CAPTIVE – CAPTOR
When we hear /ɪ/, the cohort shrinks to
CAPTAIN – CAPTIVE
With /n/, we reach a **uniqueness point**, where only one candidate is left:
CAPTAIN

In the present version of the theory, candidates are not rejected outright when they no longer match the developing signal. Instead, they lose activation. It is possible that, at the end of the process, there may be no candidates left in the cohort (for example, if the listener is trying to make a match to the *shigarette* input mentioned earlier). But the listener can still choose the most highly activated candidate as the one offering the best fit. In this way, the theory allows for the fact that an auditory signal is often less reliable than a visual one, because of external noise or the speaker's accent or a slip of the tongue.

Not as simple as it appears . . .

Activity

Here are some words that pose problems for Cohort Theory. Can you suggest why?

CAP / CAPPED / CAPTAIN – RUNNING – IMPORT – METAPHOR

❏ It was implied in this account of listening that words are accessed as a result of identifying phonemes. This is probably a simplification. It may be that we do not use the phoneme as a unit of processing at all – but recognise words instead through combinations of phonological features (+ voiced, + nasal, etc.) or syllable by syllable.

❏ It may also be that we use multiple cues to the identity of a word. The view is perhaps best illustrated by considering the reader rather than the listener. It is clear that on the page the reader has a number of different pieces of information which can assist word recognition. From smaller to larger, these are:
  – the features of the letters (curves, straight lines, etc.)
  – the letters
  – the sequence in which the letters appear
  – the word as a whole
  – the context in which the word occurs.

Interactive models of word recognition suggest that all these cues can affect activation – and can do so simultaneously.

Experimental task

Lexical items are accessed more quickly when they occur frequently. Check this frequency effect with a lexical decision test. Compile a list of 15 monosyllabic four-letter words which are very frequent in English. Choose them from different word classes. Now compile a list of 15 monosyllabic four-letter words which are infrequent. Make sure you have the same balance of word classes as in the first list. Check frequencies with a reputable database (e.g. Leech *et al.* 2001).

Add 15 four-letter non-words to each of your lists, inserting them randomly. Make sure the non-words represent possible words within the rules of English spelling (e.g. SOST or BINK but not VWOJ). Type your lists of 30 entries on to a computer, with a blank screen at the beginning of each of the lists and the distance of a screen between each entry. Ask subjects to scroll down with their right hand, pressing a buzzer with their left (or even just tapping on the desk) immediately they come across an actual English word. For half the subjects, the 'frequent' list should be presented first, and for half, the 'infrequent'. Time how long it takes subjects to complete the task for the 'frequent' list and how long for the 'infrequent'. Compare timings.

Essays, further study ➤➤➤➤

1   Read Reeves *et al.* (pp. 170–80) in Gleason, J. B. and Ratner, N. B., *Psycholinguistics*, Fort Worth: Harcourt Brace, 1998. Describe either a serial or a parallel model of lexical access and suggest its strengths and weaknesses.
2   Write a critique of Cohort Theory.
3   Does context affect lexical access? Consider the advantages of bringing context into the process at an early stage, and the disadvantages.

MEMORY AND LANGUAGE   **C6**

As we saw in Section A6, a distinction is made between:

–   Long Term Memory, holding information which is stored for long periods or permanently.
–   Working Memory, holding information which is part of a current operation. This might be information from the environment (e.g. linguistic input which we are processing) or it might be information retrieved from Long Term Memory and held temporarily for present use.

Early research also suggested the existence of sensory stores in which traces of an incoming stimulus were briefly retained. These included a visual store which held material for about 0.5 seconds and an auditory store which held material for rather longer.

Let us now review this last idea.

1 Do you think that a visual trace is strictly necessary for reading?
2 There is evidence that listening takes place **on-line**: that we process what we hear only 200 milliseconds behind the speaker. Does this suggest that an auditory trace is needed for word recognition or that it is not?

Phonology in Working Memory

Let us examine two important assumptions of the 'sensory store' theory:

– Do the processes involved in listening and reading need two separate sensory stores?
– Does sensory storage support word recognition – or does it serve some other function?

 Activity Here are some simple experiments (based on those in the literature) which may shed light on these questions.

TASK 1: Your teacher or a class member will dictate to you sixteen words from List A on page 206 (1.5–2 seconds apart). Listen and try to memorise the words. Afterwards, write down as many as you can recall (90 seconds). Now you will hear List B, also of sixteen words (1.5–2 seconds apart). Again, listen and try to memorise them. Afterwards, write down those that you recall.

Compare notes on which words you remembered. Bear in mind that the words have been controlled for frequency.

1 Did the position of the words in the list have any effect?
2 Is there any difference in the number of words recalled from List A and those from List B? If so, what is the reason?
3 Did you notice when memorising List B that some of the words begin with the same letters (RE-, COM- UN-)? Or not?

 Activity TASK 2: Now turn to page 210. Study List C for 30 seconds and try to remember the words that appear in it. Close your book and write down the words you recall.

Ask yourself: How did I commit those words to memory? Did I do so by picturing them? Or did I use some other means of support?

Now study List D in the same way for 30 seconds. Close your book and write down the words you remember.

Compare answers. Remember that the words have been controlled for frequency.

1 Were you aware of using the same memorisation strategy for List D as for List C?
2 Did you recall more or fewer words from List D than from List C?
3 Is this a similar result to the one you achieved in Task 1?
4 Look at the spellings of some of the words in List C. Do you think they affected your ability to memorise the words?

It would appear that, when trying to memorise words, we rely on some kind of 'voice in the head'. We are said to **rehearse** the words in our heads subvocally (in a way that does not involve us actually using our voices). What is important is that this occurs whether we are memorising spoken words or written words. The spoken words are already available in phonological form, but it seems that the written words are encoded phonologically so that we can rehearse them.

Two common findings in word memorisation tasks are a **primacy effect**, where the first words are remembered better and a **recency effect** where the last one or two are remembered better. The recency effect appears to be stronger with spoken lists than with written ones. This suggests that speech is more readily stored in verbatim form because it does not have to be **recoded** in the way that writing does.

There is also a well-established finding that we remember spoken lists of shorter words better than spoken lists of longer ones. What appears to make the difference is not how many syllables there are in a word, but how long it takes to say the word. It takes the listener longer to rehearse a list of trisyllabic words (like those in List B), so placing a greater burden on our memory. Again, what is significant is that this effect, associated with speech, is also seen when we try to memorise written words. Here too, subvocal rehearsal seems to be important – even when the input is visual.

In today's leading model of Working Memory (Baddeley 1990; Gathercole and Baddeley, 1993), there is a **phonological loop**, which consists of a **phonological store** plus a **rehearsal mechanism**. Spoken language has direct access to the phonological store. However, the store has a very limited capacity in terms of what it can hold. The trace of the spoken word decays very quickly (in 1–2 seconds). If we want to retain it (e.g. in a memorisation exercise), we rehearse it to prevent the verbatim form of words from fading.

From the kind of evidence discussed above, many commentators have concluded that writing as well as speech has links to the phonological store In the Baddeley model, written language feeds into the rehearsal mechanism. A second function of this mechanism is to convert written words into a phonological code. In this way, they can be rehearsed and fed into the phonological store just like spoken words. It might seem surprising that visual words are not fed into a separate visual store (there is one such in the model, termed the **visuo-spatial sketchpad**). This reflects the recognition (supported by the tasks above and by a great deal of reading research) that there is a strong phonological basis to the way in which the written word is processed and that our recall of written words depends very much upon this feature.

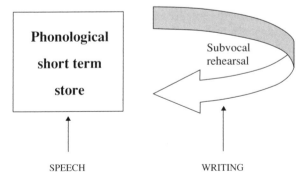

Figure C6.1   The Baddeley model of Working Memory
Source: Based on Gathercole and Baddeley (1993: Figure 1.3)

But (leaving aside memorisation) does the phonological store play any part in recognition of the spoken or the written word? It would seem that reading does not normally need such support because evidence of the written word remains on the page. Furthermore, listening has been found to be on-line, with the listener interpreting what is said only a fifth of a second behind the speaker. This suggests that the phonological store is not necessary even for recognising the spoken word.

If it is not relied on at word level, does it have other uses in supporting general comprehension? Do we need to keep some kind of verbatim form of a message in our minds while we establish understanding of a clause or sentence? The question has been investigated by means of what is known as **articulatory suppression**. This is a way of preventing rehearsal, and thus making it difficult for a subject to retain the actual words that they have read. The technique involves asking the subject to utter meaningless words (e.g. saying the word *the* repeatedly) at the same time as performing a task.

It was found that articulatory suppression does not stop readers from judging the truth of simple sentences such as

a Canaries have wings.   b Canaries have gills.

It appears that, in these cases, comprehension does *not* depend critically upon the subject being able to retain a verbatim form of the message through rehearsal. However, in other cases, articulatory suppression has been found to interfere strongly with comprehension.

Activity   Here are some examples of the kinds of sentence that might be subject to rehearsal. Suggest why it might be necessary for a listener to keep a verbatim form in their mind.

c   Mary liked John but his brother she couldn't stand.
d   Miss Peacock was murdered by Colonel Mustard.
e   Although Peter had said he'd reply, he didn't.
f   The artist I met at the party lived in Australia.
g   The point about photography – and I shouldn't really be saying this because I write books about it – is that you have to keep at it.

It would seem that we sometimes need to retain the verbatim form of a sentence when it is difficult to impose a semantic or syntactic pattern upon it until we are near the end. This seems to apply with sentences that are long or complex (e.g. (e) and (g)); with sentences with a word order that is not standard (e.g. (c)); and with sentences where it is not immediately clear what the subject is (e.g. (c) and reversible passives such as (d)). It also seems to apply when (as in (f) or (g)) there is an embedded second sentence which delays the completion of the main sentence.

Researchers do not agree about the implications. Some suggest that we rely upon the stored verbatim message to assist us when analysing a complex utterance for its syntactic structure. Others suggest that we allocate a provisional syntactic structure, then use the stored representation to check whether it is correct.

Working Memory capacity

The most important characteristic of Working Memory is that it is limited. There are limits (a) to what it can store and (b) to the amount of processing it can undertake.

On storage, an important paper (Miller 1956) suggests that Working Memory is only capable of holding about seven pieces of information (plus or minus two) at a time. This means that it is under pressure:

- to **chunk** information (combining smaller units into larger ones); we might remember an 8-digit phone number as 83-42-76-18 instead of 83427618;
- to shed verbatim information and replace it with abstract propositions (one complete idea instead of a number of words);
- to transfer important information to Long Term Memory before it decays.

On processing, Baddeley suggests that Working Memory is controlled by a **Central Executive** which determines how much **attention** a particular processing task demands (Compare the different amounts of attention involved in calculating 2 + 3 and 13497 + 56832). Sentences like (a) and (b) above demand few attentional resources whereas sentences like (g) demand more. Because our attentional capacity is limited, we may even encounter sentences which exceed it – hence the problems we find in processing a sentence such as: *The man the dog the cat chased bit died.*

Controlled vs automatic processes

On the basis of this theory of WM capacity, it is in our interests to **automatise** the processes that we engage in. If a process is automatic (e.g. if we can recognise words immediately without having to decipher them), then few demands are made upon WM and we have capacity available for other processes.

When a process is unfamiliar, it demands conscious attention and sometimes has to be performed step by step. Gradually, as we become more skilled at the process, it becomes automatised – demanding fewer and fewer mental resources. Some processes may become entirely automatic. Consider what you do when you want to go through a door. How much conscious thought (= control) do you have to apply? Or (to take a linguistic example), how much control do you have to apply to recognising the word PAGE and matching it to a meaning?

Experimental task

Use a word recall experiment to investigate the role of the phonological loop. The following lists of words have been matched for number of letters. They have also been roughly matched for frequency:

LIST A	strange	brought	sparkle	dressed	through	station	glanced
	squeeze	clothes	ground	bridge	please	scratch	flowers
LIST B	caravan	imitate	cinema	visible	satisfy	animal	economy
	educate	holiday	potato	family	occupy	another	musical

Show both sets to your subjects, with an interval between the two. With half the subjects, show List A first; with the other half, show List B first. Present one word at a time, using an overhead projector or scrolling down on a computer screen. Allow 2 seconds per word. After subjects have seen the first list, ask them to write down all the words they can recall. Repeat for the second list. Then:

a   ask subjects to report on their experience of committing the words to memory. See if they were aware of rehearsing them in their mind.
b   compare results to see if one set is more easily recalled than the other. In what way do the words in the lists differ? Can you relate this difference to the idea of verbal rehearsal, using the phonological loop? For information on this effect, see the discussion of digit recall in Section D6.

Essays, further study ➤➤➤➤

1   Read Gathercole, S. E. and Baddeley, A. D., *Working Memory and Language*, Hove: Erlbaum, 1993, Chapter 3. Examine the part played by phonological working memory. Suggest its likely role in second language learning.
2   Below is a simplified version of a figure devised by Cowan to illustrate his **'embedded processes'** model of working memory (1999: 63). The large rectangle represents all of the information in Long Term Memory. The jagged shape represents a small part of Long Term Memory, which is temporarily activated at the moment. The circle represents the part of the activated information on which attention is currently focused (e.g. a group of words whose meaning is being processed). It is shown as a subset of the activated information on the grounds that information has be activated before it can be focused on.

Attention is basically limited by capacity: only so much information can be focused on at a given moment. But activation is limited by time: it decays after a short period. How does Cowan's model differ from the Baddeley one?

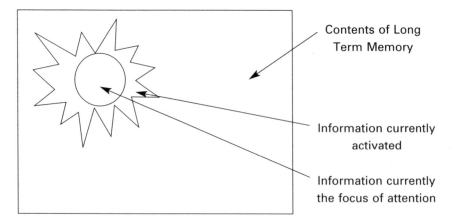

Figure C6.2   Cowan's model of memory

C

THE STAGES OF WRITING

C7

⭐ **Activity**

To understand a little more about the writing process, you are asked to write a short essay on ecology. The proposition is: 'Greedy consumers are responsible for the destruction of the earth's resources and for global pollution'.

You have five minutes to write the essay. Your teacher will ask you to pause from time to time. If you are working on your own, stop after each minute of writing. When you stop, answer the following questions.

After 1 minute of writing: 'What words / sentences / images do I have in my mind that prepare me for what I am about to write next?'

After 2 minutes of writing: 'What exactly was I doing at the moment I had to pause? What am I about to do next?'

After 3 minutes of writing: 'What decisions have I made since the last time I paused?'

After 4 minutes of writing: 'Have I thought at any stage about how this will appear to the reader? If so, what did I do?'

Stop writing after 5 minutes and review what you have written. Look at any changes you have made and decide: 'Why did I make them?' Ask yourself: 'What decisions did I make along the way? What order did I make the decisions in?'

Now compare your responses with those of your fellow students. To what extent were you aware of dealing with low level issues (spelling, letter order, vocabulary, grammar)? To what extent were you preoccupied with higher level issues (ordering ideas, planning arguments)?

The writing buffer

When you paused, you probably found that you had a general proposition in your mind which you were trying to express, and also, more concretely, some words and phrases. One set was almost certainly an immediate continuation of what you were currently writing. Ask yourself what form these words were in: did they strike you as being stored in visual form or in phonological form, like a 'voice in the head'?

It seems that, when we are in the process of writing, we need to store strings of words in a kind of **buffer** in the mind (the term comes from the information store that feeds a computer's printer). It is not possible to write without some kind of forward planning. Consider how Charles Dickens came to write the line: 'It was the best of times, it was the worst of times'. He could not have written the first part without anticipating the second. At the time he was physically producing with his pen:

It was the best of times

we have to assume that he had ready in his mental buffer the continuation: 'it was the worst of times'.

What form does this storage take? It appears to be phonological. Most writers report it in terms of spoken words – though we may only be aware of this '**voice in the head**' when we pause and reflect on our writing as you just did. But why should the buffer store words in this way? Would it not make more sense to store them in visual form? One argument might be that we originally learnt to write as an extension of learning to speak and retain vestiges of that experience. Perhaps more importantly, a phonological code is believed to be more durable than a visual one. Try to retain in your mind the physical form of the words you read in my last sentence; you will find it difficult. A further consideration is that, if words are stored in the mind in spoken form they do not interfere with the written forms that we are producing on the page.

There has been discussion about whether the complete form of words is stored in the buffer. Some writers, challenged to put down on paper what is currently in their minds, have recorded only key words or abbreviated sequences.

Higher and lower level processing

When you analysed your own writing, you probably found that you were paying very little heed to details of spelling, letter formation, letter sequencing, etc. In an experienced writer, these processes are highly automatised. There is an important trade-off at work here. We can only operate at the higher levels, planning and organising our ideas on the page, if we have developed a sufficiently automatic command of lower level activities such as spelling and letter formation. Hence the limited powers of expression of children who are learning to write and whose chief concern is legibility.

Think of it in terms of our limited Working Memory capacity. If we have to concentrate a great deal of attention upon forming letters, we do not have enough memory resources left to focus upon the higher level tasks of planning, monitoring and revising what we write.

The stages of writing

Here is a relatively simple three-stage model of writing which uses terminology proposed by Brown, McDonald, Brown and Carr (1988) and draws upon a paper by the American writing researcher Ronald Kellogg (1996). Study it and see if you can explain the arrows.

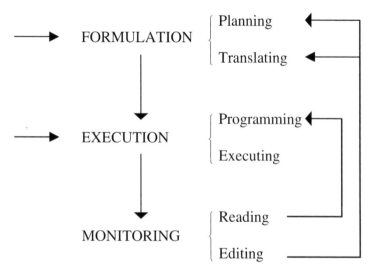

Figure C7.1 The stages of writing

The amount of processing at the **formulation** stage is one of the chief differences between a skilled and a less skilled writer. The writing specialists Carl Bereiter and Marlene Scardamalia suggest that the skilled writer takes account both of **task demands** ('What do I want to achieve? Who is my reader?') and of **text demands** ('What genre and text type is appropriate?').

Within formulation, **planning** involves setting goals, thinking of ideas to represent and organising these ideas so that they are coherently structured. **Translating** transforms these abstract concepts into linguistic form – selecting appropriate vocabulary and syntactic structure. It is then that a buffer is needed to store the products of translating.

The next stages, **programming** and **execution**, convert the phonological code of the buffer into motor instructions to the appropriate muscles, and carry out those instructions.

Monitoring, the third stage, is a further mark of skill. A good writer does not simply produce a text but reviews it both while and after writing. Reading may lead to revisions to the form of the text (for example, spelling corrections), while **editing** may involve rethinking decisions made at the formulation stage. Monitoring thus involves questions such as:

– Is the text correct (in terms of spelling and grammar)?
– Is the text **cohesive** (in terms of links between and within sentences)?
– Does the text fit my goals?
– Does it represent my arguments coherently?

An important part of monitoring is for writers to imagine themselves in the shoes of the readers. Considerations are:

– Will the words I have chosen have the desired **affective** (emotional) **impact**?
– Have I correctly identified knowledge that I share with the reader and knowledge that I have to introduce as new?
– Can the reader follow my patterns of logic?

The point made earlier about automatisation particularly applies here. The more automatic the execution stage, the more Working Memory capacity is available for monitoring and revising during the writing process.

A final point. Some writing begins not with formulation but with execution. This may be a mark of less skilled writing which omits the formulation stage. However, even skilled writers sometimes go straight to their keyboard without planning. The act of putting words on the page is sometimes found to stimulate ideas that were apparently not there at the outset. There has been interest in trying to explain how the physical act of writing can generate ideas in this way, but it remains difficult to account for. In terms of the model above, it might be that execution triggers the monitoring process and so starts off the cycle indicated by the arrows.

Experimental task

1   A method much used to investigate writing is **verbal report**, where the writer records what is foremost in their mind while they are actually writing. Ideally, this is done on to an audiocassette so that the interruption of the writing process is minimised.

The writer can either report spontaneously when they feel that they have some-thing to say – or they can be asked to pause every minute or so, as happened with you in this section.

Set a simple writing task for four subjects: ask them, for example, to write a job application to be a teacher of English. Ask two to report spontaneously and two to pause every minute. Record their comments and compare the kinds of information you derive. Consider the possible drawbacks of this experimental method.

2   Alternatively, investigate your own redrafting and editing decisions. After writ-ing a first draft of an essay or letter, pull down the Tools options on a Word for Windows program. Click on 'Track Changes' and then on 'Highlight changes'. Insert a tick for each entry. Now return to your draft and revise it. The computer screen will show in red all the changes you make. Stop after four or five para-graphs and classify the changes you made as: orthographical – lexical – syntactic – rhetorical (change of impact on reader) – change in structure of passage.

Essays, further study ➤➤➤➤

1   Read Scardamalia. M. and Bereiter, C. in S. Rosenberg (ed.), *Advances in Applied Psycholinguistics, Vol. 2*, Cambridge: Cambridge University Press, 1987. Describe the difference between knowledge telling and knowledge transforming.
2   Distinguish 'bottom-up' and 'top-down' processes in writing. Suggest how a weakness in one might affect performance in the other.
3   Contrast the psychological processes involved in using different writing systems.

C8   ## SKILLED AND UNSKILLED READERS

'Bottom-up' vs 'top-down'
Here are two views on the reading process.

> . . . nonvisual information can be employed to reduce the reader's uncertainty in advance and to limit the amount of visual information that must be processed. The more prior knowledge a reader can bring to bear about the way letters go together in words, the less visual information is required to identify individual letters. Prediction, based on prior knowledge, eliminates likely alternatives in advance. Similarly, the more a reader knows about the way words go together in grammatical and meaningful phrases – because of the reader's prior knowledge of the particular language and of the topics being discussed – the less visual information is required to identify indi-vidual words. In the latter case, meaning is being used as part of nonvisual informa-tion to reduce the amount of visual information required to identify words.
>
> (Frank Smith 1988: 155)

With respect to learning how to read, mastery of the code is essential. As development of skill increases and as text demands increase, these coding processes do not
become less important. They . . . must be executed fluently, with little effort. The increased
textual demands mean the reader must make more and more use of higher level
comprehension processes. This can be done only [provided there is not excessive]
expenditure of resources [on] low level coding skills. . . . Readers of low ability have
inefficient – slow and effortful – coding as the major obstacle to reading achievement.

(Charles Perfetti 1985: 10)

The first quote is sometimes described as a 'top-down' view. In 1967, the American
reading adviser Kenneth Goodman described reading as a 'psycholinguistic guessing
game'. He took the view that a good reader did not need to decode every word on the
page but made extensive use of context to anticipate words and thus to reduce unnecessary visual processing. This view underpins the whole word method for teaching
reading which focuses on meaningful reading tasks at an early stage instead of teaching letter-sound mappings through phonics.

The second quote could be interpreted as favouring a 'bottom-up' view (though
Perfetti's theory is considerably more complex). On this analysis, readers are only
capable of constructing higher level meaning and bringing background knowledge
to bear if they have fully mastered the mechanics of decoding. Rapid and efficient
processing of the word on the page is thus the key to skilled reading. One implication
is that it is important for children to internalise the coding system through the kind
of teaching that 'phonics' offers.

Argue for one of these views on the basis of your own experience of reading.

Evidence on context

Perfetti and Roth (1981) tested the role played by context in skilled reading. Subjects
were asked to read short texts which ended in a word that was

– highly predictable: e.g. a cooking context mentioning corned beef and CABBAGE
– not predictable: e.g. a gardening context mentioning carrots, beans and CABBAGE
– anomalous: a woman checks her handbag and finds a passport, a plane ticket and
  a CABBAGE.

The researchers classified a group of school children as high- or low-ability readers,
and asked them to read the texts. They then measured their response times to the target words. Figure C8.1 below shows their findings for fourth grade readers.

Perfetti (1985) also combined the results from a number of experiments in which
he and associates had reduced the legibility of the text by **visual degrading**. On the
horizontal x-axis, Figure C8.2 plots the extent to which contextual help was available
('none' to 'high') to counteract the poor quality of the text. The vertical y-axis shows
the time taken by subjects to identify words.

What are your conclusions on the use of context by skilled and less skilled readers?
Recall that this research focused on the way in which readers use context to support
the decoding of words. Might this be different from other uses of context?

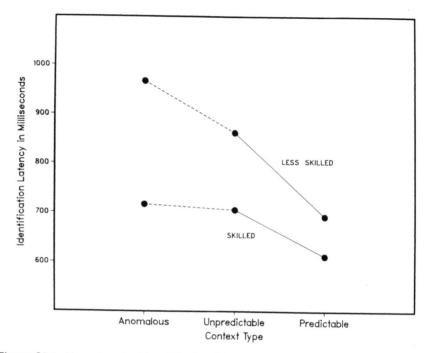

Figure C8.1 Use of context by skilled and less skilled readers
Source: Perfetti (1985: 146)

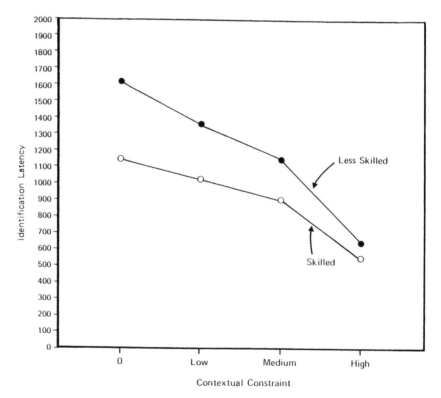

Figure C8.2 Use of context with degraded text
Source: Perfetti (1985: 147)

The role of 'context'

The reading researcher Keith Stanovich reviewed (1982) twenty-two different studies of reading, and concluded that they provided no clear evidence that good readers use context to enhance word recognition as Goodman had suggested. Stanovich's view is supported by studies of eye movements which suggest that when a word is predictable, fixation time only speeds up by about 10 per cent and there is no reduction in the number of fixations.

On the other hand, there is evidence that skilled readers are more inclined to

- recognise changes of topic in a text
- enrich their comprehension by bringing in background knowledge
- build meaning at global (text) level rather than just at local (sentence) level.

Surely all of these imply a greater use of contextual information?

Stanovich explains this by pointing out (1980) that 'context' has two distinct functions in reading, not one:

a   It can be used to supplement partial or incomplete information from the text.
b   It can be used to enrich understanding.

The evidence suggests that use (a) characterises the reading of less-skilled readers while use (b) is more likely with skilled readers.

Stanovich's **Interactive-Compensatory Hypothesis** envisages a trade-off between the quality of the incoming message and the extent to which top-down information is used to support decoding.

❏   A weak reader has to rely more heavily on information provided by context in order to compensate for poor decoding skills.
❏   A skilled reader only falls back upon top-down information to support decoding when the text is degraded through (for example) bad handwriting.

But if weak readers use context to compensate for poor decoding skills – why do they not also use it to enrich understanding? Perfetti's (1985) **verbal efficiency theory** (or 'bottleneck hypothesis') finds the answer in Working Memory.

❏   Remember that Working Memory has a limited capacity. Where (with skilled readers) decoding is **automatic**, the result is to leave a great deal of WM capacity free for considering contextual information and for constructing higher level meaning. Where (with less skilled readers) the decoding process is more **controlled** (i.e. conscious), the burden upon Working Memory is greater, leaving fewer resources for processes such as meaning building.
❏   Where (with less skilled readers) decoding is slow, it results in smaller amounts of information being supplied to Working Memory at any time. This leads to a focus upon local (small scale) rather than global (text-wide) meaning relations.

There is now evidence that training in rapid decoding does not, in fact, improve the comprehension of weak readers. What they appear to need is accurate and automatic decoding – not a higher reading speed alone. However, inaccurate decoding has the same effect as slow decoding. As we have seen (Section B8), it leads to eye movement regressions and hence slows down the supply of data to Working Memory.

Experimental task

Investigate the role of 'inner speech' in reading.

1   Devise a list of 10 monosyllabic words which are phonologically similar but not semantically related (Example: *light, height, white, night, write, tight, bite, quite, fight, might*).
2   Devise a list of 10 other words, which are similar in length, frequency and word class to those in the first list. Ensure that the words are semantically related.
3   Tell a group of subjects that their task is to recall as many of the words as possible, in the order in which they occurred. Read the first list aloud (1.5 seconds per word). After the reading, give subjects 20 seconds to write down what they recall. Repeat with the second word list.
4   Repeat the experiment with another group of subjects. This time, present the two lists visually. Use an overhead transparency, and display each word silently for 1.5 seconds, then cover it.
5   Examine the data you have collected and see which list was most accurately recalled.
    –   Is there a primacy or a recency effect?
    –   What is the effect of phonological similarity upon the process of rehearsal with the spoken items?
    –   Are the results for visual processing similar to those for auditory processing? Does this support the idea that both are subject to phonological rehearsal?

Essays, further study ►►►►

1   Study Harris, M. and Coltheart, M., *Language Processing in Children and Adults*, London: Routledge, 1986, Chapter 4. Describe the four phases of learning to read.
2   Argue for one of the following views of reading
    (a) a 'top-down' view   (b) a 'bottom-up' view
    (c) an 'interactive-compensatory' view
3   Give examples from English orthography to illustrate the difficulties of using a single approach ('whole word', 'phonics') when teaching reading.

LISTENING IN REAL TIME

Listening takes place in real time.

a The stimulus is transitory.
b We process the stimulus while the speaker is speaking. We do not wait until the
   end of a clause or sentence before constructing meaning.
   In this section, we examine the implications of these phenomena.

Verbatim recall

TASK 1

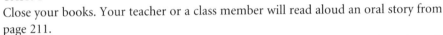

Close your books. Your teacher or a class member will read aloud an oral story from
page 211.
    Now open your books again. You will not be asked comprehension questions. Instead,
decide which of the following sequences of words appeared in the story you heard.

1 she was very fond of these animals
2 she kept talking about her little dog
3 I went into the lounge
4 there was the little dog sitting on some cushions
5 I said that I had a dog in my car
6 he goes with me wherever I go
7 my little dog died three years ago
8 we got someone to stuff him

You probably found it very difficult to recall the exact wording of what you heard.
Remember that Working Memory has a very limited capacity. So, in normal circumstances, listeners only retain the verbatim form of the words they hear for a very short
period of time. There are, of course, exceptional cases of verbatim memorisation –
such as actors who learn parts and some Muslims who can recite extensively from the
Koran. There is also a general belief that a strong oral tradition exists in some rural
communities where folk tales and songs are handed down word for word. In fact, this
seems not to be the case. Hunter (1985) studied Demo, a non-literate Yugoslavian
singer of folk songs who claimed that he only had to hear a song once to be able to
reproduce its exact wording. What he actually reproduced, however, was the gist of
the song. Hunter suggests that Demo did not have a clear idea of the notion of 'word',
which to him was tantamount to 'idea'.
    Is there a point at which a listener regularly dispenses with the exact form of words
and turns it into a proposition? Early experiments suggested that there is.
    In a well-known experiment by Jarvella (1971), two versions of a recording were
played to different groups of subjects. The recordings were paused from time to time
and subjects had to write down as much as they could remember of the preceding
text. Where the pauses occurred, the two versions of the text differed in sentence boundaries. Example:

Condition A: Taylor did not reach a decision until after he had returned to Manhattan. He explained the offer to his wife.

Condition B: With this possibility, Taylor left the capital. After he had returned to Manhattan, he explained the offer to his wife.

Correct recall for subjects in both conditions dropped sharply for words which occurred before the sentence boundary (before *He* in the Condition A example; before *After* in Condition B). In Condition B, there was also a drop in accuracy at the clause boundary (i.e. for words before the second *he*) – but this failure of recall was not for the actual words that had been heard but for the order of the words.

Activity

What does this suggest to you:

a   about the points at which we transfer verbatim words into propositional information?

b   about possible reasons for needing to retain verbatim words in Working Memory?

Consider the Condition B example again:

> With this possibility, Taylor left the capital. After he had returned to Manhattan, he explained the offer to his wife.

We can conclude that, while the second sentence is being uttered, the first is no longer stored in verbal form but has been turned into a piece of propositional information. In that case, how does the listener manage to work out what the pronoun *he* refers to? In principle, the reader can simply look back. What does the listener refer back to? One answer is that, within the propositions stored in the mind, certain features are **foregrounded**. One of those, in the example above, would be the identity of Taylor.

'Left-to-right' syntactic parsing

A major consideration in studies of listening is the fact that an utterance is processed as it is occurring. This is sometimes referred to as 'left-to-right' processing because it proceeds linearly and does not wait until a syntactic structure is complete.

Activity

TASK 2

Imagine you hear these opening words. Write how the sentences might go on.

a   The heavy fall . . .
b   The actor learnt the text . . .
c   The teachers taught by modern methods . . .
d   The rescuers discovered the plane . . .
e   The lawyer questioned . . .
f   The spokesman John . . .
g   The horse raced past the barn . . .

Here are the continuations:

a   The heavy fall clumsily.
b   The actor learnt the text amused the audience.

c   The teachers taught by modern methods had great success.
d   The rescuers discovered the plane had crashed.
e   The lawyer questioned by the judge admitted lying.
f   The spokesman John instantly distrusted.
g   The horse raced past the barn fell. (a notorious example from the literature!)

These are known as **garden path** sentences because they lead listeners and readers 'up the garden path'. In written form, they cause a reader to hesitate at the point where an unexpected word is reached (resulting in a longer fixation) and often to regress in order to check an alternative interpretation. For the listener, they pose an even greater challenge, and there may be a delay while the **syntactic parsing** of the sentence (assigning a grammatical structure) is revised. One of the reasons we briefly retain a verbatim form of the signal is to deal with cases such as these where a parse has to be rethought.

Can you decide why you chose your continuations for sentences a to g?

Bever, a pioneer psycholinguist, suggested in 1970 that certain assumptions underlie the way listeners process sentences like this. Put simply, an utterance is assumed to consist of a clause or a series of clauses, each of which follows the standard SVO (subject-verb-object) pattern. The first noun phrase in a clause is assumed to be the agent and the second the recipient of the action.

In fact, the situation is rather more complex. With sentences c and e, it would seem that world knowledge plays a part in establishing a preferred interpretation. We know that teachers teach and lawyers question. You might have decided differently if you had encountered these alternatives:

The students taught by modern methods . . .
The witness questioned . . .

Animacy also plays a part. Hearing the opening words, 'The pencil bought . . .', we assume that the word *bought* is a past participle ('The pencil bought by my daughter . . .') rather than a main verb.

Similarly, one cannot entirely ignore the effects of habit and experience – for example, the large number of sentences we have produced or understood in which the word TEACHER has been followed by a main verb TAUGHT.

The **ambiguity** of a 'garden path' sentence is not immediately obvious. But there are other cases where a listener is aware from the start that ambiguity exists which will need to be resolved at some point. The ambiguity might be syntactic, lexical or phonological.

Suggest two possible continuations for:

a I sent the boy . . .   b The bank collapsed . . .   c The /ˈweɪtəˈkʌtɪt/ . . .

Researchers disagree as to what occurs in this kind of situation. Do listeners choose the most likely or most frequent interpretation? Do listeners carry both interpretations in parallel until the ambiguity is resolved? Or do they suspend parsing until the ambiguity is resolved?

The role of prosody

The 'garden path' problem is sometimes overstated. Some of the sentences we examined above might not be ambiguous for a listener as they are for a reader. A listener has an additional resource which a reader does not have – namely **prosody** (intonation, rhythm and pausing) which often provides cues as to syntactic structure.

Activity   TASK 3

Work with a fellow student. One of you reads aloud the underlined part of one of each pair of sentences below. The other has to decide whether they are hearing part of Sentence A or Sentence B. Repeat two or three times, and try to work out for yourselves what the prosodic cues are that help listeners to assign syntactic structure.

1A <u>The actor learnt the text</u> amused the audience.
 B <u>The actor learnt the text</u> by heart.

2A <u>The rescuers discovered the plane</u> had crashed.
 B <u>The rescuers discovered the plane</u> in the jungle.

3A <u>The lawyer questioned</u> by the judge admitted lying.
 B <u>The lawyer questioned</u> the witness.

4A <u>We chose a flat with a lot</u> of care.
 B <u>We chose a flat with a lot</u> of space.

5A <u>Before she washes, her hair</u> is cut.
 B <u>Before she washes her hair</u>, it's cut.

6A <u>When they discuss college, matters</u> get complicated.
 B <u>When they discuss college matters</u>, they usually disagree.

(Loosely based on sentences used in experimental tasks)

❑ Possibly the most useful cue is the extended **duration** of a word which occurs before a syntactic boundary (strictly, the extended duration of its stressed syllable). This might affect *learnt, discovered, flat, washes* and *college* in the A sentences.

❑ **Pausing** often marks clause boundaries, though in natural speech the pauses are quite brief – much shorter than those sometimes employed by actors and newsreaders. There is also sometimes a pause between subject and verb; there might be one between *lawyer* and *questioned* in Sentence 3B.

❑ A third cue is a change in the pitch of the speaker's voice; this might particularly serve to mark the boundaries in 1A, 2A and 4A.

Experimental task

There has been much research into **lexical segmentation**: the way in which listeners manage to identify words in connected speech, despite the fact that there are no consistent pauses between them. One method (Cutler and Butterfield 1992) makes use of **faint speech**.

Record any five or six sentences from a text; these are for trialling purposes. Then record the following anomalous sequences, used by Cutler and Butterfield. Allow a pause of 5 seconds between each one.

1 dusty senseless drilling	6 never just convict them
2 achieve her ways instead	7 rings amused the sultan
3 rust presents a nuisance	8 mean baboons detained him
4 conduct ascents uphill	9 soon police were waiting
5 includes serene refrains	10 sons expect enlistment

Ask your subjects to listen to the recording though headphones. Use the trial sentences to check their hearing threshold. Keep turning down the volume of the cassette player until subjects report that they can hardly hear what is being said. Now get subjects to listen to the ten target sentences and to write down what they think they hear.

Analyse the responses and see if you can trace any consistency in where subjects choose to place word boundaries. Compare the number of boundaries inserted before stressed syllables with those inserted before unstressed. For further discussion, see Cutler and Butterfield in Section D9.

Essays, further study ➤➤➤➤

1   Read Brown, G., *Speakers, Listeners and Communication*, Cambridge: Cambridge University Press, 1995, Chapter 1. Write an analysis of the roles of listener and speaker in communication.
2   Read Werker, J., 'Cross-language speech perception', in Goodman, J. and Nusbaum, H. C., *The Development of Speech Perception*, Cambridge, MA: MIT (1994). Then write a review of the effect of Categorical Perception upon hearing phonemes in a foreign language.
3   Using examples from this section, compare the ways in which potentially ambiguous sentences are parsed in reading and in listening.

A MODEL OF SPEAKING

The most influential recent model of the speaking process is the result of many years' work by Willem Levelt at the Max Planck Institute for Psycholinguistics in Nijmegen, Holland. Levelt has produced a major work (1989) in which he explores all aspects of the speaking process.

Figure C10.1 represents what Levelt terms 'a blueprint' of the speaking process.

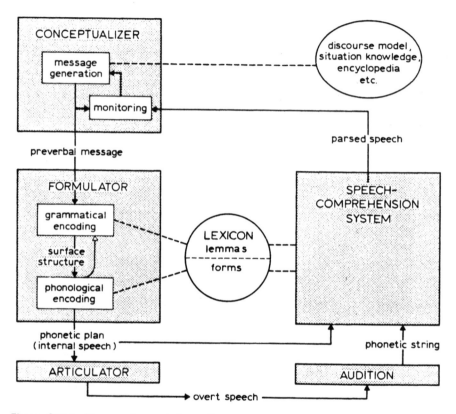

Figure C10.1 The speaker as information processor
Source: Levelt (1989: 9)

 Activity

1   Look at the circle and oval. They represent knowledge that is stored in Long Term Memory. What are these two types of knowledge? How do they feed into the speaking process?

2   Now look at the shaded boxes on the left-hand side. They represent the three main components in the speaking process. They are labelled CONCEPTUALISER, FORMULATOR and ARTICULATOR. Can you work out what these stages involve?

3   What is fed into the FORMULATOR is a preverbal message. What do you think the term **preverbal** signifies? What comes out of the FORMULATOR is a **phonetic plan**. What do you think a phonetic plan is? Can you relate the notion of **internal speech** to any phenomenon you have encountered elsewhere in this course?

4   You will recall that the SOT evidence in Section B10 suggested that the early part
     of assembling an utterance does not take the form of actual words. At what point
     in this model do you think that the message achieves phonological form? Where
     does the information come from?

     Now we come to an interesting component of the Levelt model. It recognises
     that the speaker pays close heed to what they are saying in order to check that
     the utterance conveys the message accurately and clearly. This process is termed
     monitoring.

5   Why do you think the monitoring process appears within the CONCEPTUALISER
     box?

6   Notice the way in which the message feeds back into monitoring. It emerges
     from the ARTICULATOR in the form of overt speech. It is then processed
     through AUDITION (= hearing) and the SPEECH COMPREHENSION SYSTEM.
     Explain why listening and speaking have been linked in this way.

TASK. Let us take a simple sentence through the Levelt model. Try to work out for
yourself what each stage of processing achieves, then check it against the account given
here. Capitals indicate an abstract idea and phonemic script shows phonological forms.

Activity

1   From their knowledge of PENGUINS in Long Term Memory, a speaker retrieves
     the proposition PENGUINS DON'T FLY. At the same time, they retrieve addi-
     tional stored information about PENGUINS. What kind of information would
     this be? They activate connections between PENGUIN and other entities in the
     real world. Give examples.

     ⇒ NOW GO TO 6

2   The sequences suggested by SOT data (B10) are as follows:
     a   The phonological forms are retrieved from the 'form' part of the lexical entry

          PENGUIN → /peŋgwɪn/   FLY → /flaɪ/

     b   They are inserted into the surface structure: /peŋgwɪn/ (plural) + /flaɪ/ (negative)
     c   Morpho-phonemic details are added /peŋgwɪn/ + /z/ + /dəʊnt/ + /flaɪ/

     Now the whole sentence has to be prepared for articulation. In what way might
     the phonetic plan be modified in order to make articulation easier?

     ⇒ GO TO 5

3   The speaker self-monitors – listening, at a relatively low level of attention, to their
     own speech. When the slip is heard and noticed, the information is fed back to
     the conceptualiser which can then plan a correction if it is felt necessary.

     END

4   Possible lexical entries for PENGUIN and FLY:

	PENGUIN	FLY
	PENGUIN	FLY
Concept	black/white bird	move (in air) (with wings)
Word class	N	V

Grammatical function	Countable	(SUBJ + V)
		(SUBJ + V + OBJ) (fly a plane)
Morphology	Regular plural	flies – flying – flew – flown

The speaker now forms a syntactic frame (= 'surface structure'). What will it be like?

⇒ GO TO 7

5   The instructions to the articulators must contain phonetic information. For example, the speaker might aspirate the /p/ in /peŋgwɪn/. There might also be elision to make the string of sounds easier to say: /daʊnt flaɪ/ → /daʊn flaɪ/

The speaker says the sentence. And – oh dear! – there has been a slip in 'phonological encoding'. The 'overt speech' takes the form: *fenguins don't ply.* How does the speaker detect and rectify this?

⇒ GO TO 3

6   The speaker opens up a conceptual store in Long Term Memory which includes:

a bird   black and white   lives in the Antarctic   swims

Connections may also be opened to:

emu   magpie   man in evening dress   ice floe   book publisher

These may come in handy later if our conversation about penguins takes off. Our preverbal message is PENGUINS DON'T FLY. To achieve 'grammatical encoding', we have to retrieve information from the lexical entries for PENGUIN and FLY. Remember that the entries contain information about meaning and syntax. Can you suggest what that information is likely to be?

⇒ GO TO 4

7   The surface structure might consist of meaning codes for PENGUIN and FLY plus syntactic slots which are tagged for 'plural', 'negative', etc.

NP [plural] + V [plural, neg.]

It is possibly at this point that the speaker decides what is the focal or 'new' part of the message – the part which will bear sentence stress. In this case, it is likely to be the V.

How will the structure now be given phonological form? Do you recall the order in which the elements need to be inserted?

⇒ GO TO 2

Experimental task

Record about 2 minutes of a radio discussion programme. Transcribe it, including filled pauses. Mark unfilled pauses, using + for a short one and ++ for a longer one. Time each speaker's turn. Then

- calculate the speaking rate of each speaker
- examine the pauses as evidence of planning
- establish whether there are hesitant and fluent phases
- listen for any slips of the tongue and suggest at what level they occurred.

Essays, further study ➤➤➤➤

1   Study Chapter 8 'Talking computers' in Ladefoged, P., *Vowels and Consonants*, Oxford: Blackwell, 2001. Summarise the difficulties of turning writing into speech.
2   Describe the different roles in speech production of: conceptualising, formulating, articulating and self-monitoring.
3   Discuss how the sentence 'He put the coin into the slot'. might be assembled syntactically (assuming the verb PUT is selected early in the process) and then lexically (using semantic restrictions on what types of item can go where).

INFERENCE

C11

In Section B11, we saw that skilled readers and listeners often employ inference in order to add to or enrich the literal information provided by a text. In this section, we examine the nature of inference a little more closely.

Bridging inferences

Consider the following sentences.

 Activity

a Bill had been murdered. The knife lay by the body.

Distinguish clearly (a) the propositional information that is provided for the reader; (b) the inferences that the reader is likely to draw.

The propositional information tells us simply that somebody killed Bill, that there was a knife and that its position was next to a body. It includes knowledge that is part of the meaning of the words MURDERED and LAY: namely, that Bill was dead and that the knife was not in use.

However, in order to make a connection between these sentences, the reader has to add his/her own inferences:

- The body refers to the dead Bill.
- The knife was used in the murder.

This kind of inference is necessary to an understanding of the text, and is known as a **bridging inference**.

 Can you suggest what reasons the reader might have for making the inferences described? It might help if you compare your reading of the following sentences with your reading of a.

b   Bill had been murdered. The rain fell.
c   Bill had been murdered. Our mail is delivered at 8.00.
d   Bill had been murdered. A knife lay by a body.

The reader partly makes inferences as a result of the 'effort after meaning' that we observed in Section B11. In this, they are guided by what has been termed the maxim of **relevance**: they assume that if the author follows mention of the murder with mention of rain, there must be some good reason for it. Thus, in reading example (b), you probably envisaged Bill lying in the street with the rain falling. With example (c), it is very difficult to make any such connection; we may simply conclude that the text lacks **coherence**.

The other motivation for adding inferences to example (a) is the use of the definite article. Discourse analysis tells us that the use of the article *a* is often associated with something **new** (introduced into a text for the first time) whereas the use of the article *the* is associated with something **given** (accepted by writer and reader as established by what has gone before).

So why do the words *body* and *knife* carry the definite article when it seems probable that neither word has occurred before?

–   *the* in *the body* suggests that the body in question is treated as a 'given'. The obvious conclusion (supported by the notion of relevance) is that the body is that of the dead Bill.
–   *the* in *the knife* suggests that the existence of this knife is something that we should have taken on when acquiring earlier information in the text. We assume a connection between this instrument and the current topic, the murder of Bill.

 Here are some further examples where a bridging inference is necessary. Can you explain the effect of using the definite article?

e   Sue went out walking. **The park** was beautiful.
f   We got into Cairo at 3.00 in the morning. **The flight** was late.
g   He went into the room. **The windows** were open.
h   My car needs attention. **The handbrake** isn't working.
i   I've stopped watching TV. **The programmes** are so bad.

Relate examples (g), (h), and (i) to the idea of a **schema** which you met in Section B11.

Note that making a bridging inference is not without cost. It demands extra Working Memory capacity and therefore slows down processing. Haviland and Clark (1974) found that it took longer to process *the beer* in context (j) than in (k).

j   We checked the picnic supplies. The beer was warm.
k   We got some beer out of the trunk. The beer was warm.

Elaborative inferences

The inferences we have studied so far are necessary to comprehension; they make a vital link between two pieces of information. However, not all inferences are as essential.

Consider the sentences: 'Sue cut the steak. It was too large for two people.' What do you conclude was the instrument that Sue used for cutting? How necessary is it to our understanding? Suppose that the next sentence is 'But the kitchen scissors were very blunt'. How disturbed would you be to find your inference overturned?

Activity

An inference like this – amplifying what is in a text but not essential to under-standing – is termed an **elaborative inference**. Note that an elaborative inference can easily turn into a bridging one:

l   Sue cut the steak. It was medium-rare. (Use of knife elaborative)
m   Sue cut the steak. The knife was blunt. (Use of knife bridging)

The bridging / elaborative distinction is not always an easy one to make. The reason that there has been interest in it is that some researchers believe that bridging infer-ences feed into the mental models which we construct, whereas elaborative inferences do not.

Experimental task

An important area of research in higher level processing considers how we manage to relate a pronoun to its antecedent (the entity that it refers to). The sentences below contain ambiguous pronouns. By asking subjects to complete them, we can work out which antecedent they associate the pronoun with (e.g. we can work out if *he* in sen-tence 1 is taken to refer to John or to Bill). Use these sentences in your experimental task, but randomly add ten 'foils' to them – similar sentences, also incomplete, but without pronoun ambiguity. Ask subjects to read and complete all 20 sentences.

1   John phoned Bill. The first thing he said was . . .
2   It was Mary that Anne disliked because she . . .
3   He held some bread over the fire with a fork. The problem was that it . . .
4   Jim sold his car to Nigel because he . . .
5   They bought the apples because they were . . .
6   I need a receptionist and I also need a nurse. I need her to . . .
7   The taxi driver told the passenger that she did not have . . .
8   The architect asked the builder to pick up his . . .
9   The children like visiting their grandparents when they . . .
10 Passengers can be fined by guards if they . . .

Examine answers to the ten target sentences. Establish which words your subjects associated the ambiguous pronouns with. Are there any systematic patterns based upon: similarity of position in the sentence – most recent mention – most likely interpretation of the situation – current topic – assumptions about gender?

Essays, further study ➤➤➤➤

1   Read Garnham: *Psycholinguistics: Central Topics*, London: Routledge, 1985 (pp. 156–71). Then write an account of the way in which world knowledge contributes to the meaning representation of a spoken or written text.

2   Study the way in which 'given' vs 'new' affects syntax and word order (Brown and Yule, *Discourse Analysis*, Cambridge: Cambridge University Press, 1983, pp. 169–89). Discuss the implications in terms of (a) the speaker assembling speech and (b) the listener interpreting it.

3   What do we mean by 'context'? What role do the different types of context play in the interpretation of a text?

C12   DEAFNESS: A SMALL-SCALE RESEARCH STUDY

Today, deafness is not represented as a language disorder. This is partly because some educators have emphasised the importance of equipping profoundly deaf children as early as possible with a means of self-expression in the form of sign language. Fluent signers thus acquire full competence in a first language, though it is not a language which is in spoken or written form.

Sooner or later, efforts are made to teach the signers to speak and to write English since in this way they can communicate with a wider social circle. It is at this point that problems may arise – though one can speculate that they will be different (in cause if not in type) from the problems that one might associate with deaf children who are not signers.

This was the view of Joyce Fraser in her MA dissertation project on deafness. Joyce combines a background in teaching English as Foreign Language with experience of working with deaf learners. Because of this double perspective, she concluded that a signer studying English speech and writing effectively learns English as their second language. Her impression as a teacher was that the writing of deaf learners closely resembled the writing of foreign learners of English. If she was able to demonstrate that there were indeed similarities, she would lend strength to an argument that deaf learners should be treated by educationalists much more like foreign language learners and less like sufferers from language impairment.

At the same time, certain differences could be expected. Language **transfer**, the influence of the first language (L1) on the acquisition of a second (L2), is a controversial area in Second Language Acquisition theory. But it is generally accepted that at least some of the learner's early errors in L2 will show traces of the phonology, vocabulary and grammar of L1. In the case of a signer acquiring English, we might thus expect to see some of the linguistic features of Sign affecting the forms used in speech and writing. We might also expect to see the effects of a lack of phonology just as we would with any deaf learner (Recall from Section 7A and 8A that phonology plays an important part in reading and writing skills.). The difference with a signer would be that the phonological irregularities were attributable to the fact that their first language was one without a spoken dimension. Of course, even in the case of phonology, there might be resemblances to the productions of non-native writers. The reason is that the latter would be in the course of adjusting to the phonemic categories of English (see Section B9), just as, in a very different way, the hearing-impaired have to.

Joyce's hypothesis, then, was that she would find a close resemblance between the writing of deaf learners of English and that of non-native learners. She devised her research project accordingly. She asked six subjects (two profoundly deaf learners and four EFL learners) to write a short essay based upon a series of pictures (Heaton 1975). She then submitted their work to five judges, asking them to determine which of the essays were the work of the deaf subjects. The judges were all highly experienced teachers of EFL; yet none of them succeeded in correctly identifying both the deaf writers' essays.

Joyce went on to analyse the essays qualitatively (comparing aspects of style) and quantitatively (counting instances of particular errors) – with the rider that it would be dangerous to generalise too greatly on the basis of such a small sample.

Here are the essays from a non-native writer and a deaf writer, judged to be at the same level of writing ability.

1   Can you suggest which is the deaf writer's essay? Give reasons.
2   Examine the essays and identify similarities in terms of:
    verb tenses: form and use
    the use of function words (*of, for, to*, etc.)
    word order and syntactic structure
    vocabulary.
3   Now consider the question of phonology. Remember that lack of access to a phono-logical system can lead deaf writers to learn words individually without using GPC rules. From the non-native writer we might perhaps expect over-generalisation of GPC rules. Is there any evidence of this?

Text A

One day in the evening, three children saw a train under the tunnel and waved at the passengers in the train. It had just started raining. The rain had became harder so children ran to a house for shelter.

When the rain stopped. They returned to the bridge. They saw the tunnel had been fallen down by rocks. They realised that other train will go into that tunnel at anytime. It will be a very bad accident that will kill the passengers. So children climbed down the bridge, then walked on the railway line for 5 miles for the signal tower. At last after 2 hours walk, they reached the signal tower and alerted the signal worker that the tunnel has been blocked by rocks. The worker switched the signal down to warn the train. The train stopped and was saved otherwise it will crash into the rocks by the tunnel.

Text B

In a sunny day Kate and her two brothers Tom and Peter said good bye to their father from the dyke. The children were so happy that they almost fell down from the hill.

    Although that morning started very nice and sunny when the train left the station and was gone from their eyes the weather turned discusting. Not just the weather changed to awful the events as well.

    Due to the lots of rain the hill's mud slipped down to the gateway at the tunnel and obscured the tunnel.

    Luckyly the children saw the trip on the railway when the rain passed and realised the possibility of a disaster. They hadn't too much time to do anythink so just ran down the hill to the signalbox and explained the officer what happend, who changed the sign to stop the next train.

    The driver of the train who passed this way all his life couldn't understand what happend. Tom and his crew ran to the train and told him what would have happend if they haven't been able to stop the train.

 Activity

Now look again at Text A (the essay written by the deaf subject) and compare it with Text C below, written by the second deaf writer. Consider the question of possible transfer of linguistic features from British Sign Language. BSL has the following characteristics which differentiate it from spoken English.

❑   It is a word-based system, with no sound-spelling relationships involved.
❑   It does not employ separate inflections: there are no specific signs for -*ed*, -*ing* etc.
❑   It does not use articles.
❑   Time is usually marked lexically by signs for WILL, PAST and NOW.
❑   Function words are sometimes represented by modifying the sign for a lexical item.
❑   It has flexible word order and tends to thematise, putting the current topic at the beginning of the sentence ('*London* went I'). Question words often come at the end ('Your name *what?*'). Signers seem to be aware that English is less flexible and some keep very strictly to the standard SVO order when writing.

Text C

A man, woman and boy looked at the train and waved at it. Then suddenly the rains poured and they ran into the house over the bridge. Next day, the sunny is beautiful and they were amazed to see the pile of rumbles from the top to the ground on the line. It was blocked on the bridge. They ran on the line because the train can't go through the channel and tried to warn the train 'do not disturb' because of the blockage. A man ran along the line and call the porter for help, to stop the train before it crashs! Luckily, the train was stopped. Thank god for that!

Now draw your own conclusions. To what extent does the writing of the deaf learners resemble the writing of somebody who is learning English as a foreign language? To what extent does it show the influence of Sign? What are the implications for somebody proposing to teach writing to deaf learners?

By the way, you may have noticed an apparent flaw of experimental design. Supposing that deafness incapacitated the deaf subjects, not just in terms of their writing but also in terms of their ability to tell stories? In comparing them with non-native subjects, we would thus be comparing unlike with unlike. Joyce countered this by getting the deaf subjects to tell the story again in Sign and the non-native subjects to tell it again orally in their first language. Both groups showed a high degree of fluency.

Essays, further study ➤➤➤➤

1   Study Landau, B. and Gleitman, L. R., *Language and Experience: Evidence from the Blind Child*, Cambridge, MA: Harvard University Press, 1985. Describe some of the effects of blindness on the development of language.
2   Contrast different types of developmental dyslexia and suggest where their origins may lie. Sources: Ellis, A. W., *Reading, Writing and Dyslexia*, Hove: Psychology Press, 1993, Chapter 8; Harris, M. and Coltheart, M., *Language Processing in Children and Adults*, London: Routledge, 1986, pp. 122–9.
3   Argue for or against modularity, using examples of language acquired in 'special circumstances.'

Section D

EXTENSION:
PSYCHOLINGUISTICS
READINGS

D1 THE GOALS OF PSYCHOLINGUISTICS

George A. Miller

This text is a shortened version of an important article written in the early days of Psycholinguistics. The issues it outlines are still very much the concern of the field today. Amongst the points it makes, note the concept of **levels of processing**. This assumes that readers and listeners achieve understanding by taking language through a series of stages, starting with perception and ending with evaluation.

The Psycholinguists

George A. Miller (from *The Psychology of Communication: Seven Essays.* Harmondsworth, Penguin, 1968: pp. 74–86. Abridged with permission of the author.)

Interest in psycholinguistics . . . is not confined to psychologists and linguists. Many people have been stirred by splendid visions of its practical possibilities. One thinks of medical applications to the diagnosis and treatment of a heterogeneous variety of language disorders ranging from simple stammering to the overwhelming complexities of aphasia. One thinks too of pedagogical applications, of potential improvements in our methods for teaching reading and writing, or for teaching second languages. If psycholinguistic principles were made sufficiently explicit, they could be imparted to those technological miracles of the twentieth century, the computing machines, which would bring into view a whole spectrum of cybernetic possibilities. . . .

The integration of psycholinguistic studies has occurred so recently that there is still some confusion concerning its scope and purpose; efforts to clarify it necessarily have something of the character of personal opinion. In my own version, the central task of this new science is to describe the psychological processes that go on when people use sentences. The real crux of the psycholinguistic problem does not appear until one tries to deal with sentences, for only then does the importance of productivity become completely obvious. It is true that productivity can also appear with individual words, but there it is not overwhelming. With sentences, productivity is literally unlimited.

Before considering this somewhat technical problem, however, it might be well to illustrate the variety of processes that psycholinguists hope to explain. This can best be done if we ask what a listener can do about a spoken utterance, and consider his alternatives in order from the superficial to the inscrutable.

The simplest thing one can do in the presence of a spoken utterance is to listen. Even if the language is incomprehensible, one can still *hear* an utterance as an auditory stimulus and respond to it in terms of some discriminative set: how loud, how fast, how long, from which direction, etc.

Given that an utterance is heard, the next level involves *matching* it as a phonemic pattern in terms of phonological skills acquired as a user of the language. The ability to match an input can be tested in psychological experiments by asking listeners to echo what they hear; a wide variety of experimental situations — experiments on the perception of speech and on the rote memorization of verbal

George A.
Miller

materials – can be summarized as tests of a person's ability to repeat the speech he hears under various conditions of audibility or delay.

If a listener can hear and match an utterance, the next question to ask is whether he will *accept* it as a sentence in terms of his knowledge of grammar. At this level we encounter processes difficult to study experimentally, and one is forced to rely most heavily on linguistic analyses of the structure of sentences. Some experiments are possible, however, for we can measure how much a listener's ability to accept the utterance as a sentence facilitates his ability to hear and match it; grammatical sentences are much easier to hear, utter, or remember than are ungrammatical strings of words, and even nonsense (*pirot, karol, elat,* etc.) is easier to deal with if it looks grammatical (*pirots karolize elatically*, etc.) (Epstein, 1961). Needless to say, the grammatical knowledge we wish to study does not concern those explicit rules drilled into us by teachers of traditional grammar, but rather the implicit generative knowledge that we all must acquire in order to use a language appropriately.

Beyond grammatical acceptance comes semantic interpretation: we can ask how listeners *interpret* an utterance as meaningful in terms of their semantic system. Interpretation is not merely a matter of assigning meanings to individual words; we must also consider how these component meanings combine in grammatical sentences. Compare the sentences: 'Healthy young babies sleep soundly' and 'Colourless green ideas sleep furiously.' Although they are syntactically similar, the second is far harder to perceive and remember correctly – because it cannot be interpreted by the usual semantic rules for combining the senses of adjacent English words (Miller and Isard, 1963). The interpretation of each word is affected by the company it keeps; a central problem is to systematize the interactions of words and phrases with their linguistic contexts. . . .

At the next level it seems essential to make some distinction between interpreting an utterance and understanding it, for understanding frequently goes well beyond the linguistic context provided by the utterance itself. A husband greeted at the door by 'I bought some electric light bulbs today' must do more than interpret its literal reference; he must understand that he should go to the kitchen and replace that burned-out lamp. Such contextual information lies well outside any grammar or lexicon. The listener can *understand* the function of an utterance in terms of contextual knowledge of the most diverse sort.

Finally, at a level now almost invisible through the clouds, a listener may *believe* that an utterance is valid in terms of its relevance to his own conduct. The child who says 'I saw five lions in the garden' may be heard, matched, accepted, interpreted, and understood, but in few parts of the world will he be believed.

The boundaries between successive levels are not sharp and distinct. One shades off gradually into the next. Still the hierarchy is real enough and important to keep in mind. Simpler types of psycholinguistic processes can be studied rather intensively; already we know much about hearing and matching. Accepting and interpreting are just now coming into scientific focus. Understanding is still over the horizon, and pragmatic questions involving belief system are at present so vague as to be hardly worth asking. But the whole range of processes must be included in any adequate definition of psycholinguistics.

George A.
Miller

I phrased the description of these various psycholinguistic processes in terms of a listener; the question inevitably arises as to whether a different hierarchy is required to describe the speaker. One problem a psycholinguist faces is to decide whether speaking and listening are two separate abilities, co-ordinate but distinct, or whether they are merely different manifestations of a single linguistic faculty.

The mouth and ear are different organs; at the simplest levels we must distinguish hearing and matching from vocalizing and speaking. At more complex levels it is less easy to decide whether the two abilities are distinct. At some point they must converge, if only to explain why it is so difficult to speak and listen simultaneously. The question is where. . . .

Suppose we accept the notion that a listener recognizes what he hears by comparing it with some internal representation. . . . One trouble with this hypothesis . . . is that a listener must be ready to recognize any one of an enormous number of different sentences. It is inconceivable that a separate internal representation of each of them could be stored in his memory in advance. Halle and Stevens [1962] suggest that these internal representations must be generated as they are needed by following the same generative rules that are usually used in producing speech. In this way, the rules of the language . . . need not be learned once by the ear and again by the tongue. This is a theory of a language user, not of a speaker or a listener alone. . . .

A listener's first [attempt to interpret the speech signal] probably derives in part from syntactic markers in the form of intonation, inflection, suffixes, etc., and in part from his general knowledge of the semantic and situational context. Syntactic cues indicate how the input is to be grouped and which words function together; semantic and contextual contributions are more difficult to characterize, but must somehow enable him to limit the range of possible words that he can expect to hear. . . . With an advance hypothesis about what the message will be, we can tune our perceptual system to favour certain interpretations and reject others. . . .

I have already offered the opinion that productivity sets the central problem for the psycholinguist and have referred to it indirectly by arguing that we can produce too many different sentences to store them all in memory. . . . Original combinations of elements are the lifeblood of language. It is our ability to produce and comprehend such novelties that makes language so ubiquitously useful. As psychologists have become more seriously interested in the cognitive processes that language entails, they have been forced to recognize that the fundamental puzzle is not our ability to associate vocal noises with perceptual objects, but rather our combinatorial productivity — our ability to understand an unlimited diversity of utterances never heard before and to produce an equal variety of utterances similarly intelligible to other members of our speech community. . . .

As psychologists have learned to appreciate the complexities of language, the prospect of reducing it to the laws of behaviour so carefully studied in lower animals has grown increasingly remote. We have been forced more and more into a position that non-psychologists probably take for granted, namely, that language is rule-governed behaviour characterized by enormous flexibility and freedom of choice.

George A.
Miller

Obvious as this conclusion may seem, it has important implications for any scientific theory of language. If rules involve the concepts of right and wrong, they introduce a normative aspect that has always been avoided in the natural sciences. One hears repeatedly that the scientist's ability to suppress normative judgements about his subject matter enables him to see the world objectively, as it really is. To admit that language follows rules seems to put it outside the range of phenomena accessible to scientific investigation.

At this point a psycholinguist who wishes to preserve his standing as a natural scientist faces an old but always difficult decision. Should he withdraw and leave the study of language to others? Or should he give up all pretence of being a 'natural scientist', searching for causal explanations, and embrace a more phenomenological approach? Or should he push blindly ahead with his empirical methods, hoping to find a causal basis for normative practices but running the risk that all his efforts will be wasted because rule-governed behaviour in principle lies beyond the scope of natural science?

To withdraw means to abandon hope of understanding scientifically all those human mental processes that involve language in any important degree. To [persevere] means to face the enormously difficult, if not actually impossible, task of finding a place for normative rules in a descriptive science.

Difficult, yes. Still one wonders whether these alternatives are really as mutually exclusive as they have been made to seem.

The first thing we notice when we survey the languages of the world is how few we can understand and how diverse they all seem. Not until one looks for some time does an even more significant observation emerge concerning the pervasive similarities in the midst of all this diversity.

Every human group that anthropologists have studied has spoken a language. The language always has a lexicon and a grammar. The lexicon is not a haphazard collection of vocalizations, but is highly organized; it always has pronouns, means for dealing with time, space, and number, words to represent true and false, the basic concepts necessary for propositional logic. The grammar has distinguishable levels of structure, some phonological, some syntactic. The phonology always contains both vowels and consonants, and the phonemes can always be described in terms of distinctive features drawn from a limited set of possibilities. The syntax always specifies rules for grouping elements sequentially into phrases and sentences, rules governing normal intonation, rules for transforming some types of sentences into other types.

The nature and importance of these common properties, called 'linguistic universals', are only beginning to emerge as our knowledge of the world's languages grows more systematic (Greenberg, 1963). These universals appear even in languages that developed with a minimum of interaction. One is forced to assume, therefore, either that (a) no other kind of linguistic practices are conceivable, or that (b) something in the biological makeup of human beings favours languages having these similarities. Only a moment's reflection is needed to reject (a). When

**George A.
Miller**

one considers the variety of artificial languages developed in mathematics, in the communication sciences, in the use of computers, in symbolic logic, and elsewhere, it soon becomes apparent that the universal features of natural languages are not the only ones possible. Natural languages are, in fact, rather special and often seem unnecessarily complicated.

A popular belief regards human language as a more or less free creation of the human intellect, as if its elements were chosen arbitrarily and could be combined into meaningful utterances by any rules that strike our collective fancy. The assumption is implicit, for example, in Wittgenstein's well-known conception of 'the language game'. This metaphor, which casts valuable light on many aspects of language, can if followed blindly lead one to think that all linguistic rules are just as arbitrary as, say, the rules of chess or football. As Lenneberg (1960) has pointed out, however, it makes a great deal of sense to inquire into the biological basis for language, but very little to ask about the biological foundations of card games.[11]

Man is the only animal to have a combinatorially productive language. In the jargon of biology, language is 'a species-specific form of behaviour'. Other animals have signalling systems of various kinds and for various purposes – but only man has evolved this particular and highly improbable form of communication. Those who think of language as a free and spontaneous intellectual invention are also likely to believe that any animal with a brain sufficiently large to support a high level of intelligence can acquire a language. This assumption is demonstrably false. The human brain is not just an ape brain enlarged; its extra size is less important than its different structure. Moreover, Lenneberg (1962) has pointed out that nanocephalic dwarfs, with brains half the normal size but grown on the human blueprint, can use language reasonably well, and even [Down's Syndrome sufferers, unable] to perform the simplest functions for themselves, can acquire the rudiments. Talking and understanding language do not depend on being intelligent or having a large brain. They depend on 'being human'.

Glossary

cognitive: involving the processes of thought and reasoning.

generative rules: a set of principles which enable a language user to produce (and to understand) all possible grammatical sentences of a language.

Obvious as this conclusion may seem . . . : Miller argues that a view of language as governed by rules suggests a *normative* approach to psycholinguistic research, an approach which assumes that human behaviour follows highly consistent patterns and can be accounted for by a general theory. We can contrast this with the empirical approach preferred by natural scientists, which draws upon concrete evidence and aims to attribute causes to results without any presuppositions. One alternative suggested is a phenomenological approach based on observation of events, with no conclusions reached as to external causes and influences.

nanocephalic: with a smaller brain than normal.

THE EVOLUTION OF SPEECH

Three contrasting views can be taken of how speech and language evolved.

a Evolution of the brain and body

Human beings came to need a sophisticated form of communication because they began to live in societies. Consequently, their brains and vocal apparatus evolved to support this survival need. After many generations, they evolved a capacity for language which is innate i.e. is transmitted at birth.

b Evolution of language

Language began with simple noises to express pleasure, pain, etc. It gradually evolved in ways that reflected how the human brain operates and the possibilities and limitations of the human vocal apparatus. As societies became more and more sophisticated, so did language. There were slow evolutionary modifications to the brain and the vocal apparatus in order to accommodate these new demands.

c The 'big bang'

Language came about when human brain evolution took a lucky direction and we developed an innate language faculty.

Which view do you take and why? Consider the different timescales of evolutionary change and of linguistic change.   ★ **Activity**

This article presents an overview of some issues in language evolution. In reading it, try to establish clearly:

1   What is the writer's position on the evolution of language?
2   What is the writer's view of animal cognition?
3   Why, according to the writer, have animals not developed language?

The origin of language and cognition

Ib Ulbaek (in J. R. Hurford, Studdert-Kennedy, M. and Knight, C. (eds) *Approaches to the Evolution of Language*, Cambridge: Cambridge University Press, 1998. Abridged with permission of the author).

Two kinds of theories have dominated recent discussion of the origin of language (see Pinker & Bloom 1990): a continuity approach and its counterpart, a discontinuity approach. The continuity approach has often labelled itself Darwinian and looked for predecessors of language, typically in animal communication systems. It claims that language is such a big system that it could not have evolved out of nothing (*de novo*). Just as we cannot conceive of the eye jumping into existence, so we cannot conceive of language as having no precursors.

The opposite position argues that language is unique among the communication systems of the biosphere, and that to claim continuity between, say, bee language and human language is to claim 'evolutionary development from breathing to walking' as pointedly remarked by Chomsky (1972: 68). Language is a task- and species-specific module in the human mind, a 'language organ' (1980a: 76).

Beside the Chomskyan position another anti-evolutionary and discontinuity position exists, which could be called *culturalist*. Sociological theories often separate human biological nature from human social nature. The culturalists reject Chomsky's strong innatism, arguing that, basically, humans are unconstrained learning machines who create a culture from which all relevant properties of the human mind (including language) derive. Neither Chomsky nor the culturalists have developed a detailed account of language origins, perhaps partly because their central concerns lie elsewhere. Chomsky has suggested a mutation or plain accident, whereas culturalists have sometimes hinted that a 'leap' from the natural order to the social order must have taken place. Neither explanation is satisfactory and neither will be discussed further.

. . . Some continuity theorists also emphasize learning as a fundamental aspect of human mind and language. The reasons for this are, first, their strong anti-Chomskyan attitude – some of them are learning psychologists – and second, the simple fact that language is undeniably learned. The position of these theorists was revealed most clearly in the *ape language controversy* in the 70s and early 80s. Their position was supported by experiments in which different kinds of non-spoken languages were taught to various apes, mostly chimpanzees. Researchers emphasized that even though apes do not speak in the wild, they have a mind capable of learning. By means of a sign language, apes can symbolize external (and internal) states of affairs, and can communicate about these things – primarily with the researchers and lab staff, but also with fellow chimpanzees and their own offspring (the controversy is documented in several places, including Linden 1986). . . .

. . . It is [not necessarily] contradictory to claim both continuity and innateness. These are vague (and relative) terms after all. How continuous does the continuity have to be? Some kind of discontinuity must exist if things are different and not the same. And innateness comes in degrees. Even Chomsky does not claim that language is wholly innate: to do so would fly in the face of the diversity of the world's living and extinct languages. What Chomsky *has* claimed is that without a strong innate component, language cannot be learned. To my mind his arguments are convincing. I will not defend the position extensively here. But if the child had only inductive strategies for constructing the rules of language, it would either be stuck in an enormous search space looking for consistent rules, or (perhaps) would come up with a language structure different from its parents. Some prestructuring in the child's search lightens the burden of induction and explains why parents and children speak the same language after all.

1 From cognition to language

Ib Ulbaek

The correct theory of evolution of language, in my opinion, is this: *language evolved from animal cognition not from animal communication*. Here lies the continuity. Language grew out of cognitive systems already in existence and working: it formed a communicative bridge between already-cognitive animals. Thus, I not only reject the seemingly natural assumption that language evolved out of other communication systems, but I adopt the far more radical assumption that cognitive systems were in place before language. Although times are changing this has not been the most popular point of view in this century – quite the contrary. . . . The traditional stance is that the hallmark of human rationality, thinking, is not only strongly influenced by language, but is even determined by language, or exists solely in language. . . . I cite Saussure because he is clear: 'Without language, thought is a vague, uncharted nebula. There are no pre-existing ideas, and nothing is distinct before the appearance of language' (Saussure 1966: 112). . . .

[I suggest that] we need a theory that does not rule out animal thinking *a priori*. Animals are not just instinctual machines or learning machines . . . : they are thinking creatures. . . . Wolfgang Köhler demonstrated elaborate problem-solving behaviour in the chimpanzee as early as the beginning of this century. Even rats evidently do more than just learn a route when running a maze. . . . Especially in the apes, many findings point to their high intelligence, and therefore support a view of these animals as cognitive creatures beyond . . . behavioural modification through learning. I do not have space to go through the data in detail, and so simply note some of the relevant areas.

1.1 Tool-using and making
Apes not only use tools, but also make them. They prepare sticks for fishing for termites (and are seen carrying around 'good sticks'). . . .

1.2 Cognitive maps
Apes show a sophisticated knowledge of their territory and use this knowledge to plan routes between food areas (Menzel 1978).

1.3 Learning through imitation
Primates are virtually the only order that learn by (social) imitation (Passingham 1982: 176). Ladder-climbing in an enclosure spread rapidly in a group of captive chimpanzees; the spreading of potato-washing from one individual, Imo (a Japanese macaque), to its group is another example (Passingham 1982: 182).

1.4 Social knowledge
Monkeys and apes conform to a pecking order in their groups, with a dominant alpha male and lower-ranking males and females, and they know each other's place within the hierarchy. . . .

Ib Ulbaek

1.5 Deception

Cheating, or feigning, is known throughout the animal kingdom by the name of mimicry and camouflage. Birds of some species will feign a broken wing to get rid of an unwelcome predator, but this is probably a non-conscious, non-cognitive program, rather than problem-solving behaviour. Anecdotal evidence does exist, however, pointing to deliberate, intentional lying among apes and monkeys (Whiten & Byrne 1988).

1.6 Theory of mind

One question is whether the ape itself is an intentional animal, creating and acting on goals; another is whether it treats its fellow apes as intentional. David Premack has answered the second question in a series of experiments by showing that a chimpanzee can treat others as having intentions (Premack & Woodruff 1978). His chimp, Sarah, could watch a videotape of a person trying to solve a problem and then find among alternatives the right tool to solve the problem. Here it is important to remember that the problem could not be described in purely physical terms, so that the chimpanzee could not solve it merely by looking. It had to 'imagine' the person (not another chimpanzee) as having a problem and trying to solve it. Since it did so, we can conclude that the ape has a theory of mind.

1.7 Capable of learning a language-like system?

Apes in the wild do not speak, but several experiments have tried to teach them language. . . . Although chimpanzees have not been able to learn any sophisticated language (say, beyond the stage of a two-year-old child) they have demonstrated a degree of language capacity by using arbitrary symbols to denote physical objects. Evidently apes can encode mental content into physical tokens (manual signs, plastic symbols, pictograms) but do not have the syntactic machinery for stringing words into sentences. If human language does indeed comprise an innate module for processing syntactic information, it is hardly remarkable that apes cannot do syntactic processing. Otherwise, they would have a complete language faculty that they never use – which is scarcely plausible.

On the basis of these diverse indications of ape intelligence, I conclude that, if language developed from cognition, the ape has the means to fulfil the role, and *so had the last common ancestor between ape and man.*

2 The function of language

The scenario is this: in some distant past (approximately 6 to 8 million years ago) an apelike primate existed which became the last common ancestor between apes and humans. The two lines separated. In one, language evolved, in the other it did not. Why? In the *Homo* line several things happened, while the apes remained relatively static. The ape's brain, for example, seems to have changed and grown very little since the split, suggesting that the ape was already well adapted to the pressures of its habitat. Not so for the line of *Homo*, where many things changed, even though they took several millions of years to happen: upright walking, freeing of the hand and changing manual function (especially of the thumb), handedness, lateralization

Ib Ulbaek

and rapid growth of the brain, conquest of fire, toolmaking, weapons, changing social structure, culture. All these things surely contributed to the origin of language, and a total account of language origins would have to take all these things into consideration. I have not tried to do that and will not do so here. Instead I have asked why humans, but not apes, have language. This question can be given a plausible answer if we understand correctly the biological role of language. What is its survival value? My answer is that language had – at the time it began to evolve or get a foothold – the function of communicating thoughts among group members. To use language is to share information as deliberately as the sharing of food is deliberate, and contrasts with the involuntary giving away of information of, say, a monkey displaying that it is scared when approached by an aggressive male. . . .

If we can substantiate [this] functional view, some of the answers to the question of language origin may fall into place. We can ask: why did chimps not get a language? We now know that they have enough intelligence to use simple symbols. Either they did not need a language or they were prevented from getting it. . . . The need is indeed there today, as is shown by apes patrolling, hunting, moving to new food sites, and so on. We may expect the same need in prehistoric times. So they were prevented – by whom or by what?

3 Sharing of information from a Darwinian perspective

Presumably, language was blocked in the chimpanzee by the impersonal forces of Darwinian evolution. Every trait that enhances one's fitness enhances (by definition) one's chances of survival and chances of reproduction and so of passing one's genes to the next generation. [L]anguage would seem to be such an improvement for us that we are tempted to extrapolate into thinking that language would be an advantage for every species . . .

It is easy to see that this should not be generalized: a bee talking would have such a big head that it could not fly! In other words, having a language is a question of cost and benefit, or, in Darwinian terms, of losing and gaining fitness. We are so used to focusing on the benefits that we tend to forget the costs.

Loosely speaking, some of the costs are: extra brain tissue, reorganization of the brain, changes in the respiratory system, and many more. What are the benefits? The one benefit that we tend to take for granted is that language enables us to co-operate, to speak to and help each other. From a Darwinian perspective, this is also, paradoxically, its main cost. . . . Why should we share information in the first place, if evolution demands that we enhance *our* fitness, not our neighbors'? If we look at animal communication, it seems that most of it has a selfish purpose. If territorial songs are an easier way of keeping competitors away, it seems preferable to patrolling and beating up other male[s]. . . . Mating calls have a similar selfish purpose. . . . Perhaps indeed selfishness has kept animal communication at a minimum. . . . Wilson (1972) finds the static nature of animal communication striking: 'By human standards the number of signals employed by each species of animal is severely limited. One of the most curious facts revealed by recent field studies is that even the most highly social vertebrates rarely have more

Ib Ulbaek

than 30 or 35 separate displays in their entire repertory' (p. 56). It is striking indeed: both compared to human language and to the evolution of intelligence.

4 The last obstacle

To co-operate, as we all know, is often more efficient than letting each work on his own. But working together and cheating the others out of their fair share is even better – except for those who are cheated . . .

Luckily, we have a loophole: *reciprocal altruism* (Trivers 1971). Through reciprocal altruism, co-operation becomes possible, but at a price, the price of keeping track of cheaters and freeriders . . . The good side is that a favour is returned by another favour, a friend can always trust a friend. The point is that, although some form of reciprocal altruism is found in many species, including primate species, it is of particular and fundamental importance to the working of a social system [like the human one] based on co-operation. . . .

. . . [T]he impetus for sharing information is small in chimpanzee society, except for occasional sharing and reciprocal altruism based on friendship. As Jane Goodall observed, young chimpanzee males have the patience and ingenuity to open boxes of bananas laid out by researchers, but the older and stronger males take the bananas, leaving little incentive for the youngsters to go on (Goodall 1972).

So this is the whole story: language is cognitive whereas animal communication is not. Cognitive intelligence is an earlier and more widely spread property of mind than language because evolution selects for effective information-gathering. Language's proper function is to communicate, which here means sharing of information. But information-sharing would seem to be prohibited by natural selection, except in extraordinary conditions. Only under the extraordinary conditions of reciprocal altruism can information-sharing take place without loss of fitness to the speaker. In the human lineage, social co-operation based on obligatory reciprocal altruism has evolved, a system which rewards people for co-operating and punishes them (morally and physically) for cheating. In such an environment language is finally possible.

Glossary

innatism (also **nativism**): a view that a capacity for language is born within us.

induction: working out general rules from examples.

cognition: thinking and reasoning.

theory of mind: the ability to identify with the point of view of another. To give a simple linguistic example, if somebody says: *The newspaper's here*, the listener has to recognise that the HERE in question relates to the speaker's position and not to the listener's own.

fitness: in the Darwinian sense means 'suitability'.

reciprocal altruism: being good to another person in the expectation that they will be good to you.

LOCALISATION AND LATERALISATION REVISITED

Do all speakers (no matter what their language) employ a similar set of psychological processes for dealing with grammar? Consider these questions in the light of
the following:

❏ Different languages use different types of sentence structure. While English uses
   an SVO (subject-verb-object) order, Japanese uses an SOV and Welsh uses a VSO.
❏ Different languages make varying use of inflection. While a language like Italian
   is highly inflected, one like Chinese has virtually no inflections. This means that
   Italians have to reserve attention for the ends of words, whereas the Chinese have
   to rely to some extent on context.

Differentiated syntactic processes

Terrence Deacon (from *The Symbolic Species*, London: Penguin, 1997: 306–8. Abridged with
permission of the author.)

[W]hat parts of the brain should we expect grammatical and syntactical information processing to recruit? As with simple word association processes, the answer
to this probably depends on processing demands, and not on some grammar-
processing center. Syntactic operations and grammatical judgments can involve many
different syntagmatic and paradigmatic processes, and these can differ from language to language. In languages like English and German, for example, word and
phrase position in a sentence are used to determine many grammatical functions,
such as relationships of possession or subordination, the difference between state-
ments and questions, and certain changes in tense such as the passive tense. But
in highly inflected languages, like Italian or Latin, affixes, suffixes or systematic
changes in phonemes tend to signal these functional roles. If grammatical operations were handled by some central processor we should not expect to observe
neural variations correlated with language variations, but since grammatical relationships are symbolic relationships, they are probably no less distributed and task-
dependent in their localization in the brain than are word retrieval processes. Even
within bilingual individuals different languages may be organized differently and
separately, sometimes in ways not even restricted to cortex. For example, bilingual
patients with subcortical . . . damage are often paradoxically more impaired in their
native language than in their secondary one.
    The clearest demonstration of the variable relationship between language struc-
tures and brain structures has recently come from studies of acquired agrammatism: loss of grammatical analytic abilities due to focal brain damage in adults.
Though it's long been unclear whether grammatical ability could be linked to specific
brain damage, English speakers appear to be especially susceptible to disruption of
grammatical abilities as a result of damage associated with Broca's area. Thus,
patients who have significantly impaired speech fluency also tend to show difficulties interpreting sentences that depend critically on grammatical function words,

Terrence
Deacon

and particular difficulties interpreting sentences that depend entirely on transforma-
tions of word order (like the passive [forms] in English). Such problems might
suggest that this grammatical function is located in this part of the brain, and many
have suggested just this. Curiously, however, a generalized grammatical deficit is
not consistently associated with damage to Broca's area, and specifically, in speakers
of highly inflected languages where word order is more free and where the
passive [form] is marked by grammatical words, morphemes, or inflections, there
appears to be far less agrammatism associated with Broca's area damage. In these
languages (such as Italian), Wernicke's aphasics, who also show disturbances
of semantic analysis but not speech fluency, are more impaired in producing and
analyzing the corresponding grammatical transformation than are patients with Broca's
area damage. So if there is a grammar module, then the parts of this module
map in very different ways to different grammatical operations, depending on
the relative importance of positional or inflectional tricks for cuing grammatical
decisions in different languages. . . .

   Probably the crucial factor behind this difference is the need to use very
different sorts of neural computations and mnemonic tricks to analyze word order
as opposed to individual words, suffixes, prefixes, and sound changes. Both
coding methods offer viable means for marking the same grammatical distinctions,
and are quite variably employed in different languages. Those languages that extensively utilize change in word form to mark grammatical functions tend correspondingly
to allow considerable freedom of word order, and vice versa. English, for example,
makes minimal use of inflection and extensive use of word order and special
'function words' to mark word-order interpretations. Italian and Latin, in contrast, rely almost exclusively on inflections and function words that change the
grammatical function of content words they modify. If we took the view that a
particular language function (e.g., the passive transformation) was a distinct primitive operation that was 'computed' by brain regions specialized for it, then we
would be forced to conclude that English and Italian speakers have different kinds
of brains with different types of language regions that make this possible. This, of
course, is absurd. What happens is that in the process of learning one of these
languages, particular syntactic functions tend to demand most from areas of the
brain that were previously specialized to perform [other] similar manipulations
of the signal. . . . Over the course of maturation and in response to constant
language use, the development of a certain degree of skill in this process is
accompanied by progressive specialization of this region. . . .

   Thus, a particular class of syntactical operation . . . can come to 'reside' somewhere in the brain, so to speak, and can be selectively lost due to focal damage,
particularly in mature brains, and yet be located differently in the brains of
speakers of different languages.

Glossary

syntagmatic and paradigmatic processes: terms that are paradigmatically related can
substitute for each other (e.g. *afraid – terrified – scared*); those that are syntagmati-
cally related occur in conjunction with each other (e.g. *afraid + of* or *heavy + smoker*).

neural variation: different patterns of activity in the nerve connections in the brain.
a semantic analysis: ability to assign a meaning.

Briefly look back at Section C2. Do you conclude that the right hemisphere plays any role at all in language processing? If so, what?

★ **Activity**

Lateralisation as competition

Terrence Deacon (from *The Symbolic Species*, London: Penguin, 1997: 311–15. Abridged with permission of the author.)

It might seem odd that in a book on language and the brain, whole chapters haven't been devoted to lateralization – the difference in functional representation between the two cerebral hemispheres. This is in part merely a stylistic choice. But it is also a reflection of the fact that I consider this to be a side issue (bad pun) that is not an essential feature of language processing, only an incidental feature of the way human brains have adapted to the computation problems of language use. The fact that many specialized language functions are strongly lateralized to the left hemisphere in the vast majority of human brains has been a major impetus for theories suggesting that lateralization might have been a precondition for language evolution. Many argue that this robust side-to-side difference reflects some major organizational logic underlying language. But . . . [l]ateralization is almost certainly an effect and not a cause of brain-language co-evolution. Indeed, I think it is largely an effect of language development in an individual's lifetime. The structure of languages has probably evolved to take advantage of intrinsic subtle biases in developing brains to break up and distribute their component cognitive computations so that they can most easily be processed in parallel, and one important way this can be accomplished is by 'assigning' functions to either side of the cerebral hemispheres.

Unfortunately, the study of lateralization has been afflicted with the problem of being an interesting topic for popular psychology, and of offering an attractive source of analogies for theorizing about almost every aspect of the mind. As a result, everyone's favorite complementary pair of mental functions can be mapped onto a brain whose functions differ on opposite sides. Since the middle of the nineteenth century, physicians and psychologists have argued over whether the left was female and the right male, the left verbal and the right nonverbal, the left linguistic and the right spatial, the left rational and the right irrational, the left differentiated and the right undifferentiated, the left localized and the right holistic, the left positive emotion and the right negative emotion, the left ego and the right id, the left dominant and the right subordinate, and even the left human cognition and the right primate cognition, to describe a few of the more prominent dichotomies. The attraction of discovering the most elegant way of dividing up the mind into two major complementary cognitive systems is almost irresistible. . . .

The representation of language functions probably develops primarily in response to the need to perform simultaneous but competing operations when speaking or listening to speech. This is supported by the fact that lateralization is

Terrence
Deacon

not so much a commitment of one side to language and the other not, but rather a segregation of component language functions . . . to the two sides. . . .

[I]t is important to get one thing straight. The right hemisphere is not the non-language hemisphere. It is critically and intimately involved in language processing at many levels during both development and maturity. Perhaps most importantly, it is critical for the large-scale, semantic processing of language, not word meaning so much as the larger symbolic constructions that words and sentences contribute to: complex ideas, descriptions, narratives, and arguments. Symbol construction and analysis do not end with the end of a sentence, but in many regards begin there. The real power of symbolic communication lies in its creative and constructive power. . . .

The best evidence for this right hemisphere language involvement comes from analysis of how right hemisphere damage affects such abilities as story and joke comprehension.[1] Patients who have suffered extensive damage to their right but not left hemispheres are generally able to speak well, without any unusual increase in grammatical errors or mistakes in choice of words; but when required to follow and interpret a short narrative, they seem to fail to grasp the logic of the whole. For example, they do not recognize when important steps in a story have been left out or inappropriate or anomalous events have been included, though they can recount the details. They seem to be unaware of the constraints of the context. Jokes provide another window into this difficulty. Humor depends crucially on understanding both what should ordinarily follow, and how the insidious twist of logic of the punch line undermines our expectations. Assessment of what makes something funny depends on an awareness of two conflicting contexts: an expected, 'appropriate' context, and a logically possible but very odd one. The aptness of the shift in contextual logic, the extent to which it effectively catches us off guard even when we know it is a joke, the way it caricatures what in a 'straight' context might be serious or threatening, all these are the ingredients of good jokes. . . . Well, anyway, this poses a serious problem for someone unable to construct the appropriate narrative context in the first place. Patients with right hemisphere damage seem to rank jokes as funny based solely on the extent to which the punch line contains material that is different from what preceded it. . . .

[A]s language abilities become progressively more sophisticated with age and experience, the need to analyze symbolic relationships at many levels simultaneously grows. The highly automated interpretation of symbolic relationships encoded in word combinations and sentence structure requires a strategy of one rapid interpretation followed by another. It demands both rapid implementation and an ability to keep previous operations from interfering with subsequent operations. The same neural systems that subserve sentence-length analysis would probably also be critical for maintaining long-term [recall] of symbolic information. These simultaneous demands would thus likely conflict or interfere with one another, and so limit the efficiency of both processes. But because right and left brain structures are paired, it is possible to keep the processes from interfering with one another by compartmentalizing them to opposite hemispheres.

The right hemisphere also subserves another important language function that is nonsymbolic, but . . . probably is competitive with phonological analysis and word pro-

Terrence Deacon

cessing. It is the processing of prosodic features of speech. Prosodic features are the rhythmic and pitch changes that we generally use to convey emotional tone, to direct the listener's attention to the more and less significant elements in a sentence, and in general to indicate how aroused we are about the contents of our speech. . . .

Here again, language production and analysis effectively require that we implement two different modes of phonetic analysis and vocal control simultaneously: prosodic and phonemic processes. These tasks would tend to compete for recruitment of the same brain structures (probably the classic Broca's and Wernicke's areas), and as a result would probably interfere with each other. It would be . . . inefficient to trade off use of the same cortical system for both. . . . [T]he monitoring of prosodic information tends to operate against a foreground attention to specific words and phrases. . . . [Extending] the representation of this background function to the right hemisphere, and phonemic and word analysis to the left, . . . may similarly provide a means for processing these sources of information in parallel with minimal cross-interference. . . .

But the right hemisphere may be far more capable of full-scale linguistic functions than we normally imagine. . . . Data from schools that train simultaneous translators . . . suggest that under the special demands of this difficult language task, both hemispheres can to some extent become language hemispheres. The problem for the simultaneous translator is to keep the two languages from getting in each other's way. Listening to one while producing the other is like that old problem of patting your head and rubbing your stomach with opposite hands, and then reversing what each hand is doing but leaving them in place; or chewing gum while playing the drums or dancing or just walking out of sync with each chew. The direct competition of simultaneous similar language functions is often further coupled with a consistent asymmetry of auditory input: most translators develop an ear preference for listening to the source language. Studies before and after training demonstrate that most students begin with a right ear (left hemisphere) preference for both languages, but may develop an opposite ear advantage for each language by the end of their training.

Thus, the two languages can come to be preferentially represented in opposite hemispheres. This is all the more remarkable since the shift . . . can be induced in young adults, not infants. . . . This special case nonetheless demonstrate the general principle: when sensorimotor or cognitive operations tend to compete simultaneously for the same neural substrates, there is strong developmental . . . pressure to segregate the competing operations to counterpart structures in the opposite hemispheres. . . .

In general, then, it is misleading to think of language as though it is all in the left hemisphere. The right side is neither primitive nor mute. Both hemispheres contribute essential and complementary functions. These develop in tandem, and the biases for a particular pattern of asymmetry evolved with respect to this complementarity of functions. Lateralization is not so much an expression of evolutionary adaptation as of adaptation during one's lifetime, biased so as to minimize any neurological 'indecisions' about what should go where.

[1] For an interesting example of right hemisphere language comprehension, see Gardner *et al.* (1983); also see Larsen *et al.* (1978, 1980) for evidence of right hemisphere functions contributing to speech.

Jean
Aitchison

Glossary

difference in functional representation: differences in which language functions are dealt with.

processed in parallel: with several operations taking place at one and the same time.

ego: sense of self, in relation to the external world.

id: instincts and innate needs.

representation: distribution.

As language abilities . . . Deacon argues that we need to do two things in order to achieve understanding. We need to analyse what we hear in terms of phrase and sentence structure (i.e. syntax). This demands 'one rapid interpretation followed by another'. At the same time, we need to build up meaning on a larger scale, adding what we have just heard to our understanding of the whole conversation so far. These simultaneous demands potentially conflict. But, because the left hemisphere deals primarily with syntactic processing and the right hemisphere deals primarily with larger-scale representation, we are able to keep them apart.

prosodic features of speech: intonation, rhythm, stress.

prosodic and phonemic processes: a speaker has to supply an overall intonation pattern. At the same time he/she has to produce the basic sounds of the language. These two are seen as potentially in conflict.

asymmetry of auditory input: heavy reliance on one ear rather than the other.

sensorimotor: related to movement or sensation.

neural substrates: nerve connections.

FORMING LEXICAL CATEGORIES

Activity ★

One of the easiest ways of getting to grips with the notion of a lexical category is to look at what we know of how infants acquire such categories when they are in the process of developing their first language. Suggest how an infant might form the concept associated with the word DUCK. Remember that the infant has to learn to relate the word to a whole class of entities in the real world, not just to a single example.

How children learn the meaning of words

Jean Aitchison (from *Words in the Mind*, Chapter 15, London: Blackwell, 2nd edn., 1994, pp. 169–180, Abridged with permission of the author.)

Essentially, children are faced with three different but related tasks: a labelling task, a packaging task and a network-building task. In the labelling task, youngsters must discover that sequences of sound can be used as names for things. In the packaging task, they must find out which things can be packaged together under one label. In the network-building task, they must work out how words relate to one another. . . .

The packaging task

There is quite a lot of difference between applying a label such as *penguin* to one toy penguin and the ability to use that label correctly in all circumstances. How does a child come to apply the name *penguin* to a wider range of penguins? And how does she learn to restrict it to penguins alone, and not use it for puffins and pandas, which are also black and white? . . . By adult standards, both under-extensions and overextensions occur: sometimes children assume that a word refers to a narrower range of things than it in fact does, whereas at other times they include far too much under a single name.

Underextensions seem quite understandable, as when 20-month-old Hildegard refused to accept that the word *white* could be used of blank pages, since she her-self associated it only with snow [Leopold in Bar-Adon & Leopold, 1971: 98]. She had acquired the word in a particular context, and it took time for her to realize that the word had a wider application. Similarly, a child quizzed on the words *deep* and *shallow* 'might respond correctly if he happens to be probed about ends of swimming pools. . . . But if shown a picture of a deep puddle . . . and asked "Is this a deep puddle?" the child might answer, "No, a big one" ' [Carey, 1978: 288]. And in cases where words have abstract as well as concrete physical applications, it may be years before the child fully understands the range of mean-ing covered: in one experiment three- and four-year-olds readily called milk *cold*, water *deep*, boxes *hard* and trees *crooked*, but had no idea that these words could be extended to people, and some even denied that it was possible: 'I never heard of deep people anyway!' 'No people are cold!' [Asch & Nerlove, 1960]. A period of underextension for a word, then, is quite normal, and the gradual enlarging of meaning to include an increasingly wide range does not seem particularly puzzling.

Overextensions are less common than underextensions, but are more notice-able, as the effects may be bizarre. . . . Three main types of explanation have been proposed for overextensions: gap-filling, 'mental fog' and wrong analysis. The first of these suggests that . . . [the child] might recognize the difference between [a] duck and a peacock but say *duck* for both because he doesn't yet know the word *peacock*. Or she might know the name *peacock*, but be unable to pronounce it, since some children consciously avoid sounds they find difficult to cope with. Gap-filling explanations are possibly correct for some overextensions, but are unlikely to account for all of them, especially the more bizarre ones such as using the same word for a duck and a mug of milk.

'The child unquestionably perceives the world through a mental fog. But as the sun of experience rises higher and higher these boundaries are beaten back.' This statement by [Chambers] an early twentieth-century psychologist typifies the 'mental fog' viewpoint. Its proponents argue that meanings are necessarily hazy and vague in the early stages, and that they gradually become more precise as children learn to discriminate more finely. . . .

A more recent version of this theory suggests that 'when the child first begins to use identifiable words, he does not know their full (adult) meaning: he has only partial entries for them in the lexicon. . . . The acquisition of semantic knowledge, then, will consist of adding . . . to the lexical entry of the word until the child's . . . entry for that word corresponds to the adult's' [Clark, 1973: 72]. The child might have learnt the word *dog* but only noticed certain outline characteristics: 'dogginess' might have been identified with 'being four-legged'. In that case, cows, sheep, zebras and llamas would wrongly be included in the category *dog*. But each of these lexical items would gradually be narrowed down. To the lexical entry for *dog* the child might attach the additional specifications 'makes barking sounds', 'is fairly small', while to *zebra* it might add 'striped' and 'fairly large', so distinguishing one from the other. Eventually, the child's lexical entries would have all the details filled in, and so be comparable to those of an adult.

This gradual narrowing down may apply to some words. But there are two facts which this type of theory does not explain. First, relatively few words are overextended – perhaps less than a third. If the mental fog viewpoint was correct, one would expect many more words to start out by being too wide in their application. Second, many of the overextensions are bizarre and cannot easily be related to a lack of subdivisions in the adult word. This suggests that the child is not simply operating in a mental fog, in which he can only see broad outlines. Instead, he has made an analysis of the items concerned, but a wrong one by adult standards.

The Russian psychologist Vygotsky [1962: 70] discusses a child who used *qua* ('quack') for a duck swimming on a pond, a cup of milk, a coin with an eagle on it and a teddy bear's eye. In his view, children are perfectly capable of analysis, but they tend to focus on only one aspect of a situation at a time and to generalize that alone. The child began with *qua* as a duck on a pond. Then the liquid element caught the youngster's attention, and the word was generalized to a cup of milk. But the duck had not been forgotten, and this surfaced in *qua* used to refer to a coin with an eagle on it. But then the child appeared to ignore the bird-like portion of the meaning and focus only on the roundness of the coin, so reapplied the word *qua* to a teddy-bear's eye. Vygotsky calls this a 'chain-complex', because all the usages of *qua* are linked together in a chain. Each one is attached to the next, with no overall structure.

A more recent 'wrong analysis' theory suggests that children are working from prototypes. Like adults, they learn the meaning of words by picking on a typical example or 'prototype' which they analyse. They then match other possible examples of a category against the characteristics of the prototype, and if there is sufficient agreement, they assign the new object to the same category. According to this viewpoint, discrepancies between child and adult language occur because children analyse the prototype differently from adults. For example, between the ages of 16 months and 2 years, Eva used the word *moon* to refer not only to the moon but also to a slice of lemon, a shiny green leaf, curved cow horns, a crescent-shaped piece of paper and pictures of yellow and green vegetables on the wall of a store [Bowerman, 1980]. Most of these objects are crescent-shaped, which seemed to be an important property of moonhood for Eva. At first sight this observation supports mental fog theories: perhaps Eva simply thinks that *moon* means 'crescent'. But on examination there is more to it than this. First, Eva was able to recognize the moon in all its phases, when it was a full moon, a half moon or a quarter moon. So moons were not inevitably crescents, they were just typically crescents. Second, each of the objects labelled *moon* had something else apart from shape in common with the moon, though something different. The lemon slice shared its colour with the moon. The shiny green leaf shared the property of being shiny. The curved cow horns were seen from below. The green and yellow vegetables on the chart were seen against a broad expanse of background. So Eva had apparently identified several characteristics of the moon, the most crucial of which is its shape. Something was likely to be labelled *moon* if it shared both the shape and one other characteristic with the real moon.

Similarly, at around the same age, Eva took someone kicking a ball as a prototype for the word *kick* [Bowerman, 1978]. She seems to have analysed this action as possessing three main characteristics: first, a waving limb, second, sudden sharp contact between part of the body and an object, third, propulsion forward of the object. This analysis could account for her labelling as *kick* a kitten with a ball of wool near its paw, dancers doing the can-can, a moth fluttering on a table, pushing a bottle with her feet and pushing a teddy bear's stomach against her sister's chest. All these things share characteristics with the prototypical *kick* but not the same ones. . . .

Prototype theory therefore accounts for children's broad mental fog-type generalizations as well as the strange chain-complex ones. And it ties in with the way in which adults assign words to categories. Children, like adults, look for clusters of properties which belong to a prototype.

Children differ from adults, however, in that they may not focus on the same features when they analyse words. In the early stages, they are over-influenced by appearance, especially shape. When asked to name an object that was a crayon shaped like a car, younger children tended to call it a *car*, and older ones a *crayon* [Merriman *et al.*, 1993].

Kindergarten-age children concentrate on superficial characteristics. A child was asked if a friendly and cheerful woman who disconnected and removed a toilet bowl could be a robber. The reply was: 'No . . . 'cause robbers, they have to have guns and they do stickups, and this woman didn't do that, and she didn't have a gun, she didn't do a stickup' [Keil & Batterman, 1984]. Another child argued that a hut containing dirty clothes which people paid to see couldn't be a museum, because 'a museum is something with dinosaur bones'. As children get older, they gradually alter their analyses to fit in with those of the people around them – though this can go on into the teenage years. . . .

Network building

Somehow, words have to be fitted together into a semantic network. How does this happen?

The evidence is sometimes confusing. . . . Brian [at two and a half] would not believe that a horse was an animal [Macnamara, 1982]. . . . This seemed to be the reaction of around half of the two-year-olds tested. They reserved the word *animal* for a bunch of assorted animals. And the 'one name only' preference has been confirmed by other researchers.

The evidence, then, can be difficult to interpret. Apparent backward steps may be the best guide that network-building is taking place. Two-year-old Christie used the words *put* and *give* appropriately, as in 'I *put* it somewhere', '*Gimme* more gum'. Then, when she was three, she started to use them interchangeably: 'You *put* ("give") me bread and butter', 'Whenever Eva doesn't need her towel, she *gives* ("puts") it on my table' [Bowerman, 1978]. Perhaps, suggested Christie's mother, she had suddenly discovered that *put* and *give* had very similar meanings, but had not yet realized that one *puts* something on to a thing, but *gives* something to a person. Two more years elapsed before Christie used *put* and *give* correctly by adult standards.

Network-building takes place slowly. . . . Words which an adult would regard as related take time to get linked in the child's mind. This fits with the evidence from underextensions, the fact that children often learn a word in a particular context and only gradually extend it to a wider situation. Even fairly old children may find it hard to detach words from specific contexts. A group aged between eight-and-a-half and ten-and-a-half correctly guessed that the nonsense word *lidber* meant 'collect' from the sentence 'Jimmy lidbered stamps from all countries'. But when asked to interpret 'The police did not allow the people to lidber on the street', a typical response was that the police did not allow people to collect stamps on the street [Werner & Kaplan, 1950]. . . .

The tortoise-like progress of network-building is confirmed by the literally dozens of studies which have explored how children cope with overlapping words, such as *tall, big, fat, high* and opposites, such as *big–small, deep–shallow, tall–short* [Richards, 1979]. All the studies reported that these words acquire their adult meaning only gradually, sometimes with backward steps. . . .

Collocational links appear to have priority for children, while those between co-ordinates lag behind. This is shown by word association experiments: young children are likely to respond to 'table' with *eat*, to 'dark' with *night*, to 'send' with *letter* and to 'deep' with *hole*, whereas typical adult responses to these would be *chair, light, receive* and *shallow*. As children get older, the more likely they are to give an adult-like response. A suggested explanation is that 'this change in word associations is a consequence of the child's gradual organization of his vocabulary into the syntactic classes called parts-of-speech' (Brown and Berko 1960: 14). Another explanation is that children may take time to discover the criteria by which adults classify items as co-ordinates. A study conducted with a group of three- to five-year-olds showed that they were quite happy to agree that prototypical birds, such as sparrows or robins, were birds, but often argued that ducks or hens were not birds, they were ducks and hens [White, 1982]. It is unclear whether the children had come to this conclusion by themselves or whether they were simply reflecting the speech of their parents, since the same experimenter noted that parents tended to refer to typical birds as *birds* more often than atypical ones: 'Oh, look there's a bird, it's a robin'; 'That's a turkey, like the ones we saw at the turkey farm'.

Efficient retrieval may be another explanation for the importance of co-ordinates in adult speech. Fast word-finding is a skill that has to be acquired, and young children can be quite slow at naming objects such as *ice-cream, lion* and *bed*, whose names they know very well. Perhaps the gradual shift-over comes in response to a need to organize and retrieve words quickly as the overall vocabulary gets larger.

LEXICAL PROCESSING

D5

You may find this extract quite challenging. First skim it to find out:

- what are the four parallel sources of information in a connectionist model?
- what is a logogen?
- what two features characterise a connectionist model?
- what is the author's chief argument in favour of a lexical search theory?

Before reading the article as a whole, look through it and gather more information about

- logogens
- connectionism
- search models

Lexical processing

Kenneth I. Forster (in Oscherson, D. N. and Lasnik, H. (eds), *An Invitation to Cognitive Science: Volume 1, Language*, Cambridge, Mass: MIT, 1990. Abridged with permission of the author).

5.3.1 Word-Detector Circuits

It may be useful to begin by considering how we might design a simple circuit that could perform the lexical decision task. Suppose we had six switches, a battery, and 32 light bulbs. The light bulbs correspond to word detectors, and the switches correspond to letters (for instance, switch 1 being ON means the letter A is present). With six switches, we have 64 possible combinations, of which [let us say] only 32 correspond to actual words. The task is to design the circuit so that a different bulb lights up whenever one of the 32 'permissible' combinations of switches is selected; otherwise, nothing happens. The system could now be used for [word recognition]. We observe which letters are present in the target

**Kenneth I.
Forster**

stimulus, we press the appropriate switches, and if a bulb lights up, we say 'Yes,' and if no bulb lights up, we say 'No.'

The obvious first step in solving this problem is to construct AND gates for each bulb so that they are connected to the battery only when a particular combination of switches is ON. But what happens if some other switches are also ON? The AND gate will ignore this information, and the bulb will still light up. This . . . would mean that the input BEARD would light the bulb not only for the word *beard*, but also for the word *bear*. Similarly, the *bear* bulb would be lit by the nonword input BEARF. We must therefore complicate the circuit and connect all switches that should be OFF to the bulb so that if any one of them is ON, the circuit connecting the bulb with the battery is broken. These could be described as having an *inhibitory* effect on the lighting of the bulb.

Another factor that needs to be taken into account is letter position. In the example just given the *bear* bulb would also be lit by the stimulus AREB, since the switches code only for the presence of a letter and ignore its position. We must therefore distinguish between 'B-in-first-position' and 'B-in-fourth-position,' which means having separate switches. To be able to recognize words up to 10 letters in length, then, we need 260 switches (26 letters × 10 positions). . .

5.3.2 Activation Models

Two influential models of word recognition use word-detector circuits similar to the example we have just discussed: the *logogen* model of Morton (1970) and the network approach of McClelland and Rumelhart (1986), which is now perhaps better known as a *connectionist* model.

In Morton's theory, logogens are word detectors, just like the bulbs in our example, except that they do not use AND gates. Instead, they sum the activation received from letter detectors, and if the sum of the activation exceeds the threshold for that logogen, it fires. Logogens also receive activation from other systems. . . . [I]n order to explain the effect of a sentence context on word recognition, Morton proposes that the cognitive system (which is responsible for comprehension) is able to direct activation back to the logogen system, so that words appropriate to the context receive activation and hence are detected more readily. Similar accounts can be offered for semantic priming effects of the *doctor-nurse* variety.

Very similar assumptions are involved in the connectionist models of word recognition (see McClelland and Rumelhart 1986 for a general survey of network models). The network consists of a series of layers, each layer in turn consisting of a bank of . . . detector units. Each unit in the network is connected to each unit in the adjacent layers, and also to each other unit within its layer. These connections vary in strength, and they are of two types. Connections *between* layers are excitatory, whereas connections *within* a level are inhibitory (see Figure 1).

For word recognition, four layers are appropriate: one layer each for detecting visual features, letters, words, and semantic features. As the network gradually learns to recognize printed words, the connections change strength. . . .

Kenneth I.
Forster

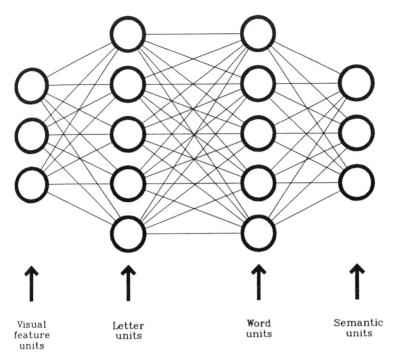

Visual	Letter	Word	Semantic
feature	units	units	units
units			

Connectionist network for word recognition. Connections between levels are excitatory. Initially every unit is connected to every unit at the next level, but as a function of experience some of these connections are weakened and others are strengthened.

Figure 1

The major feature of this model that distinguishes it from the logogen model . . . is this assumption of varying strengths of connection. A further feature is the existence of inhibitory connections between units within a layer. . . . Basically, the units within a layer compete with each other. Thus, at the word level units receive activation from both the letter level and the semantic level, but they also receive inhibitory inputs from neighboring word units.

When a word is initially presented, the activation pattern is relatively diffuse, since there is a great deal of *cross-activation*. With an initial input B-E-A-R, for example, the units corresponding to these letters will be most strongly activated, but units corresponding to other letters will also be activated. Thus in addition to the 'B1' [B in first position] unit, . . . the 'P1' unit will also be activated, because 'B' and 'P' resemble each other. All of these cross-activation effects will be passed on to the next highest level. At the word level, the unit for the word *fear* will receive strong activation because it shares three letters with the input, as will the unit for *pear*. The latter unit, however, might receive a higher amount of activation because of the extra effect of the similarity of its first letter to B. . . . If this

Kenneth I.
Forster

process were allowed to continue unchecked, eventually every unit in the network would become active. This is where the inhibitory connections play an important role. For example, if the unit for *bear* has strong inhibitory connections to the unit for *pear*, then the more strongly *bear* is activated, the more effectively it suppresses activation in the *pear* unit. Thus, competition between units reduces the amount of cross-activation, making the activation pattern sharper and less diffuse. . . .

With such a network, deciding what word has been presented involves waiting until the network reaches a state of equilibrium, with just one word unit being strongly activated. If no unit remains active, then the input most likely was a nonword. Thus, making a lexical decision would involve somehow monitoring the distribution of activation across all word units, waiting until some . . . criterion of equilibrium is reached. If, after a [set] interval of time, this criterion is not met, then [a] deadline . . . become[s] effective, and a 'No' decision would be reached.

Frequency effects are readily explained in the network model in terms of connection strengths. Each time a word is recognized, it is assumed that the strengths of the active connections are all incremented slightly. . . .

[E]xplanation[s] of the frequency effect run into interesting problems when we consider the case of two words with substantial graphemic overlap but marked difference in frequency. For example, take the relatively high-frequency word *bright* and its low-frequency competitor *blight*. When the stimulus input is actually the low-frequency alternative BLIGHT, substantial activation is going to be produced in the unit for *bright*. . . . If all connections were of the same strength, then activation from the 'L2' [L in second position] unit would be enough to tip the scales in favor of *blight*, but once frequency is taken into account, this result is not guaranteed.

To be sure, there will be some occasions where this is [what happens]. For example, if we flash BLIGHT onto a screen very briefly, it might be misread as BRIGHT. But what about the occasions where it is correctly perceived . . . ? How is it guaranteed that the changes in connection strengths induced by frequency are never sufficiently large to prevent a low-frequency word from being perceived?

The problem here is that frequency is assumed to produce changes that are indistinguishable from those produced by [the] stimulus. . . . A network theory has little choice, however, since its only commodity is strength of activation, and every feature of performance must be explained in these terms. . . . Hence, we need some principle that limits the influence of frequency so that this type of problem does not arise. . . .

5.3.3 Lexical Search Theory

Rather than trying to describe the operations of the lexical processor in terms of simple network circuits, lexical search theory moves to a more abstract level and defines the operations of the lexical processor in terms of information retrieval. . . . The basic assumption is that information about words is stored in a way comparable to that of a random-access mass storage device in a digital computer.

Kenneth I.
Forster

Each word is associated with a lexical entry, which is like a data file that specifies all the necessary linguistic properties of the word, such as its pronunciation, spelling, part of speech, and meaning. The collection of all such entries defines the mental lexicon for a given person. Lexical access involves comparing the letter pattern of the stimulus with the orthographic specification of each lexical entry in turn, until an exact match is found. . . .

The most important difference between this kind of model and the activation models in the preceding section is that here the input stimulus is compared serially with each lexical entry in turn, whereas in the activation models all entries are compared with the stimulus *simultaneously*. Thus, lexical search theory is a serial-comparison theory, whereas an activation theory is a parallel-comparison theory.

The first model to explicitly consider the nature of the search process was developed by Rubenstein (Rubenstein, Garfield, and Millikan 1970). In this model it was suggested that the search process was literally a random search of a limited subset of the total lexicon (this subset being defined by a preliminary examination of the letters in the input word). . . . [However,] the common assumption . . . [today] is that the search is *frequency-ordered*. That is, the entries for high-frequency words are compared to the stimulus before the entries for low-frequency words. This has the effect of minimizing the average search time.

It is also assumed that the lexicon can be accessed in several different ways. When we read, we have a visual display to recognize, but when we listen, we have a sequence of speech sounds. On the other hand, when we talk or write, we have some kind of meaning in mind, and we need to find a word that will express that meaning. Obviously, the same organization of entries is unlikely to serve the requirements of all three modes of access. Rather than have three totally different lexicons, Forster (1976) proposed three different access files: an orthographic access file, a phonological access file, and a semantic access file. Each such file consisted of a set of pointers to the actual lexical entries, plus an *access code*. For the orthographic access file, the access code would be some aspect of the spelling of the word – say, the first three letters. For the phonological access file, the access code would specify some aspect of the phonological specification of each word. Similarly, an access code in the semantic access file might specify the general semantic category to which a word belongs. Access now consists of first selecting the right access file (depending on what input mode we are in) and then comparing the properties of the input stimulus with the access codes in a strict frequency-ordered manner.

Once a match is found (for instance, in the orthographic case, the access code matches the first three letters of the input word), then the pointer to the location of the real lexical entry can be extracted from the access file. . . . The full orthographic specification of the word can now be retrieved and compared with the original letter input. This is referred to as a *postaccess check*. If this check reveals a match, then the correct entry has been found. If not, then the search of the access file must continue. In the now familiar terms of personal-computer data base systems, the set of lexical entries is the data base, and the access files are

Kenneth I.
Forster

index files, where indexing has been carried out on something less than the total spelling of the word.

A relevant question to ask at this point is, 'Why have a serial search procedure?' The implication of search is that the location of some desired piece of information is unknown. To set up an information retrieval system where the precise location of every conceivable piece of information is known in advance is extremely expensive. In practical terms, it is usually easier to have the general location known, but not the precise location. Consider a conventional printed dictionary as an example. Since words are listed in alphabetical order, we can predict the relative locations of pairs of words very precisely. However, from the spelling alone, we cannot predict which line a given word should appear on, or even which page. Hence, we still need to use search procedures even with alphabetized entries. Note that it is not *impossible* to design a system that would permit accurate prediction of location. In theory, we could print the dictionary according to a rule that assigned a line number to each word. But such a dictionary would at least have to reserve a separate line for every distinct combination of letters, whether a word is formed or not. Even if we ignore words over 10 letters in length, we will still have 26^{10} lines in the dictionary, with the overwhelming majority of those lines having no word listed. Allowing a generous 100 lines per page, this produces a mammoth book with more than one trillion mostly empty pages. Obviously, such a dictionary would be quite impractical, so much so that one wonders whether even the brain with its billions and billions of cells could afford such an extravagance.

What kinds of phenomena does the notion of search enable us to explain? First, it accounts for the frequency effect . . . Frequency works by establishing a rank order across all lexical entries, so that the search process compares the entries for high-frequency words with the input first . . . This theory also accounts nicely for the consequences of an *exhaustive search*. Consider what happens when a nonword is presented. Before we can say that it is a nonword, we must wait until all entries have been scanned. This predicts a longer decision time for nonwords than words, which is the case.

Glossary

lexical decision task: an experiment in which subjects have to identify actual words in a list of words and non-words.

AND gates: so that (e.g.) the bulb for BEAR would only light up when B + E + A + R were all present.

inhibitory: evidence not only supports a word that appears to fit the signal; it also suppresses the activation of words that do not.

exceeds the threshold . . . , it fires: when activation reaches a particular level, the word is treated as recognised.

the cognitive system . . . : the logogen system is responsible for recognising words, but is influenced by general cognition which handles 'context' (world knowledge and our memory of the text so far).

Connections between layers . . . : evidence accumulates from layer to layer (letter features, letters, whole words, etc.). But as the activation grows for one particular interpretation, it is reduced for other interpretations *at that level*. As it becomes more and more likely that what we see is an A, the activation for competitors such as H or E declines. As the evidence builds up for BEAR, so support for HEAR or BEAT is suppressed.

frequency is assumed to produce changes: clues provided by frequency are mixed with clues based on what is actually physically present on the page.

this subset being defined, . . . : words are grouped in subsets by their first letters.

expensive: demanding in terms of the resources involved.

WORKING MEMORY: AN OVERVIEW

Before reading this extract, jot down what you can recall of Working Memory from Section C6. What is the phonological loop? What is its function?

Check your recollections as you read.

Working Memory

Robert H. Logie (from *The Psychologist*, 13/4 (1999). Abridged with permission of the author.)

There is fairly widespread, although not universal, agreement among researchers that working memory is a useful concept, and interest in its characteristics has grown dramatically in the last few years. The result is something of a debate as to its characteristics (Miyake & Shah [1999] . . .), but I will focus on one particularly successful theory that has been developed largely in Britain and was inspired by the work of Alan Baddeley and Graham Hitch (Baddeley, 1986). . . .

One version of this theory is illustrated in Figure 1 (adapted from Logie, 1995). A key feature of the model shown in Figure 1 is that it contradicts the typical view, in most contemporary introductory psychology textbooks, of short-term memory or working memory as the gateway between perception and long-term memory. The reasons for this change should become clear as the article progresses.

Also immediately apparent from the figure is that working memory comprises a coherent collection of specialised cognitive functions. One group of functions enables temporary storage of the visual appearance of objects and scenes (the visual cache), a second group likewise offers temporary retention of verbal material in terms of sounds or 'phonology' (the phonological loop), while a third offers a co-ordinating executive function which enables the conscious manipulation of

Robert H.
Logie

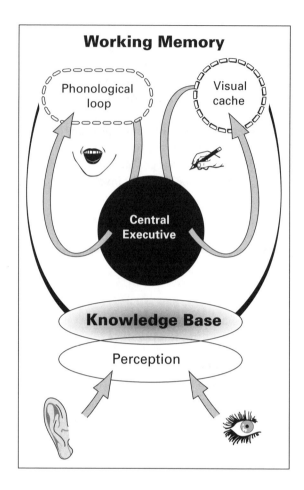

Figure 1

information (central executive). All of the components draw on prior knowledge (the 'knowledge base') and on the products of moment-to-moment perception (interpreted via the knowledge base).

The model as a whole is derived from experimental work with normal adults and children, from studies of individuals who have suffered brain damage, from computational modelling, and from recent work using brain imaging techniques. I will start with a description of what might be some basic requirements for a respectable theory of working memory. . . .

Basics of working memory

Clearly, there are some basic features of a usable working memory. One such feature is its limited capacity. Therefore, only some of our immediate past experience is retained, with the selection based at least in part on task demands. However, despite its limited capacity, working memory has to deal with the products of perception from vision, hearing, taste, smell and touch.

Robert H.
Logie

An additional feature is the temporary nature of working memory. This is essential for updating moment to moment, and to avoid crowding our mind with irrelevant information. Nevertheless, it is useful to be able to extend the retention of crucial information when necessary.

The use of the descriptor 'working' implies that this is not simply a passive, temporary deposit box for the left luggage of perception (as was one suggested role for the old concept of short-term memory). The contents of working memory can be combined with stored knowledge and manipulated, interpreted and recombined to develop new knowledge, assist learning, form goals, and support interaction with the physical environment.

The theory of working memory outlined in Figure 1 offers a conceptual tool with which to understand the nature of the mental apparatus and of the activity that might support at least some of its basic features.

Visual appearance and location

. . . [I]t is not difficult to describe, from memory, many of the core features of a scene that we have glanced at a few moments before. Nor is it overtaxing mentally to count the number of doors in your house by recalling a few details of the layout of each room.

One way to account for this form of mental ability is to suggest that we have a temporary memory that can hold information about where objects are and what those objects are, thereby allowing us to guide hand and arm movements to the correct location and to pick up the objects in the absence of vision.

This ability is highly adaptive, in that it allows us to recall the location of objects in our immediate environment that are not currently in view (e.g. behind us, occluded by larger objects, or in the dark), and to recall those locations when we change our location or orientation. We can still remember the layout if we turn around or leave the room.

This temporary memory also allows us to recall and describe the physical appearance or layout of familiar environments, such as the inside of our living room or the main square of our home town. The details are drawn from our knowledge base and become available in the temporary memory for the period that the task requires. . . .

Memory span, counting and language acquisition

Thus far, I have said very little about the more verbally oriented functions of working memory. At one level, these can be seen primarily as a means to store phonological properties of words for brief periods. Yet it turns out that the characteristics of this temporary memory for words – the phonological loop – have significant implications for a wide range of everyday activities. Any activity that requires retention of a verbal sequence such as remembering a new telephone number long enough to dial it, repeating a foreign word or counting objects would rely on this aspect of working memory.

There is now a large literature on this topic suggesting that verbal temporary memory is closely linked with the speech system. So, for example, immediate

Robert H.
Logie

memory span for digits (such as a telephone number) is severely disrupted if the experimental participant is required to repeat aloud an irrelevant word, such as 'the the the' – a technique known as articulatory suppression.

Moreover, sequences of words that take longer to say, such as 'hippopotamus, university, parliament', are more difficult to remember than are sequences of short words, such as 'zebra, school, policy' (Baddeley et al., 1975). Closely linked to this finding is the observation that people who can speak quickly tend to have longer digit spans than do people who speak more slowly (Nicolson, 1981).

This link between speaking rate and memory span has important practical implications. For example, Ellis and Hennelley (1980) observed that digit span in Welsh-speaking children was poorer than in English-speaking children. This was attributed entirely to the fact that the words for digits in Welsh take longer to pronounce than do the digits in English.

Similar results have been reported showing shorter digit spans in Italian, where again the words for digits take slightly longer to pronounce than in English (Della Sala & Logie, 1993), and longer digit spans in Chinese where digit words are very short (Stigler et al., 1986). In other words, digit span is language specific, and we should be cautious when interpreting digit span scores across languages and cultures.

In terms of Figure 1, overt speaking rate appears to act as a constraint on the rehearsal rate of the phonological loop rehearsal component (indicated by the 'mouth' and the looped arrow in the diagram). Longer words take longer to rehearse, therefore the information in the phonological loop begins to decay before it can be reactivated by rehearsal of the items.

A second important application for working memory is in counting and mental arithmetic. For example, when counting we have to keep track of where we are in the counting sequence at any one time. If we are counting objects, such as coins or number of events, we continually have to update our mental record of where we are in the counting sequence. If we are counting an array of objects, such as words on this page, then we have in addition to keep track of which words have been counted and which have not. This is particularly important if the items are scattered randomly in front of us.

Some years ago, Alan Baddeley and I (Logie & Baddeley, 1987) examined whether the working memory theory could shed any light on how normal adults accomplish such tasks. We asked participants to repeat aloud an irrelevant word (articulatory suppression) while they were counting a series of flashes on a computer screen.

Because we already knew that articulatory suppression affects verbal working memory, we were interested to find out whether normal counting would also be affected. It would be affected if the phonological loop were crucial to the counting process.

Articulatory suppression had a dramatic effect on counting. Participants rarely achieved the correct total, although they could do so if they were not repeating an irrelevant word. The disruption did not arise because participants had to do two things at once, because asking these same people to repeatedly tap their hand on the table or presenting them with random words or numbers had virtually no effect on counting. It was the requirement to generate repeated speech that was crucial for the interference to appear.

Robert H. Logie

Therefore, mentally repeating the numbers is crucial for keeping track in a counting task, and this mental repetition comprises the subvocal rehearsal component of the phonological loop.

Given that the phonological loop system had been shown to provide an explanation for important aspects of verbal immediate recall, it appeared that the system could also enable the process of keeping track moment to moment of where we are in a counting sequence.

More recent work has shown that a similar account can be given for mental arithmetic, particularly for sums such as $5 + 3 + 6 + 8 + 2 = ?$, in which a cumulative total is repeatedly updated (Logie *et al.*, 1994). Each [time the] total is updated, it is repeated subvocally, and this capitalises on the memory function of the phonological loop.

Clearly, a large part of mental arithmetic relies on a knowledge base of known solutions (McCloskey *et al.*, 1991), but mental rehearsal within the phonological loop appears to offer an account of how we keep track of intermediate totals as we progress through a sum, as well as where we are in a counting sequence.

The phonological loop component of working memory has proved useful in studies of language acquisition in young children. Susan Gathercole, Alan Baddeley and others (e.g. Gathercole & Baddeley, 1989) have shown that young children's ability to repeat a series of nonsense words at age 3 or 4 predicts their language ability several years later.

This suggests that the ability to repeat an unfamiliar speech sound (a feature of the phonological loop) is important for acquiring vocabulary and other language skills, both in young children and in adults learning a second language.

The loop has also been found invaluable in interpreting the pattern of difficulties encountered by brain-damaged patients who show deficits of one component of working memory while having other components intact (for a review, see Della Sala & Logie, 1993).

Recent developments in neuroimaging techniques offer further converging evidence for the concept of a phonological loop that has both a memory store and a rehearsal system. Paulesu *et al.* (1993) used positron emission tomography (PET) to measure regional Cerebral Blood Flow (rCBF) during a series of tasks that systematically varied whether participants had to store a series of letters or mentally repeat the letter sounds.

By contrasting rCBF observed during the performance of each task, Paulesu *et al.* identified mental rehearsal of letter sounds with an area of the brain known as Broca's area. This area is more commonly associated with aspects of speech production, but appears also to be involved in 'mental speech' or the rehearsal component of the phonological loop. The letter memory task was associated with [a different] area known as the supramarginal gyrus. This pattern supported the idea that the phonological loop comprises separate components for phonological storage and for mental rehearsal.

Robert H. Logie

Long-term working memory

In the spirit of the examples given above, working memory should offer temporary memory for immediate past experience, plus some means to mentally represent the immediate environment and to manipulate and continually update the contents of that mental representation. Also it should support the acquisition of new knowledge, problem solving and decision making (for recent reviews, see Logie & Gilhooly, 1998). However, none of this can happen in isolation from past experience.

Knowledge accumulated over our lifetime is clearly available to each of us. When we think of castles in Scotland, colleges in Cambridge, or television soap operas, our accumulated knowledge becomes readily available to us. . . .

Having activated such knowledge, we can then manipulate it and extract novel information that had not been explicitly stored away, such as whether King's College Chapel in Cambridge is larger or smaller than Crathes Castle in Aberdeenshire. Similar questions about television soap operas would bring nothing to mind for some, or richly endowed memories of plots and characters for others.

Ericsson and colleagues (e.g. Ericsson & Delaney, 1998) distinguish between a short-term working memory – on which I have focused thus far – and a long-term working memory that accounts for the ease with which we can access highly familiar stored knowledge. The greater our expertise in a particular domain, the greater is our working memory capacity for information in that domain.

Thus, chess experts can retain details of chess games played simultaneously even when blindfold (Saariluoma, 1995), and avid soccer supporters can remember scores from matches more accurately than can the more casual fan (Morris *et al.*, 1985).

Even experience in crime leads to a form of, albeit undesirable, expertise: experienced burglars can remember details in photographs of houses seen a few moments before better than can samples of police officers or householders (Logie *et al.*, 1992).

In each case, the expert knowledge allows very efficient coding and retrieval of information within the area of expertise. These memory skills clearly do rely on the short-term working memory, but expertise greatly facilitates activation of relevant information in the knowledge base, and this activated knowledge can offer significant support for the more limited temporary working memory system.

Glossary

overt speaking rate: the rate of actual speech as compared with the rate at which speech is **rehearsed** (repeated) in the mind.

FACTORS IN SKILLED WRITING

D7

⭐ **Activity**

Consider the situation of a child learning to write. As compared to an adult:

Carl Bereiter and Marlene Scardamalia

a   The child might spend a great deal of time forming letters and recalling spellings.

b   The child might produce very basic texts consisting of only a few simple sentences with no clear connections between them.

Can you account for what is going on? In what ways does the whole process of writing differ from that of a skilled writer?

The role of production factors in writing ability

Carl Bereiter and Marlene Scardamalia (from *The Psychology of Written Composition*, Hillsdale, NJ: Erlbaum, 1987, Chapter 4: pp. 100–13. Abridged with permission of the authors.)

To start with a concrete example, consider a normal third-grade class engaged in a writing assignment. Almost all the children will write very slowly and many with obvious labor, some more drawing than writing the letters. There is likely to be audible sounding of words or at any rate lip movement as the children write (Simon, 1973). Even without direct evidence it seems reasonable to infer two things: (a) that handwriting is taking up considerable attention, which accordingly must be taken away from other aspects of the writing task such as content planning (Graves, 1978b); and (b) that the slow rate of production must create problems of remembering – not only problems in remembering immediately forthcoming words but also problems in remembering higher-level plans and intentions.

In more mature writers, of course, handwriting is fluent and automatic enough that production problems associated with it should be greatly reduced. But writing remains a complex activity in which many different processes must compete for limited attentional capacity and it remains slow enough that writers . . . frequently . . . complain that they cannot keep up with their thoughts. It seems reasonable to suppose, therefore, that how well a person writes will continue to depend not only on what conceptual and procedural knowledge the person has available but also on how successfully the operations involved in using it are coordinated.

Research on speech production has revealed the elaborate orchestration of mental functions that must go on in this apparently effortless activity. . . . While part of the cognitive system is concerned with articulation and coordinating speech with gestures and eye contact, another part is occupied with planning ahead. These processes use some of the same resources, however, so that finely organized time sharing is required, and even at that the system is frequently overtaxed, with the result that speech is filled with errors and unplanned pauses (Butterworth & Goldman-Eisler, 1979).

Written language production differs from conversational speech production in several ways that should make production factors less problematic. Writing is less time-constrained and there is not the immediate social situation that requires

Carl Bereiter
and Marlene
Scardamalia

monitoring. (Butterworth and Goldman-Eisler, 1979, note, for instance, that during planning phases of speech production the speaker is vulnerable to interruption and will therefore often break eye contact with listeners so as to keep the floor.) The absence of incoming social stimuli may also, however, create serious problems.

A key factor in fluent language production seems to be temporal organization of subprocesses. By this we mean the fine-grain (small fractions of a second) distribution of time among various levels of planning so that language production both proceeds steadily and maintains purposefulness and high-level organization.By the time children begin learning to write, they already speak fluently and coherently so that it seems that the major temporal organization of language-production processes must already have been achieved. This organization has developed through conversational experience, however. It would be reasonable to expect, therefore, that the programing of production factors would be keyed to conversational events. . . . [T]here is substantial evidence that metacomponents of the composing process still bear the stamp of conversational circumstances in young writers. It therefore seems worth investigating the possibility that some of the difficulty children have in writing production has a more profound basis than the slow and demanding qualities of handwriting, that it reflects breakdown in the organization of subprocesses when language production must go on in the absence of signals from the conversational milieu. . . .

This intuitive analysis of the act of writing depicts it as a complex, internally regulated process characterized by slow and attention-demanding output. The analysis has suggested three production difficulties that we shall explore further . . . : (a) short-term memory loss, to which slow rate of production could be a contributing cause; (b) interference from mechanical demands of the written medium that compete for mental resources with the higher-level demands of content planning and the like; and (c) general discoordination of language production resulting from the lack of external signals.

Short-term memory loss due to slow writing rate

. . . The most obvious place to look for an effect of production factors on written composition is at the interface between the mental process of language generation and the physical process of transcription. Models of language production generally place at this interface a buffer, a short-term memory store, that holds language already composed while it awaits translation into physical speaking or writing responses (e.g., Fodor, Bever, & Garrett, 1974). Such temporary storage is a necessity, even if we imagine the slowest of planners. Even someone who planned only a single word ahead would need to hold that word in mind long enough to write it. But no one could produce coherent language without planning farther ahead than that, and so somehow the products of planning must be held in mind while transcription goes on.

In writing, because of its slowness, the products of planning must often be held in mind for some seconds, an appreciable period of time by short-term memory standards. This raises the possibility that 'forgetting what one was going to say' may be a more significant factor in writing than in speaking. Some relevant data on memory loss in writing comes from a study by Bereiter, Fine, and Gartshore (1979).

Carl Bereiter and Marlene Scardamalia

This was an exploratory study, using a very simple methodology. Students wrote, in the presence of an experimenter, on any subject of their choice. At irregular intervals the experimenter would halt the writing process by suddenly placing a screen over the writing paper. Students were then to report any words they had already formed in their minds, but they were urged not to make up any new material. After each forecast, the screen was removed and subjects resumed writing where they had left off. After a paragraph was completed, the students were asked to repeat from memory, as exactly as they could, the paragraph they had just written. . . . The study was conducted on 14 children in fourth grade and 14 in sixth grade (mean ages approximately 10 and 12 years).

The experimental procedure made it possible to compare at certain points in each composition (a) what students reportedly intended to write; (b) what they actually did write; and (c) what they remembered having written.

The number of words per forecast – that is, the number of words children supposedly already had formed in their minds in advance of the last word they had written – averaged five to six. There was great variability, however, the forecast tending to run to the end of a clause regardless of the number of words that took. . . .

The average number of discrepancies between forecasts and actual writing was .5 per forecast. Thus, for about half of the forecasts children subsequently wrote exactly the words they had claimed to have in mind. Furthermore, of the discrepancies, 78 per cent were stylistic variations that carried the same meaning in writing as in the forecast. (More about these variations presently.)

In 17 per cent of the discrepancies, however, significant words uttered in the forecast failed to appear in writing. In about half of these cases the result was a syntactic anomaly – for instance, the forecasted phrase *on the way to school* was written *on the to school*. Lapses of this kind clearly indicate language getting lost somewhere between its storage in an output buffer and its translation into handwriting movements. But, just as clearly, these lapses cannot be described as 'forgetting what one was going to say.' For one thing, the lapses were almost invariably repaired on recall: in the case of *on the to school*, for example, the author not only intended to write *on the way* but claimed later to have written it.

Lapses of this kind are common in first-draft writing by experienced writers (Hotopf, 1980). They probably represent a lack of monitoring of the written output, the result of devoting conscious attention entirely to planning ahead, while leaving the process of transcription to run 'on automatic.' If this is what children are doing as well, then it is a sign that temporal organization of the writing process is already well advanced for them, making it possible for them to carry on planning and transcribing operations in parallel.

Such a speculation gains interest when related to the developmental observations of Simon (1973). Simon observed that primary-grade children tended to dictate to themselves, mouthing each letter or syllable as they wrote it. This activity would

Carl Bereiter
and Marlene
Scardamalia

bespeak a heavy investment of conscious attention in the process of transcription, making it unlikely that any planning ahead could occur while the child was transcribing. This simultaneous mouthing of the words was observed to give way after the first couple of years, however, to the practice of mouthing a string of words and then writing them. This latter practice would clear the way for planning while transcribing. . . .

The existence of such parallel or overlapping processes means that we cannot look for a simple connection between production rate and short-term memory or other production factors. A variety of mental activities may be going on while the writer's pencil is in motion. Some of these may interfere with retention of language in the buffer and its translation into writing, others may have no such effect, and still others might provide rehearsal of buffer contents, thus reducing the effects of delay in transcription. It remains, however, a question of some interest whether, on the whole and for whatever reasons, loss of information from short-term storage may be a significant factor in written language production. The previously cited study of discrepancies between what children say they are about to write and what they do write provides evidence that short-term memory losses may be significant, at least for elementary school children . . .

Interference from mechanical requirements of written language

Although ideas about production factors tend to be esoteric, there is one such idea that seems already to be firmly established in conventional wisdom. This is the idea that having to attend to low-level considerations such as spelling and punctuation interferes with attention to higher-level concerns of composition. Some teachers operate on this idea by urging their students to pay no attention to correctness, at least until after a first draft has been produced. Others take the approach of stressing early mastery of these mechanical aspects of writing so that they need no longer demand much attention. The policies are different, but the underlying psychological premise is the same, that the writer has a limited amount of attention to allocate and that whatever is taken up with the mechanical demands of written language must be taken away from something else.

This premise cannot be accepted in so simple a form, however. We must ask what gets interfered with and when. Although language production is often a rapid process, the development of an utterance through stages of intention to choice of syntactic frame to construction of constituents to overt output covers a time span that is not trivial in the time scale of cognitive operations. What gets interfered with when a writer is caught up by a spelling problem is the other cognitive activity going on at that moment. If the meaning of the sentence being written has already been fully constructed in the writer's mind, then *ipso facto* attention to a spelling problem cannot interfere with construction of *that* unit of meaning –

By mechanics of writing we do not mean merely handwriting or other means of transcription. Mechanics also includes spelling, capitalization, punctuation (for the most part), hyphenation, indentation, etc. . . .

although it could interfere with construction of some other unit of meaning – if the writer was thinking about it at the time. Thus we must consider possible interference in relation to the temporal unfolding of the composing process, which, as we have already noted, is greatly complicated by the existence of parallel or overlapping mental activities. We must furthermore take account of the possibilities of time sharing. In an unhurried activity such as writing, it seems likely that a writer with a well-developed executive system for sharing time among different activities could tolerate all sorts of additional attentional burdens without reducing the total amount of attention devoted to any one of them. Additional burdens would simply call for filling in spare time-slots or extending total time (cf. Spelke, Hirst, & Neisser, 1976).

In the forecasting study (Bereiter *et al.*, 1979), discussed in the preceding section, we have indicated that the small amounts of information loss observed between forecasts and actual writing might reflect interference from the attentional demands of mechanics. This would not show interference with higher-level composing processes, however, simply interference with short-term storage of language already composed. Consequently we would expect this type of interference to have only minor effects on the composing process. We also noted evidence of a different kind of interference resulting in syntactic anomalies. But this phenomenon seemed attributable to *high-level* processes interfering with *low-level* ones–the very opposite of the phenomenon we are concerned with here. . . .

On the basis of these theoretical considerations, it seems that we must reject the commonplace idea that attention to how written language is to be spelled or punctuated will interfere with its content. If concerns about mechanics only enter after the original intention has already been shaped into propositions, then it is too late for them to interfere with the construction of meaning. The meaning of the sentence in question will already have been constructed.

There remain, however, three ways in which attention to low-level aspects of writing could interfere with the higher-level metacomponents.

1.   It could lead to forgetting high-level decisions already made. In the preceding section we considered only forgetting of material that was already at an advanced stage of shaping into utterance. We did not consider and have no direct evidence bearing on the possibility of forgetting less-developed intentions and meanings – for instance, concentrating on details of expression and in the process forgetting what purpose a sentence was intended to serve. We have introspective reason to believe that this occurs, from everyday experience. Consider, for instance, pausing to consult a dictionary and finding, on return to writing, that although we can recall the rest of the interrupted sentence, we have forgotten what it was supposed to be leading up to. . . .

2.   Concern with mechanics could interfere with high-level planning of the *next* unit of discourse. This could happen if people are simultaneously expressing one unit and planning another, and we have already noted indications that even children as young as 10 years old do this. The result of this kind of interference would be that whereas individual sentences are well expressed,

Carl Bereiter and Marlene Scardamalia

overall coherence and the complexity of content integration suffer. Thus evidence on the low level of content integration in children's writing could be taken to suggest interference of this sort.

3. Finally, attention to problems of mechanics could interfere with consideration of intentionality *at the point of utterance*.

This last possibility has interesting implications, but it is one for which systematic evidence is entirely lacking. Bracewell (personal communication) has observed that skilled writers make, as they go along, small changes in wording that seem to an observer to have no point to them. One word or phrase is replaced by another that has no discernible semantic or stylistic claim to preference. Leaving aside the possibility that the writer has more refined sensibilities than the observer, we may speculate that the writer makes such changes in order to make the expression more closely fit his or her intentions. Having no independent knowledge of those intentions, the observer cannot judge one expression to be more appropriate than the other, as the writer can. But, considering that the writer has already written one thing and then changed it to another, it seems that this very precise fitting of expression to intention goes on into the very latest stage of written language production. Consequently, if this stage is being occupied with concerns about spelling, capitalization, or even penmanship, there will be little opportunity for this fine fitting to occur. . . .

Discoordination resulting from lack of external signals

The discussion so far has presupposed a model of the composing process that consists of a number of subprocesses governed by an executive system (or monitor, as it is called in the Hayes and Flower [1980] model). . . . We assume that the child develops an executive system to control everyday speech production and that, in learning to write, the child does not construct a whole new executive system but instead tries to adapt the existing one to the new requirements. But the existing system is an interactive one, designed to respond to signals from the external environment, specifically signals from conversational partners. Without such inputs, it has trouble functioning, much as typists have trouble functioning without a keyboard to provide cues for programming their motor output. . . .

[Here] we focus on what is perhaps the most elemental feature of conversation from the standpoint of executive system functioning. This is *production signaling* — that is, signaling that simply activates the executive system to produce another unit of language. In conversation, we assume, the executive system is attuned to such signals; it normally responds to them when they are presented and does not respond without such signals, since to do otherwise is to violate conversational etiquette. In composition, however, there is usually neither a partner nor anything else in the environment to provide production signals. Therefore, in order to produce continuous discourse, the language production system must somehow provide its own means of sustaining production.

Glossary

metacomponents: higher level operations which organise and co-ordinate the process.

a well-developed executive system: a system which controls and allocates attention to cognitive processes.

mechanics: the mechanical processes involved in writing (forming letters, sequencing letters, inserting punctuation).

the complexity of content integration: how well the parts of a text are related to each other.

consideration of intentionality: the writer's awareness of his/her overall intentions.

DECODING VERSUS 'WHOLE WORD'

D8

 Activity

In Section C9, we encountered two opposed views of skilled writing:

- a 'top-down view', involving the use of context
- a 'bottom-up' view, stressing the importance of decoding.

Before reading this extract, jot down what you can remember of each. Decide which account you personally think is the more convincing and suggest why.

Constructing meaning: the role of decoding

Philip B. Gough and Sebastian Wren (in J. Oakhill and R. Beard (eds): *Reading Development and the Teaching of Reading*, Oxford: Blackwell, 1999. Abridged with permission of the authors.)

The idea that reading is a process of constructing meaning is gaining popularity among reading educators. This is a useful metaphor. It reminds us of the fact that all that exists on the printed page is dried ink, so that meaning must emerge in the mind of the reader. It also suggests that the reader actively contributes to this process, that what he or she knows and thinks will contribute to that meaning.

But as a description of reading, the metaphor is obviously incomplete. For one thing, it tells us nothing of *how* meaning is constructed. In particular, it makes no mention of the role of the printed word in constructing meaning. . . .

The reason, we suspect, is that advocates of this view (largely proponents of Whole Language) would de-emphasize the role of decoding (word recognition) in the reading process. They tend to believe that print is only one of several cueing systems which the reader makes use of in constructing meaning. The standard view

Philip B.
Gough and
Sebastian
Wren

(Goodman, 1993) has it that there are three cueing systems, the semantic, the syntactic, and the graphophonic. . . .

Empirical support for this position can be found in a large body of research on *miscue analysis* (e.g., Goodman and Burke, 1973), that is, the qualitative and quantitative description of oral reading errors. What we take to be the central result of this research is that oral reading errors (miscues) are often syntactically and semantically appropriate, even though they may depart wildly from the text, indicating that they must have been derived from the syntactic and semantic cueing systems.

This is important evidence; in fact, it provides the cornerstone of research support for the Whole Language position. But it should be noted that it depends upon the existence of miscues. To obtain miscues, the miscue analyst will routinely ask the student to read a passage which is challenging (i.e., slightly too difficult) for him or her. This led us to wonder how common miscues are among college students reading college-level materials.

The miscues of skilled readers

As part of a larger study of the miscues of skilled readers . . . , we asked 101 students in introductory psychology to read aloud the first page of [Goodman, 1993]. We recorded their miscues (defined as an uncorrected departure from text; if the reader corrected his or her error, we did not consider it a miscue), and timed their reading of the passage with a stopwatch.

On average, our 101 students read the 259 words in 106 seconds, an oral reading rate of approximately 147 words per minute. The 101 readers made a total of 223 miscues. . . . The lion's share of them (76 per cent) were substitution errors (e.g., the student read 'reach' when the word was *read*). Of these substitution errors, the vast majority were orthographically similar to the target (e.g., 'word' for *work*, 'phonetics' or 'phonemics' for *phonics*, or 'definition' for *definitive*). Orthographically dissimilar words (e.g., 'anyone' for *everybody*) constituted only 4 per cent of the substitution errors (and 3 per cent of all errors). The next most common error was omission, accounting for 16 per cent of all miscues; the remaining 8 per cent were insertions.

We also categorized the miscues as meaning-preserving or meaning-changing. We were surprised to see (given previous miscue research) that nearly half (48 per cent) of the miscues were meaning-changing. Most of these were substitutions (e.g., 'equator' for *educator*, 'insensitive' for *intensive*); omissions and insertions tended not to change meaning. . . .

But what impressed us more than the quality of our readers' miscues was their quantity: there were very few of them. Our 101 college students each read aloud 259 words . . . a total of 26,159 words. They made a total of 223 miscues, an error rate of 0.0086. Looked at positively, they correctly named 25,797 of the 26,020 words, an accuracy rate of 0.9914. . . .

It appears that college students reading college-level material make very few miscues. Clearly, we could induce more miscues by using more demanding material. But as we see it, this would be inauthentic. The fact seems to be that skilled readers, reading a text like those they usually read, do so very accurately.

Philip B.
Gough and
Sebastian
Wren

How are we to account for this amazing accuracy? . . . Supporters of Whole Language would presumably argue that it was the skilful integration of the multiple cueing systems which led to this success. In particular, they would downplay the role of print in this process. As Ken Goodman (1993, p. 97) describes it, 'The brain, the organ of human intelligence, is engaged in far more than recognizing known entities. It actively seeks meaning. It controls the sensory organs and uses them to select and sample from available input, print in the case of reading.'

Thus the Whole Language advocate underplays the recognition of letters and words ('known entities') in constructing meaning. As Goodman (1996, p. 91) writes, 'An *efficient* reader uses only enough information from the published text to be *effective*.' This led us next to wonder how well readers would recognize words if the 'information from the published text' was reduced.

In previous research (e.g., Gough, Alford and Holley-Wilcox, 1981; Gough, 1983) we . . . have provided the prior context and asked readers to predict the next word. In the case of function words (articles, conjunctions, prepositions, auxiliary verbs, and pronouns, which account for roughly half the words in running text), readers can correctly anticipate roughly 0.4 of them. With content words (adjectives, nouns, and verbs, which account for the remaining half), our subjects could manage only 0.1 . . .

[However,] [t]his condition is clearly too extreme. Goodman concedes that readers do 'select and sample' from the print, so that depriving them of all print is unfair. But what would give them a fair shot? If we knew what the reader would 'select and sample', we could provide that and see if the other letters are irrelevant (as Goodman's model would predict). But we obviously cannot anticipate this, so we decided to examine the effect of two graphophonic cues which we believed (along with many teachers) must be useful cues: the word's first letter, and its length.

We asked 60 readers to anticipate (predict) each of the first 119 words of Ray Monk's (1996) fascinating biography of Bertrand Russell by typing it into a computer. The computer recorded their responses, applauding them if their response was correct, and replacing it by the correct word in the event they were wrong; the computer also provided all punctuation. Thus the reader had, at every point, the entire preceding context (i.e., both the syntactic and semantic cueing systems) to aid him or her in anticipating the next word. Half of our readers were also provided with the first letter of that word; orthogonally, half of our readers were given the length of the word. Thus one-fourth (15) of our readers had only the prior context, one-fourth had the prior context plus the first letter of the word to be predicted, one-fourth had the prior context plus the word's length, and the remaining fourth had the prior context plus the word's first letter and its length.

The proportions of correct identifications in each of the four conditions are presented in Table 1, divided into content words and function words.

As we have repeatedly observed, function words were more identifiable (across all conditions, mean = 0.51) than content words (0.23), and this held true in each of the four conditions as well. Without any cues except prior context, our students correctly predicted 0.34 of the function words and 0.11 of the content words, a

Philip B.
Gough and
Sebastian
Wren

Table 1 The proportions of correct identifications in each of the cue conditions
(no cue, first letter cue, word length cue, and both word length and first
letter cues)

Function Words			
	No length hint given	Length hint given	Average
First letter hint given	0.57	0.69	0.63
No first letter hint given	0.34	0.43	0.38
Average	0.455	0.56	0.51

Content Words			
	No length hint given	Length hint given	Average
First letter hint given	0.25	0.40	0.325
No first letter hint given	0.11	0.17	0.14
Average	0.18	0.285	0.23

result similar to what we have previously reported. But with both content and
function words, adding the first letter significantly increased their identification,
by about 20 per cent. Providing the word's length increased its predictability another
10 per cent . . . Yet even with both cues, the readers averaged only 70 per cent
correct identification of function words, and only 40 per cent of the content words,
far short of the 99.14 per cent they averaged (across all words) when given the
full word. . . .

These results suggest to us that the reader relies on the printed word far more
than Goodman and other advocates of Whole Language would lead us to believe.
Our results seem to indicate that the graphophonic system plays a central role in
constructing meaning. How else are we to explain why the speed and accuracy
of reading isolated words (and even *pseudowords*) correlates almost perfectly with
reading comprehension in the early grades (Gough, Hoover and Peterson, 1996),
and still substantially in college students (Cunningham, Stanovich and Wilson,
1990)? . . .

We are inclined to agree with Marilyn Adams (1990, p. 105), who asserts that
'the single immutable fact about skillful reading is that it involves relatively complete
processing of the individual letters in print.'

Ken Goodman (1993, p. 94) completely disagrees. He holds that this claim was
refuted by an experiment conducted by Frederick Gollasch (1980). Gollasch asked
seventh-graders and university juniors to read the passage presented in Figure 1.
Half the readers in each group were told in advance that there were errors in the
text; the other half were not. After reading the text, all readers were asked to
write down the story, and list any errors they had noticed in the text.

Philip B.
Gough and
Sebastian
Wren

The Boat in the Basement

A woman was building a boat in
her basement. When she had finished the
the boot, she discovered that it was
too big to go though the door. So he
had to take the boat a part to get
it out. She should of planned ahead.

Figure 1 passage used by Gollasch in a study of error identification

There are six errors in the passage. According to Gollasch, the college students found more errors (42 per cent) than did the seventh-graders (32 per cent). But in both groups, those readers who had been warned that the passage contained errors reported only slightly more than three (none found all six), while those who had not been informed found even fewer. Evidently only about half of the errors were noticed. Importantly, despite the presence of these errors the readers still understood the story.

Goodman's reasoning seems to be that since the readers did not report the errors, those errors did not affect their reading. We wondered whether this was correct. So we decided to compare the reading times on Gollasch's error-filled passage with reading times on an error-free ('clean') version of the same text.

We . . . asked 65 undergraduates to read the Gollasch passage, and 65 others to read an error-free version of the same passage. The passage was presented line by line on a computer screen. The subject advanced from one line to the next by pressing the space bar and the computer recorded how long the reader spent on each line. When the reader finished the passage, he or she was given a copy of the Gollasch version of the text and asked to indicate any errors he or she had noticed. . . .

Our students reading Gollasch's passage noticed even fewer errors (mean 1.56) than his did. . . . But our reading-time data (Figure 4.5) indicated that the errors did have an effect on the reading process. While readers of the Gollasch passage read the error-free title and first line of the passage slightly faster than the controls, on each line containing an error they were slower.

It might be objected that these differences could be attributed to those readers who noticed the errors. To eliminate this possibility, we examined the reading times on each line only of those readers who failed to report that error, and compared them to the reading times for the error-free passage. Again, we compared each difference with any difference observed on the first two lines of the passage (which contained no error in either version). These data are presented in Table 2.

What we found was that in every case, reading times were greater on the erroneous line than on its error-free counterpart; five of these differences were statistically significant, and the sixth approached significance.

Philip B.
Gough and
Sebastian
Wren

Table 2 A comparison of the reading times on each line of text, comparing only the reading times of those readers who failed to report each error with the reading times for subjects reading the same line of the error-free passage

	Clean	Gollasch	N in Gollasch condition
Title line (clean)	1459	1406	68 subjects
First line (clean)	1549	1547	68 subjects
THE THE line	1579	1760	64 subjects
BOAT BOOT line	1625	1742	28 subjects
TH(R)OUGH line	1723	2132	64 subjects
(S)HE line	1723	1942	38 subjects
A()PART line	1661	2145	54 subjects
SHOULD. HAVE/OF line	1916	2256	58 subjects

What these results indicate is that, whether or not an error is reported, it slows down the reader. While they still are able to see past (or through) those errors and arrive at a correct interpretation of the story, those errors do make meaning construction more difficult.

We conclude that decoding – word recognition – is an important component of reading. It is important to note that we are not equating reading with decoding. Having recognized the words, the reader must then comprehend them. Thus we see reading as the product of two dissociable factors, decoding and comprehension. If we think of reading (R), decoding (D), and comprehension (C) as variables ranging from 0 to 1, then R = D × C. Both decoding and comprehension are necessary; neither is sufficient. We have defended this Simple View elsewhere . . . , arguing that it provides a very parsimonious description of reading skill and reading disability.

Glossary

proponents of Whole Language: those who favour the idea that a good reader uses context so as to minimise their dependence upon decoding. They conclude that the most important goal of early reading instruction is to encourage learners to seek meaning in a text rather than to develop letter recognition skills.

graphophonic: the relationship between graphemes and phonemes.

sensory organs: the eyes and ears.

the syntactic and semantic cueing systems: information provided by the current syntactic structure and by the context.

orthogonally: dividing each of the first two groups into two.

significantly, statistically significant: statistically, not likely to have happened by chance.

LOCATING WORD BOUNDARIES

⭐ **Activity**

**Anne Cutler
and Sally
Butterfield**

Natural speech only has occasional pauses; there are no consistent gaps between words as there are in writing. Suggest how a listener might identify individual words in a sequence like:

thecasesarelightandportable

In theory, they could simply match a word at a time on the basis that where one word ends, the next begins. But then how are they to deal with these alternatives:

case#is vs *cases – are#* *light* vs *alight* – *light#and* vs *lighten* – *port* vs *porter* vs *portable*

In theory, they could use context – but then how do they know whether to expect an adjective after /keɪsɪz/ or a plural verb?

Rhythmic cues to speech segmentation: Evidence from juncture misperceptions

Anne Cutler and Sally Butterfield (*Journal of Memory and Language*, 31: 218–38. Abridged with permission of the authors.)

Finding where new words begin in continuous speech is a problem, since word boundaries are rarely reliably marked. Cutler and Norris (1988) proposed that speakers of English use the rhythmic patterns of utterances to guide hypotheses about where new words begin. In English, which is a stress language, speech rhythm has a characteristic pattern which is expressed in the opposition of strong versus weak syllables. Strong syllables bear primary or secondary stress and contain full vowels, whereas weak syllables are unstressed and contain short, central vowels such as schwa. (Although there are levels of stress within strong syllables, the only difference which matters for metrical rhythm is the binary opposition of strong versus weak.) . . .

The statistics of the English vocabulary show that assuming strong syllables to be word-initial will be a pretty good bet. Cutler and Carter (1987) found that in a computer-readable English dictionary containing over 33,000 entries about 12 per cent of the words were monosyllables (such as *camp* or *lodge*), just over 50 per cent were polysyllables with primary stress on the first syllable (such as *camphor* or *cycle*), a further 11 per cent were polysyllables with secondary stress on the first syllable (such as *campaign* or *psychological*); while the remaining 27 per cent were polysyllables with weak initial syllables (in which the vowel in the first syllable is usually schwa, as in *camellia*, but may also be a reduced form of another vowel, as in *illogical*). All of the first three categories have strong initial syllables, and these categories together account for 73 per cent of the words in the list. . . .

Cutler and Carter [also] examined a natural speech sample consisting of approximately 190,000 words of spontaneous British English conversation. Almost 60 per cent of the lexical words in this corpus were monosyllables. 28 per cent were polysyllables with initial primary stress, and a further 3 per cent were poly-

Anne Cutler
and Sally
Butterfield

syllables with initial secondary stress. Most noticeably, . . . less than 10 per cent of the lexical words were polysyllables with weak initial syllables. In other words, the three categories with strong initial syllables accounted, together, for over 90 per cent of the lexical word tokens.

However, this lexical word count disguises one important fact: the majority of words in the corpus were, in fact, grammatical words. But because hardly any grammatical words had more than one syllable, the lexical word total nevertheless accounts for 51 per cent of all *syllables*. In fact, with some reasonable assumptions, it was possible to compute the probable distribution of syllables in this speech sample. Cutler and Carter assumed that grammatical words such as *the* and *of* were in general realized as weak syllables. In that case, about three-quarters of all strong syllables in the sample were the sole or initial syllables of lexical words. Of weak syllables, however, more than two-thirds were the sole or initial syllables of grammatical words.

Thus a listener encountering a strong syllable in spontaneous English conversation would seem to have about a three to one chance of finding that strong syllable to be the onset of a new lexical word. A weak syllable, on the other hand, would be most likely to be a grammatical word. It would appear, therefore, that English speech indeed provides a good basis for the implementation of a segmentation strategy which assumes strong syllables to be the onsets of lexical words. . . .

We can make two general classes of prediction, which arise directly from the hypothesis about lexical segmentation proposed by Cutler and Carter (1987) and Cutler and Norris (1988). . . . The first type of prediction concerns what kind of [word boundary] errors occur before what kind of syllable. . . . The obligatory initiation of a new lookup process occasioned by every strong syllable . . . will tend to induce errors in which strong syllables are erroneously taken to be word-initial; likewise, the obligatory attachment of weak syllables to preceding syllables wherever possible . . . will tend to induce errors in which boundaries preceding weak syllables are overlooked. In brief, therefore, errors involving insertion of a word boundary before a strong syllable or deletion of a boundary before a weak syllable should prove to be relatively common, whereas errors involving insertion of a boundary before a weak syllable or deletion of a boundary before a strong syllable should be relatively rare.

The second type of prediction arises for the word class correlates of the strong/weak distinction. . . . All strong syllables initiate lookup processes in the main lexicon whereas when a weak syllable initiates lookup process, it is in [a separate closed set of function words]. This should lead to strong syllables being interpreted as [beginning] new lexical words, while weak syllables are interpreted as grammatical words. . . . When boundaries are inserted prior to strong syllables, the word following the boundary should be taken to be a lexical word, whereas when boundaries are inserted prior to weak syllables the word following the boundary should be taken to be a grammatical word.

Spontaneous misperception

Anne Cutler
and Sally
Butterfield

Procedure

The psycholinguistic literature contains a number of studies of spontaneous misperceptions or 'slips of the ear'. . . . We examined all the published error examples we could find, plus all the slips of the ear included in a speech error collection assembled over several years by the first author. Finally, we asked other researchers in the field to send us slips of the ear. . . .

Bond and Garnes (1980) report that misperceptions of juncture are relatively common and accounted for about 18 per cent of their corpus of spontaneous slips of the ear. Among the slips that we analysed, we found in all 246 which involved misplacement of a word boundary across at least one syllable nucleus. . . . Some slips in fact involved more than one misplaced boundary (such as 'for an occasion' → 'fornication,' in which boundaries before two weak syllables have been deleted); the 246 misperceived utterances contained a total of 310 juncture misplacements.

Some example errors are shown in Table 1. We found that in this set of naturally occurring errors all possible types of word boundary misplacement appeared: insertions of a word boundary before a strong syllable (e.g., 'analogy' → 'and allergy'); insertions of a boundary before a weak syllable (e.g., 'effective' → 'effect of'); deletions of a boundary before a strong syllable (e.g., 'is he really' → 'Israeli'); deletions of a boundary before a weak syllable (e.g., 'my gorge is' → 'my gorgeous').

Table 1 Examples of spontaneous slips of the ear

Input		Error
She'll officially	→	Sheila Fishley
She's a must to avoid	→	She's a muscular boy.
How big is it?	→	How bigoted?
By loose analogy	→	By Luce and Allergy
The parade was illegal	→	The parade was an eagle
into opposing camps	→	into a posing camp
My gorge is still rising	→	My gorgeous . . .
I'm not sure about this yet, but . . .	→	I'm not sure about this shepherd
Is he really?	→	Israeli?
I can't fit any more on	→	I can't fit any, moron
in closing	→	enclosing
the effective firing rate	→	the effect of . . .

The rhythmic segmentation hypothesis predicts first that insertion errors will occur more often before strong syllables than before weak, while deletion errors will occur more often before weak syllables than before strong, and second that insertions

Anne Cutler
and Sally
Butterfield

before strong syllables will tend to postulate lexical words while insertions before weak syllables will tend to postulate grammatical words. . . . But note that Cutler and Carter's (1987) corpus analysis suggests that both types of prediction are counterintuitive. Cutler and Carter estimated . . . that among [. . .] syllables [that are not word-initial], weak syllables on average outnumber strong syllables by more than three to one. This makes the opportunity for erroneous word boundary insertions much greater before weak syllables than before strong. . . .

Results and discussion

Table 2 shows the distribution of the 310 boundary misplacements across the four possible categories of insertions before strong versus weak syllables. It can be seen that, as predicted, erroneous boundary insertions occur more often before strong than before weak syllables, while erroneous boundary deletions occur more often before weak than before strong syllables. The interaction is highly significant (with correction for continuity, χ^2 [1] = 22.48, $p < .001$). Binomial tests on boundary insertions versus deletions show that each difference is separately significant: $z = 3.79$, $p < .001$ for insertions, $z = 2.87$, $p < .005$ for deletions.

Table 2 Word boundary insertions and deletions before strong versus weak syllables in spontaneous slips of the ear

	Before strong	*Before weak*
Boundary insertions	90	45
Boundary deletions	68	107

Table 3 Occurrence of lexical versus grammatical words following inserted word boundaries before strong versus weak syllables in spontaneous slips of the ear

	Before strong	*Before weak*
Lexical	85	16
Grammatical	5	29

Table 3 shows the distribution of word types following erroneously inserted boundaries. As predicted, when boundaries are inserted before strong syllables, the strong syllable is nearly always taken to be the beginning of a lexical word; but when boundaries are inserted before weak syllables, the weak syllable is more often interpreted as a grammatical or function word. Again, the difference is significant (with correction for continuity, χ^2 [1] = 52.13, $p < .001$), and the word class dif-

Anne Cutler and Sally Butterfield

ference is separately significant for insertions before strong versus weak syllables: $z = 8.33$, $p < .001$ for strong syllables, $z = 1.79$, $p < .04$ for weak syllables.

Thus, both types of prediction from the rhythmic segmentation hypothesis are supported by the data from spontaneous slips of the ear. Word boundaries tend to be inserted more often before strong syllables than before weak, but deleted more often before weak syllables than before strong; boundaries inserted before strong syllables produce lexical words, while boundaries inserted before weak syllables produce grammatical words.

As we pointed out above, both these findings are counterintuitive given the relative proportions of strong and weak syllables indicated by Cutler and Carter's corpus analysis. Moreover, note that just over half of all errors occurred before strong syllables, although Cutler and Carter estimated that only 39 per cent of all syllables in typical English speech are strong. This again is consistent with the hypotheses that speech segmentation is primarily driven by hypotheses about strong syllables, with the interpretation of weak syllables being to a certain extent subordinate (cf. the even more radical proposals to this effect made by Grosjean & Gee, 1987).

Glossary

schwa: the sound /ə/ as in <u>a</u>bout or pap<u>er</u>.

word class correlates of the strong / weak distinction: this refers to the fact that strong syllables occur almost entirely in content words, while many weak quality syllables (/tə/, /fə/, /ðə/) turn out to be monosyllabic function words.

juncture: word boundary location.

significant: statistically likely not to be the outcome of chance. The probability of a chance result is shown by the symbols $p <$ ('probability is smaller than . . .'). $p < .001$ means that the likelihood of a chance result is only 1 per cent. Two statistical tests are used here. The first (χ^2) compares figures representing four factors: insertions / deletions / strong syllables / weak syllables. The second (z score) examines separately insertions (strong vs weak) and deletions (strong vs weak).

D10 **SELF-MONITORING IN SPEAKING**

Activity

Willem
Levelt

You will recall that part of Levelt's model of the speech process (Section C10) showed the speaker monitoring their own words to make sure they had not made errors.

What kinds of error do you think a speaker listens for?

Do you think that they correct everything? What errors do you think are given priority?

One could represent the monitoring process in two ways:

a   The speaker monitors at every level of assembling the message: checking first lexis, then syntax, then phonology, then articulatory plans.

b   The speaker only monitors the articulatory plan, immediately before speaking.

Which do you think is the more plausible?

Self-monitoring

Willem Levelt (from *Speaking*, Cambridge, MA: MIT, 1997: 460–71. Abridged with permission of the author.)

What Do Speakers Monitor for?

That speakers can attend to various aspects of the action they are performing is apparent from the kinds of spontaneous self-repairs speakers make. Some major targets of monitoring seem to be the following.

Is this the message/concept I want to express now?

[A] particular message may, on closer inspection, not be correct or adequate with respect to the intention. This seems to have been the case in the following utterance (from Schegloff 1979):

(1) Tell me, uh what – d'you need a hot sauce?

Here the speaker probably started to say *what do you need?*, but it was apparently more . . . [effective] to issue a different directive, a Yes/No question. The original utterance was interrupted on the fly, and a somewhat different speech act was performed.

   In these and similar cases the speaker's trouble is at the conceptual level. The speaker can directly monitor the messages he prepares for expression, and he may reject a message before or after its formulation has started. In the former case no overt repair will result, though there may be some hesitation. In the latter case the original utterance will sooner or later be replaced by a formulation of the alternative message.

Is this the way I want to say it?

Even if the speaker is sure about the information to be conveyed, he may get second thoughts about the way it should be expressed, given the discourse record –

Willem
Levelt

i.e., given the topic and content of previous discourse, given what was literally said earlier, and so on. Consider the following example . . . :

(2) To the right is yellow, and to the right – further to the right is blue

Here the speaker started expressing the intended concept, but then realized that the move described previously had also been to the right. By adding *further* the speaker made his utterance more cohesive with previous discourse.

The speaker may also realize that what he is saying involves a potential ambiguity for the listener. Again, the intended concept was expressed, but it was, in retrospect, not sufficiently contextualized. The following example from Schegloff *et al.* 1977 is a case in point:

(3) Hey, why didn't you show up last week. Either of you two.

Here the speaker . . . realized that the communicative situation could be ambiguous. That ambiguity was taken away by the repair. . . .

Is what I am saying up to social standards?
One's choice of words will, normally, depend on the level of formality required by the context of discourse. In court one will say *policeman* rather than *cop*; this is a choice of *register*. There is some evidence that speakers monitor their speech for unacceptable deviations from standards of formality and decency. In particular, Motley, Camden, and Baars (1982) have shown experimentally that speakers are very good at catching taboo words before they are uttered.

Am I making a lexical error?
The speaker's message may be as intended and contextually appropriate; still, flaws of formulation may appear. . . . The most frequently caught error of this kind is the *lexical error*. Consider [this] example:

(4) Left to pink – er straight to pink

Here the speaker almost certainly intended to express the concept 'straight'. Still, the wrong lemma, *left*, became activated. . . . The speaker caught the error and corrected it. Here is another case, from Levelt and Cutler 1983:

(5) Well, let me write it back–er, down, so that . . .

Are my syntax and my morphology all right?
Certain formulating errors are due not so much to lexical access as to other trouble in grammatical encoding; and sometimes speakers do become aware of deviant syntax or morphology, as is evident from their repairs. Note the following instances:

(6) What things are this kid – is this kid going to say incorrectly?

(from Levelt and Cutler 1983)

Here the speaker noticed an error of agreement and corrected it.

(7) Why it is – why is it that nobody makes a decent toilet seat?

(from Fay 1980)

Here an ordering error, either an error of syntax or a shift, was caught and immediately corrected.

Am I making a sound-form error?

Trouble in phonological encoding is often recognized by speakers, as is apparent from spontaneous repairs. Cases 8 and 9 are examples of segmental and supra-segmental phonological trouble that was apparently quickly noticed by the speaker.

(8) A unut – unit from the yellow dot (from Levelt 1983)

(9) . . . from my prOsodic – prosOdic colleagues (from Cutler 1983)

Has my articulation the right speed, loudness, precision, fluency?

There is some minimal evidence that speakers monitor their speech delivery for parameters of this sort, but it does not stem from spontaneous self-corrections. It is exceptional indeed for a speaker to spontaneously repeat a word with more precision, or more slowly, or more loudly. Such corrections are typically induced by the interlocutor, who says *what?*, knits his brows, or otherwise signals that the speaker's delivery was not optimal. There is some experimental evidence for self-monitoring of loudness. Speakers immediately increase the loudness of their speech when it becomes masked by loud noise – this happens naturally at cocktail parties, but it can also be provoked experimentally (Siegel and Pick 1976). . . .

Selective Attention in Self-monitoring

Do speakers actually attend simultaneously to all these aspects of their speech? This is most unlikely, and there are data to support the view that (i) much production trouble is not noticed by the speaker, that (ii) monitoring is context-sensitive, i.e., contextual factors determine which aspects of speech will be given most scrutiny by the speaker, and (iii) a speaker's degree of attention for self-generated trouble fluctuates in the course of an utterance.

There is both indirect and direct evidence that the meshes of a speaker's trouble net are too wide to catch all queer fish in his own speech. Nooteboom (1980) analyzed Meringer's (1908) corpus of speech errors and found that 75 per cent of the registered phonological errors and 53 per cent of the lexical errors were repaired by speakers. This is indirect evidence, because a speaker may detect all errors but still not bother to correct each and every one of them.

More direct evidence can be found in Levelt 1983, which reports on color-naming errors in a pattern-descriptions task. The subject's task was to give a description that would allow another subject to draw the pattern. It was, therefore, essential for a speaker to give correct color names in all cases. All 2,809 pattern descriptions, produced by a total of 53 subjects, were checked for errors in color naming. There were 472 such errors. A speaker would occasionally say *yellow* instead of *green*, *orange* instead of *pink*, *green* instead of *blue*, and so forth. Of these errors, only 218 were repaired by the speaker. That is 46 per cent, which corresponds well to Nooteboom's 53 per cent for lexical errors. So, even where it is a speaker's given task to produce the correct color name, only about half of the errors are caught. This is most probably due to failures in detection.

Not all sources of trouble are given equal attention. The context of discourse is an important determinant of the kind of flaws a speaker will try to prevent, intercept, or correct. One would expect a speaker to attend most carefully to trouble that is potentially disruptive for the ongoing discourse. Evidence pointing in this direction was provided by Cutler (1983), who analyzed a corpus of lexical-stress errors (such as the one in example 9 above). About 50 per cent of these errors were spontaneously repaired. The likelihood of repair depended on how disruptive the error might be for the listener . . .

There is, further, evidence that a speaker's attention to his own output fluctuates in the course of an utterance. The evidence proceeds from an analysis of the 472 color-name errors mentioned above (Levelt 1983). For each of these errors . . . , it was determined how many syllables separated the erroneous color word from the end of the syntactic constituent (usually a noun phrase) to which it belonged. For example, the erroneous color words in examples 10, 11, 12, and 13 are zero, one, two, and three syllables away from the end of the phrase (which is marked by a slash).

(10) And then you come to *blue/* – I mean green

(11) There is a *yellow* node / to the right of the red one

(12) To the right is a *black* crossing/ from which you can go up or down

(13) You enter at a *green* nodal point /

It was then determined how many color-name errors in these different positions were noticed by the speaker and repaired (as in Example 10). The results . . . [show] clearly that the error-detection rate increases sharply toward the end of the phrase. Of the phrase-final color-name errors, 57 per cent were detected and repaired; for non-phrase-final errors, the percentage was no greater than about 15. In other words, a speaker's selective attention to his own output increases toward the ends of phrases. During speech a speaker's attentional resources are mainly used for message planning, but by the ends of phrases attention can momentarily shift in order to evaluate the current speech output.

Editor Theories of Monitoring

The major feature of editor theories is that production results are fed back through a device that is *external* to the production system. Such a device is called an *editor* or a *monitor*. This device can be distributed in the sense that it can check . . . results at different levels of processing. The editor may, for instance, monitor the construction of the preverbal message, the appropriateness of lexical access, the well-formedness of syntax, or the flawlessness of phonological-form access. There is, so to speak, a watchful little homunculus connected to each processor.

A major problem with distributed editing is reduplication. . . . A more restricted editing device was proposed by Motley, Camden, and Baars (1982). It

Willem
Levelt

cannot inspect all intermediary output in the generation of speech, but only the prearticulatory output. Editing follows phonological encoding, according to these authors. The editor can intercept or veto troublesome output before it becomes articulated – hence the notion of 'prearticulatory editing.'. . .

Unlike distributed editors, the prearticulatory editor [does not operate at every stage of language production. So how can it pick up potential errors at semantic, syntactic or phonological levels?] . . .

An obvious solution is to identify the editor with the language-understanding system. A speaker can attend to his own speech in just the same way as he can attend to the speech of others; the same devices for understanding language are involved. In Levelt 1983 I elaborated this proposal by supposing that there is a double 'perceptual loop' in the system – that a speaker can attend to his own *internal* speech before it is uttered and can also attend to his self-produced *overt* speech. In both cases the speech is perceived and parsed by the normal language-understanding system. It should be noted that the language-understanding system is not only able to derive a message from its speech input, it is also able to detect deviations from linguistic standards. When we listen to the speech of others we can discern deviant sound form, deviant morphology, and deviant syntax. According to the perceptual-loop theory, the same mechanism is involved in monitoring one's own internal or overt speech.

The major advantage of this approach is that no *additional* editing devices have to be conjectured. There are no special-purpose editors to check the outputs of lemma access, of grammatical encoding, of segmental spellout, and so forth. Only the final (prearticulatory) phonetic plan or internal speech and the overt speech produced can be attended to by the language-understanding system. The aspects of the self-produced speech to which a speaker will be especially sensitive will then depend on the context. . . .

This is important, because MacKay (1987) has argued against editor theories on the ground that the errors one detects in one's own speech are different *in kind* from those one detects in the speech of others. MacKay compared Nooteboom's (1980) counts in the Meringer data on self-correction and in Tent and Clark's (1980) data on error detection in other-produced speech. As mentioned, Nooteboom found a 75 per cent correction rate for phonological errors and a 53 per cent rate for lexical errors. Tent and Clark, who asked their subjects to exactly transcribe the sentences they heard (and these sentences could contain various kinds of errors), found that a phonemic mispronunciation was noticed far less often than a morphemic or a syllabic error.

But this argument is invalid. Apart from the fact that the two data sets are highly incomparable (for instance, white noise was added to Tent and Clark's experimental sentences), it is obvious that the attentional criteria are quite different in listening and speaking. A listener's first concern is to extract meaning from the speech signal, even in spite of ill-formedness. A speaker, however, must guard not only the meaningfulness of his speech but also its satisfaction of grammatical standards. His attention will be tuned accordingly.

Glossary

self-repairs: corrections of speech errors that one has made oneself.

distributed: able to operate at any one of several different levels of processing (at phoneme level, syllable level, word level, syntactic level etc.).

homunculus: a hypothetical 'person in the brain'.

reduplication: the fact that speakers have to keep matching their plan against their intentions at so many different levels.

prearticulatory output: the fully-constructed phonetic plan, just before it is articulated.

white noise: a hiss added to recorded material which reduces audibility.

ANAPHOR RESOLUTION

D11

⭐ Activity

An important higher level skill is the ability to process anaphors efficiently. An anaphor is a word that refers back to some previously mentioned entity, action or idea. It might be a personal pronoun (*her*, *him*), a demonstrative pronoun (*this*), a pro-verb (*did so*), an adverb (*there*) or an expression like *the latter*.

The process of linking an anaphor to its antecedent (what it refers to) is known as **anaphor resolution**. How might the process differ for a reader and for a listener?

It seems that weaker readers often have problems in relating anaphors to their antecedents. Can you suggest why this might be?

1. Read the extract below to establish what the experiment demonstrated. Do not worry about the statistics on a first reading.
2. There are usually the following sections in a research paper: background – method – results – discussion. Locate them in this paper (even where they are not subtitled).
3. Consult the notes below on statistics and read the 'results' section again.

Understanding anaphoric devices

Nicola Yuill and Jane Oakhill (From *Children's Problems in Text Comprehension*, Cambridge: Cambridge University Press, 1992: 86–94. Abridged with permission of the authors.)

Halliday and Hasan (1976) provide a taxonomy of types of cohesive ties that appear in text. . . . . *Reference* includes links such as personal pronouns, . . . and demonstratives, such as *this* and *that*. Like other cohesive ties, references can be used to point back to a previous item in text. For example, in the sentences.

(a) Mary Jane Wilson went for a walk. She found 10p on the ground.

Nicola Yuill
and Jane
Oakhill

she stands for Mary Jane Wilson. The pronoun could be replaced by *Mary Jane Wilson* and the sentence would still mean exactly the same as it did before. *Substitutions* and *ellipses* are rather similar to each other. In both cases, a noun phrase, verb phrase or clause is replaced. This replacement can be marked by the substitution with a word such as *one* and forms of the verb *do*, such as *do so, has done*.

Examples of substitutions are:

(b) John has an ice cream and I want one too.

(b′) Has the plane landed? Yes it has done.

where *one* replaces *an ice cream* and *has done* replaces *has landed*. In other cases a gap (*ellipsis*) can be left:

(c) Has the plane landed? Yes it has.

Lexical ties are rather more diverse and subtle in nature. They involve semantic links that run through a text. These can include word reiterations and the use of synonyms, but the links can also be more nebulous associations of meaning. For example, in:

(d) Mary was in her garden. The flowers smelt lovely.

the words *garden* and *flowers* are connected by being related to the same general topic, and we understand the flowers to be the ones in Mary's garden. . . .

We know that text comprehension is guided by anaphors (Hirst and Brill, 1980), but our studies of pronouns suggest that less-skilled children are rather poor at resolving anaphors. If their performance in our experimental tasks is an indication of how they normally read, the results suggest that they could fail to resolve around 25 per cent of such anaphors.

Many studies of anaphor resolution, including our own, test children by asking a question about the text . . . Moberly (1979) devised a rather more difficult task: after reading a story, children were given a fresh copy of it with certain anaphors underlined, and had to insert after each one the words in the text that each anaphor 'pointed back to'. Thus, they were required to identify which words in the text an anaphor replaced, or referred to. Despite extensive practice on this task, fourth- and sixth-grade children were correct for only an average of 62 per cent and 72 per cent of anaphors respectively.

A further problem in resolving anaphors may arise if, as we have suggested, less-skilled children process information less efficiently during reading than do skilled ones. Anaphors refer to other words elsewhere in the text, but these words may be at some distance from the anaphor. The less-skilled children, particularly if they are not building an integrated representation of the text as they read, may be unable to retrieve the preceding text containing the referent, and so have difficulty in resolving the anaphor. For example, if a long description of Mary's walk intervened between the two sentences in (a), the reader may forget the name of the person who was taking a walk, and be unable to give the referent of *she*.

. . . [T]here has been some research showing that anaphors are harder to resolve as distance increases, particularly for people whose working memory is relatively

Nicola Yuill and Jane Oakhill

inefficient: Light and Capps (1986) found that the greater the person's working memory span, the greater the distance across which they could link pronouns with their antecedents. We expected that less-skilled comprehenders would be at a particular disadvantage as the distance between anaphors and antecedents increased.

Method We wrote a 700-word story, attempting to adopt a relatively naturalistic style, and selected from it six examples of each of the four types of anaphor described above: reference, substitution, ellipsis and lexical ties. Within each of these types, there were two examples at each distance. The anaphor was either *immediate* – the antecedent was in the sentence immediately preceding the anaphor, or *mediated* – more than one sentence distant, but with an intervening mention of the item, or *remote* – more than two sentences distant, with no direct mediating reference. There were two types of task for each anaphor: saying which words the anaphor 'stood for', or 'pointed back to' (Meaning question), and answering a question about the anaphor (Text question).

After all sixteen children in each skill group had been given practice with examples of each anaphor type, each child was tested individually. The experimenter read the story aloud, aiming to produce as relaxed and natural a situation as possible. Then she read through a new copy of the story, with the target anaphors underlined in red, and the text visible to the child. As each marked anaphor was encountered, the child was asked the Meaning question. If a wrong answer was given, the Text question was also asked, to check whether the child had at least formed an appropriate mental model of the text, even if they did not have an explicit awareness of how links are made in text. If children correctly answered the Meaning question, though, the Text question was not presented, because this would imply that the first answer was wrong. In such cases, we considered that the Text question would have been answered correctly.

Results We classified answers to each of the two questions as correct if the relevant piece of text, or the gist of it, was given. We analysed the results for the two question types separately because the tasks were not independent, for the reasons described above. For each question type, we performed an analysis with skill group between subjects and distance and anaphor type within subjects, as well as separate analyses for each type of anaphor, with skill group and distance as factors.

The performance of the groups on the two types of question (pooled over anaphor type) is shown in Table 1. In an analysis of performance on the Meaning question, the less-skilled comprehenders performed more poorly than skilled comprehenders overall, $F (1, 30) = 26.63$, $p < .0001$. This difference was also apparent in the separate analyses for each type of anaphor, as shown in Table 2: all $Fs (1, 30) > 5.5$, all $ps < .025$.

Performance on the Text questions (also shown in Table 1) was almost perfect for the skilled children (90 per cent correct), whereas the less-skilled ones were poorer overall on these questions (72 per cent correct). The difference between groups was significant in the overall analysis, $F (1, 30) = 20.94$, $p < .0001$ and for all four types of anaphor analysed separately, all $Fs (1, 30) > 5$, all $ps < .05$

Nicola Yuill and Jane Oakhill

Table 1 Mean percentages correct at each distance for the two question types and two skill groups

	Distance			
	Immediate	*Mediated*	*Remote*	*Mean*
Meaning question				
Less-skilled	65.6	46.9	38.6	50.4
Skilled	81.3	68.7	61.0	70.3
Text question				
Less-skilled	83.6	75.8	57.0	72.1
Skilled	97.7	92.2	80.5	90.1

Table 2 Mean percentages correct for each anaphor type at each distance for the two skill groups (Meaning questions)

	Distance		
Anaphor type and skill group	*Immediate*	*Mediated*	*Remote*
Reference			
Less-skilled	65.6	40.6	21.9
Skilled	90.6	65.6	25.0
Difference	25.0	25.0	3.1
Ellipsis			
Less-skilled	90.6	50.0	43.8
Skilled	93.8	65.6	87.5
Difference	3.2	15.6	43.7*
Substitution			
Less-skilled	81.3	81.3	20.1
Skilled	96.9	96.9	43.8
Difference	15.6	15.6	23.7
Lexical			
Less-skilled	25.0	15.6	68.8
Skilled	43.8	46.9	87.5
Difference	18.8	31.3	18.7

Note: * = planned comparison significant at $p < 0.05$.

(see Table 4.12). This result suggests that the poor comprehenders were worse at scanning the text for an answer.

The . . . performance [of all children] also varied according to the distance between an anaphor and its antecedent, as shown in Table 1. Anaphors that were further

Nicola Yuill
and Jane
Oakhill

from their antecedents were in general harder to resolve, in both of the tasks, and these differences were significant in the overall analysis of the data: [(2, 60) = 30.32, p < .0001 for Meaning questions and F (2, 60) = 30.08, p < .0001 for Text questions]. Separate analyses of the Meaning questions for the different types of anaphor also showed a main effect of distance in all cases: all Fs (2, 69) > 16.00, all ps < .0001. However, there was only one instance of an interaction between skill group and distance, in the case of the ellipses, F (2, 60) = 5.33, p < .01. . . .

There is, therefore, little support for our idea that less-skilled children are particularly hampered in establishing links between parts of a text as the load on memory is increased. Although the less-skilled children were poorer overall at understanding the anaphors, the effects of distance, where present, were usually apparent for both groups.

To investigate further their understanding of anaphors, we looked at the *incorrect* responses that children gave, as opposed to correct or 'don't know' responses. Twenty per cent of the less-skilled comprehenders' error responses were wrong choices . . . (as opposed to 'don't knows'), compared with only 9 per cent of the skilled comprehenders' answers. The less-skilled children showed two types of mistake demonstrating apparent misunderstandings of how to interpret cohesive ties, which we will describe in turn.

Part of the story went as follows: *Bill was proud of his new fishing rod and reel. His mother had given it to him for his birthday. On Saturday morning, Bill was going on a fishing trip with his Uncle, the Captain. As he carried his rod to the bus stop, he met Mrs Tripp from next door.* The children were required to say who the first *he* in the final sentence referred to. So far in the story, four people have been mentioned, two male (Bill and his uncle, the Captain), and two female (Bill's mother and Mrs Tripp). The female characters can be ruled out (although one poor comprehender did give a female as the answer), and several features of the context suggest that Bill is the answer: he is the main character, mentioned in the title, he has just been given a fishing rod, he was going on a trip. If the reader has built up a model of the story so far, it will be easy to find the correct answer. Even so, four poor comprehenders said that *he* referred to Bill's uncle, the most immediately preceding plausible response. So it looks as though less-skilled children may sometimes look for the nearest plausible response, whereas skilled children are more likely to use a mental model of the text.

The less-skilled children also made another sort of mistake: they sometimes referred outside the text to find a response. Four less-skilled children answered the above question with *John*, the name of a character who appeared in the training sentences, although they then corrected themselves. A further example of this tendency occurred in response to the sentence, *That is where I am going now*, where *now* refers to the time of the story, Saturday morning. Nine less-skilled comprehenders gave incorrect responses for the Meaning question on this item, compared to only two skilled comprehenders. While these wrong responses were usually plausible, in that children named a day of the week, they picked a different day from the one mentioned in the story. The way they did this suggested that they just 'picked a day, any day': they often did not scan the text, and some gave

**Nicola Yuill
and Jane
Oakhill**

'pseudo-explanations' for their answers. For instance, one child said that *now* was the day of the interview. She had made the mistake of referring to the real world, rather than the world of the text, and compounded these two worlds in her explanation that the characters would have had time to go fishing 'today' (real-world time) because, like her, they started school late on that day. This error is particularly striking, in that this child could have scanned the text for the single instance of the name of a day, and thus answered correctly but, rather than looking back to the text, she used her own knowledge inappropriately. It also indicates that the less-skilled comprehenders sometimes realise that it is appropriate to use general knowledge to help understand a text, but that they may not realise what aspects of their knowledge are appropriate or the constraints on its use. Such errors suggest that some children, even at the age of 7, still have difficulty in coordinating information in the 'two worlds', the real world and the text world. . . .

Given these results, it is not surprising that some children show poor comprehension. Often, an incorrect assignment of an anaphor can change the whole sense of a story. In our story, a crucial anaphor, *that*, referred to a fish given to the main character in return for some bread, which satisfies one of the boy's main goals of providing some fish for the neighbour's cat. Fourteen of the sixteen skilled comprehenders showed that they understood the meaning of this anaphor, but only eight of the less-skilled comprehenders did so. Informal questioning at the end of the story suggested that many of the latter group had missed the main point of the story, which depended on successful resolution of this particular anaphor.

Glossary

referent: the entity to which a pronoun or other type of anaphor refers.

analysis with skill group between subjects . . . : comparing skilled and less-skilled subjects. . . . **and distance and anaphor type within subjects**: examining the way in which the results of individual subjects varied according to (a) the distance between the anaphor and its antecedent, and (b) what type of anaphor was involved.

separate analyses for each type of anaphor: results for each type of anaphor were analysed separately with a view to seeing what part was played by skill group and distance from antecedent.

an interaction between skill group and distance: evidence that the less-skilled became especially disadvantaged (relative to the skilled) as the distance became more remote.

A note on statistics in Psycholinguistics

When you read a research article, you will encounter a number of abbreviations

N=   giving number of subjects
x̄=   giving mean (average) of a set of results
SD= giving Standard Deviation (average divergence of the responses from
     the mean)

It is important to establish whether a result is **significant** (i.e. whether we can discuss it as demonstrating some kind of effect) or whether it might simply be the outcome of chance. For this, we use the letter p (= probability):

$p < 0.05$ indicates a probability of less than 5 per cent that a result occurred by chance
$p < 0.01$ indicates a probability of less than 1 per cent that a result occurred by chance

The symbol < means 'is smaller than' and the symbol > means 'is bigger than'.

A number of different statistical tests are used to demonstrate whether a result is significant or not. These tests can be **within subjects** (comparing the way each subject responds to different types of task) or **between subjects** (comparing the way different groups of subjects respond).

❏ To establish if two sets of results *vary together* (i.e. when one changes, so does the other), researchers use a test of **correlation**. This gives a correlation coefficient, a figure between 0 and 1.
❏ To establish if two independent sets of results *diverge enough* to suggest that they come from two different groups, researchers might use a **t-test**. The figure is shown as t = . . .
❏ An **ANOVA** (Analysis of Variance) is a more sophisticated test, used to establish if three or more sets of results diverge sufficiently to suggest that they show different effects at work. In the experiment described in the extract, the data was divided up in a number of different ways: by skilled vs. less-skilled, by distance of anaphor from antecedent, by type of anaphor and by Meaning question vs Text question. ANOVAs allowed the researchers to establish which of these had a **main effect** (i.e. an effect that was independent of other factors) and which of them produced an effect in conjunction with other factors (**an interaction**). The resulting figures are shown as F = . . .

Statistical tables tell us if the above figures are significant, taking account of the number of subjects or results that have been studied.

D12

**Dorothy
Bishop**

TWO VIEWS OF SPECIFIC LANGUAGE IMPAIRMENT

Modular theories of grammatical deficits in SLI

Dorothy Bishop (from: *Uncommon Understanding*, Hove: Psychology Press, 1997, 133–36. Abridged with permission of the author.)

Whichever approach we adopt to explain language acquisition, we need to explain why some children fail to learn language normally. One influential view, based in the Chomskyan tradition, maintains that language acquisition depends on innate grammatical modules that are defective (or even absent) in SLI. As a consequence, it is argued, one sees very selective problems with particular components of the grammar. This is an extreme type of theory that maintains that a biological system that is crucially important for language learning is defective in children with SLI, so that their grammatical knowledge is qualitatively different from that seen in normal children. This approach has appealed to theoretical linguists, who see the study of SLI as having the potential to throw light on fundamental issues of what it is about language that is innate.

The 'feature-blindness' hypothesis

In 1990, Gopnik published an account of a fascinating three-generation family, of which about half the members were affected by a severe form of SLI. One reason why this family was of particular interest to linguists was because their impairment appeared to be genetic. . . .

In early accounts of the family, Gopnik proposed just such a theory, affecting one component of the grammar. She reported striking deficits in the ability of affected individuals to mark features such as number, gender, animacy, mass/count, proper nouns vs. common names, tense, and aspect. These features are usually marked by inflectional endings and they also constrain the form of other items in the sentence. . . . Extracts from notebooks kept by some of the family members illustrate their problems with features such as number ('All the children got present'), aspect ('Carol is cry in the church'), and proper names ('A Patrick is naughty'). To investigate mastery of the plural feature, Gopnik administered an experimental task in which the tester presented a nonsense creature and said, for example, 'This is a zoop'. The testee was then shown several such creatures and asked: 'These are——?' She found that people with SLI were poor at this task and did not appear to have an internalised, unconscious set of rules for forming plurals. . . .

Of course, if a person lacks grammatical features in underlying representations, there should be problems not just in producing grammatical inflections, but in understanding their significance. In another test, Gopnik (1994) used a grammaticality judgement task. Family members with SLI could judge as correct those sentences that were correct. However, they tended also to accept as correct sentences that had errors in feature-marking, and if they did detect the error they had difficulty in correcting it.

Dorothy Bishop

. . . A different type of comprehension test yielded findings that were problematic for the theory: affected individuals showed good understanding for some items on a task testing understanding of inflectional endings, and were able, for instance, reliably to select the picture of several books (rather than a single book) when asked 'point to the books'. Gopnik accounted for this by suggesting that a word like 'books' might be rote-learned to refer to a group of objects. Just as the young child might learn 'cornflakes' without realising this is the plural of 'cornflake', so the child with SLI might learn a wide range of plural or other inflected forms, without appreciating their morphological composition. Unfortunately, a critical test of this hypothesis, i.e. checking whether the affected individuals could understand the plural '-s' in a nonsense word context (e.g. 'show me the zoops') was not conducted. Subsequent studies, however, have led to the abandonment of the 'feature blindness' hypothesis as too extreme an account of the impairment in SLI. Rather than supposing that such children have no representation of grammatical features in the grammar, Gopnik and her colleagues proposed a new hypothesis, that their problem is with the rule-based nature of learning that is involved in building morphological paradigms.

Rule learning in morphological paradigms

Gopnik and Crago (1991) proposed that the problem for children with SLI is that, in effect, they approach the language-learning task as if all words were irregular. The child with SLI is aware of the grammatical features that need to be marked, but does not realise that the appropriate marking for a specific word can usually be derived by rule, rather than rote-learned. . . . [This recalls] Pinker's (1984) proposal that, in normal development, children initially place each inflected form in a word-specific paradigm, but then come to recognise the regularities in inflectional morphology, creating a differentiation in the lexicon between the storage of regular and irregular forms. Pinker (1991) argued that different processes are implicated in producing a regularly inflected word, which involves assembling the word from stem and inflection, and in producing an irregularly inflected form, which is retrieved directly from long-term memory. If, as proposed by Gopnik and Crago, the child with SLI lacks the specialised system for learning morphological rules, then this differentiation between regular and irregular inflected forms will not be made; both will be learned by associative processes. This will have two consequences. First, it means that inflected forms will take up far more space in long-term memory, because a great deal of redundant information will be stored. This is likely to make word retrieval more difficult. Second, it follows that these children will not be able to use inflections spontaneously and creatively, although they will be able to produce and understand those that have been rote-learned and which have a lexical representation.

However, as with the original 'feature blindness' account, any theory that maintains that children with SLI are completely deficient in building morphological paradigms is hard to sustain. Leonard, Bortolini *et al.* (1992) noted that children with SLI, like normally developing children, sometimes made over-regularisation errors, producing

Dorothy Bishop

forms such as 'comed' or 'goed', which provide evidence of rule application. . . . In addition, studies have demonstrated that children with SLI are impaired at producing irregular as well as regular inflections (Bishop, 1994; Ullman & Gopnik, 1994). . . . Vargha-Khadem *et al.* (1995) assessed the same family as had been studied by Gopnik and colleagues, and reported that they made over-regularisation errors and had difficulties with irregular inflections.

In response to such findings, research on SLI has moved in several directions. Some researchers have rejected altogether the notion of an impaired language module. However, others have continued to pursue this line of explanation. Gopnik's team at McGill University have pushed the rule-abstraction hypothesis to the limit, noting the importance of looking at the data in detail, and arguing that use of compensatory strategies, especially by older individuals, may cloud the picture. For instance, Goad and Rebellati (1994) noted that the apparently correct use of noun plural inflections seemed to be achieved in some cases by the explicit application of the taught rule: 'add -s to form a plural'. Not only did this lead to slow and effortful production, but detailed phonetic analysis showed that the apparently correct plural '-s' forms produced by language-impaired individuals lacked voicing assimilation; for instance, when asked for the plural of 'wug', the response was /wʌgs/ rather than /wʌgz/. Gopnik (1994a) further argued that individuals with SLI appeared to treat past tense marking on a verb as a semantic means of referring to an earlier point in time, rather than as a syntactic feature. On this view, an '-ed' marker on a verb expresses a similar meaning as terms such as 'yesterday' or 'then'. Most critically, if a sentence does include such temporal adverbs, then there is no semantic motivation for using the past tense; for the person with SLI, a sentence such as 'then the branch fall off' is acceptable, because the past time is expressed by the adverbial 'then'; there would be more reason to use the past tense 'fell' if the adverbial were omitted. The point stressed by these researchers is that correct performance on a language test need not necessarily reflect true competence in underlying ability. Grammatical morphemes might be used without appreciation of their syntactic significance, either as semantic markers, or applied consciously after explicit instruction in their use.

Glossary

modules: components that are independent of general cognition.

animacy: whether an entity is animate or inanimate.

aspect: the way in which an event is presented by the speaker. In English, this covers progressive aspect (*I am waiting*) and perfect aspect (*I have waited*).

grammaticality judgement task: a task in which subjects have to say whether sentences are grammatical or not.

morphological paradigms: systematic patterns of inflection.

over-regularisation: extending a rule too far.

compensatory strategies: ways of achieving the right word without using the normal procedure.

A nonmodular explanation: perceptual deficit

Dorothy
Bishop

Dorothy Bishop (from: *Uncommon Understanding*, Hove: Psychology Press, 1997, 149–52
Abridged with permission of the author.)

How far could a perceptual deficit account for grammatical impairment? In 1989, Leonard proposed what he termed the 'surface hypothesis', which maintained that it is the perceptual and articulatory characteristics of grammatical morphemes that make the task of morphological paradigm building unduly difficult for children learning English. The precise details of the hypothesis have changed somewhat over the years, but in the earliest accounts, Leonard emphasised the evidence for auditory processing deficits in children with SLI, implying that there might be a straightforward link between ease of perceiving phonological material and its incorporation into a morphological paradigm. Many grammatical morphemes are brief, unstressed, and tend not to occur in a salient word-final position (e.g. past tense '-ed', plural '-s'), and the kind of auditory perceptual impairment proposed by Tallal [Tallal & Stark, 1981] could conceivably make such morphemes hard to detect. Thus, formation of morphological paradigms could be unduly difficult and protracted, not because of any impairment of the innate language-learning module itself, but because of inadequate perception of language input.

. . . Leonard *et al.* (1987, 1988) compared expressive difficulties of SLI children in two different languages, English and Italian. In English, many grammatical contrasts are marked by morphemes that are unstressed, brief, and of low perceptual salience (e.g. -s or -ed). In contrast, in Italian, grammatical morphemes are often syllabic and much more salient. In the study by Leonard *et al.*, eight English-speaking children were contrasted with eight Italian-speaking children, all diagnosed as cases of SLI. The English children all used word final /s/, /z/, /t/, and /d/ in singular nouns such as *bus*, and *bed*, so any failure to produce plural or past tense morphemes could not be attributed to difficulty in articulating these phonemes. The two groups of children were matched in terms of mean length of utterance in words. Samples of their language were collected, using pictures to elicit examples of grammatical forms of interest. Italian children did not show striking differences between regular noun plurals and third person singular verb inflections: both were produced in obligatory contexts at a much higher rate than was observed in English children. While there was no overall difference between Italian and English children in the production of articles, the Italian children used the feminine forms of the definite and indefinite articles, *la* and *una*, significantly more often than the corresponding masculine forms, *il* and *un*. Given that the number of obligatory contexts for *il* and *un* was as high as for *la* and *una*, it is difficult to explain this difference except in terms of phonological structure. Most errors with articles involved omission of the article rather than substitution of an alternative. Finally, Leonard *et al.* (1987) also noted that Italian children with SLI correctly marked gender agreement of possessive pronouns and adjectives in nearly all instances where this was required. . . .

Leonard and his collaborators have gone on to investigate production of grammatical morphemes in a wide range of languages. They conclude that many, but not all, of their findings fit the hypothesis that children with SLI have particular difficulty in learning morphemes of weak perceptual salience.

There are three lines of evidence that have been advanced against perceptual deficit explanations for morphosyntactic deficits in SLI.

1. First, it has been noted that grammatical problems can be seen with written as well as spoken language. For instance, in the study of comprehension of sentences with postmodified subjects, Bishop (1982) found that children with SLI actually performed more poorly with written input than with spoken input, even though they could read all the individual words. If an auditory processing problem is at the root of a comprehension difficulty, then wouldn't we bypass the problem by using the visual modality, i.e. written presentation? . . .

[Against this argument, we should bear in mind that] written language is parasitic on oral language; the child must have some understanding of the language that is represented by the written word in order to make sense of it. This is why children with severe congenital hearing loss have so much difficulty in learning to read: their mastery of the phonology, syntax, and semantics of oral language is severely compromised by the auditory deficit, and this hampers learning of written language.

2. A second objection to an auditory processing account is that children with SLI can discriminate very accurately between inflected and uninflected forms (Gopnik, 1994). This demonstration, however, is not very convincing. The critical issue is not whether the child is capable of discriminating between different phonological forms, but whether auditory discrimination is impaired relative to other individuals when listening under non-optimal conditions, i.e. when words are spoken rapidly, in the context of a sentence, and against competing noise. The evidence . . . strongly suggests that, for many children with SLI, discrimination between certain speech sounds is not at chance, but is below normal levels.

Furthermore, . . . there is more to auditory perception than the ability to discriminate. Classification of speech input is also important, so that the child learns to recognise acoustically different stimuli as exemplars of the same phoneme. . . . This ability to perceive phoneme constancy might pose a more severe problem for children with SLI than the ability to tell two speech sounds apart. . . . In order to detect similarities between inflected forms, the child must be able to segment the inflectional ending and appreciate that this is equivalent for different words such as 'book+s', 'cat+s', and 'ship+s'.

3. The final objection to perceptual deficit accounts is that there is no direct correlation between the perceptual salience of a morphological marker and its risk of being impaired (e.g. Gopnik, 1994), as the difficulty of a particular phonological form varies with its grammatical function. Watkins and Rice (1991), for instance, found that children with SLI had much more difficulty in producing prepositions such as 'over' or 'on' when these were in the role of verb particle (e.g. 'put on the hat', 'kick over the fence') than when they functioned as prepositions (e.g. 'sit on the chair', 'jump over the fence'). To take another example, children with SLI were far less accurate in their use of the morpheme '-s' in possessive

**Dorothy
Bishop**

contexts or to mark third person singular than when it served to mark a noun plural (see, e.g. Bishop, 1994; Rice & Oetting, 1993). Evidence such as this has been used to conclude that difficulties with auditory perception of speech input are not adequate to explain syntactic problems in SLI.

Furthermore, children with SLI have difficulty with some morphemes that can by no stretch of the imagination be regarded as phonetically weak, e.g. in English, irregular past tense forms, and the distinction between nominative and accusative pronouns (he/him; she/her). These types of error, it is argued, cannot be attributed to auditory perceptual difficulties.

The question one has to ask of this line of explanation is whether it is safe to assume that a problem in perception at an early stage of input will simply interfere with acquisition of those parts of syntax signalled by hard-to-perceive elements, leaving the rest of the system to develop normally. This ignores interdependence of components of the grammar. For a start, there is ample evidence that function words such as 'the' and 'a' and inflected endings such as '-s' or '-ed' are important cues to children about the grammatical category of words with which they are associated. Thus, for instance, if I tell you that 'the zod prungled a verd' you will be able to deduce that 'zod' and 'verd' are nouns and 'prungle' is a verb, just on the basis of the related function words and inflections they occur with. Problems in perceiving grammatical morphemes should, therefore, not just affect morphological skills, but will also have a more pervasive impact on grammatical knowledge, making it harder to establish grammatical category information when learning new lexical items (Leonard & Eyer, 1996). Poor perception of phonologically weak morphemes could also delay acquisition of a wide range of syntactic structures by increasing the ambiguity not just of structures where inflections are important, but also those which they usually contrast with. Consider the following example: suppose a child has perceptual problems such that the sentence 'The boy is hit by the girl' will sometimes be heard as 'Boy hit girl'. Clearly, such a child will find it difficult to learn passive constructions, which are characterised by unstressed morphemes '-ed' and 'by'. . . .

'Perceptual deficit' explanations of impaired grammatical comprehension have relatively few contemporary adherents among those interested in formal linguistics, but it may be that the rejection of this line of explanation has been premature and is based on a limited view of the nature of perceptual impairment, together with inaccurate assumptions about what the consequences of a perceptual deficit should look like.

Glossary

mean length of utterance: progress in developing a first language is often measured in terms of the average number of syllables in the infant's utterances.

obligatory contexts: sentences where the grammar obliges the speaker to use the item.

non-optimal conditions: conditions which are less than ideal.

MATERIAL FOR ACTIVITIES

SECTION A8

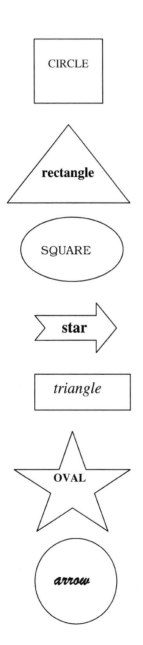

CIRCLE

rectangle

SQUARE

star

triangle

OVAL

arrow

SECTION B11, TASK 1

Read aloud the following text.

How did the body of the murder victim come to be found in a locked room? Hercule Parrott, the famous detective, was called in to investigate.

He examined the layout of the ground floor where the crime had taken place. The body had been found in the library. The only door into the library was from the hall, and it had been locked on the inside. The library was between the dining room and the sitting room. Several guests had come out of the dining room and gone into the sitting room, but nobody reported hearing voices from the library.

The body was discovered when a cleaner wanted to get into the library. The door had to be forced open as nobody had a spare key. There was a large fireplace in the library and the body was lying to the right of it. It was face downwards, with the legs towards the door and the left arm outstretched. Blood from the wound to the head had soaked into a valuable Persian rug. There had clearly been a violent struggle. A table had been overturned and a vase knocked on to the tiled floor. A lamp had been smashed.

Parrott pulled back the heavy curtains in front of one of the two windows in the room, and examined the window closely. His brain was working fast. Outside the window, a terrace ran alongside the house. It was still wet from the rain, and there were muddy footprints visible on it.

SECTION B11 TASK 2: TEXT A

You are a burglar. You have 15 seconds to read this text.

Two boys play hooky from school. They go to the home of one of the boys because his mother is never there on a Thursday. The family is well off. They have a fine old home which is set back from the road and which has attractive grounds. But since it is an old house, it has some defects; for example, it has a leaky roof and a damp and musty cellar. Because the family is wealthy, they have a lot of valuable possessions such as a ten-speed bike, a colour television and a rare coin collection.

(Anderson and Pichert, 1978)

SECTION C6

List A
Dictate the following words (1.5–2 seconds per word).

clear   stay   name   back   seem   view   down   health   wrong   most   world
such   life   course   move   each

List B
Dictate the following words (1.5–2 seconds per word).

afternoon   government   important   already   together   everything   understand
company   yesterday   family   possible   interesting   remember   certainly
difference   national

(The two groups have been roughly balanced for imageability – the ease with which
a word can be pictured. They have frequencies of between 140 and 300 words per million in the spoken subset of the British National Corpus (Leech, Rayson and Wilson
2001) – with one higher-frequency exception in the second group.)

List C (for visual memorisation)	List D (for visual memorisation)
smell	introduce
edge	animal
worst	somebody
really	computer
choose	disappear
straight	seventeen
twelve	underneath
part	enormous
cheap	continue
both	expensive
plant	cinema
throw	recognise
science	company
break	beautiful
quiet	generally
lunch	impossible

(All words are shown in the spoken subset of the British National Corpus as of relatively high frequency.)

SECTION B11 TASK 2: TEXT B

You are looking for a house to buy. You have 15 seconds to read this text.

Two boys play hooky from school. They go to the home of one of the boys because his mother is never there on a Thursday. The family is well off. They have a fine old home which is set back from the road and which has attractive grounds. But since it is an old house, it has some defects; for example, it has a leaky roof and a damp and musty cellar. Because the family is wealthy, they have a lot of valuable possessions such as a ten-speed bike, a colour television and a rare coin collection.

(Anderson and Pichert, 1978)

SECTION C9 TASK 1

Read aloud the following text.

She was very fond of these animals and always talking about her little dog. I went into the sitting room and there was the little dog sitting on the cushion looking at me and I said that my dog was in the car because he goes with me wherever I go. And then she said 'Well, of course, my little dog's been dead for three years', and I felt quite cold! There I turned and saw this little dog sitting on the settee. 'Oh,' she said, 'yes, we had him stuffed'.

(From Underwood: *Listen to This* (1975: 152))

FURTHER READING

(* = good starting point)

REFERENCES

Aitchison, J. (2003) *A Glossary of Language and Mind*. Edinburgh: Edinburgh University Press.
Field, J. (2004) *Psycholinguistics: the Key Concepts*. London: Routledge.

INTRODUCTORY READING

Carroll, D. W. (1999) *Psychology of Language*, Pacific Grove: Brooks/Cole, 3rd edn, Chapter 1, pp. 3–17.
Garnham, A. (1998) *Psycholinguistics: Central Topics*, London: Routledge, Chapters 1–2, pp. 1–41.
*Libben, G. (1997) 'Psycholinguistics', in W. O'Grady, M. Dobrovolsky and F. Katamba (eds) *Contemporary Linguistics: An Introduction*, London: Longman, pp. 438–62.
Ratner, N. B., Gleason, J. B. and Narasimhan, B. (1998) 'An introduction to Psycholinguistics: What do language users know?', in J. B. Gleason and N. B. Ratner (eds) *Psycholinguistics*, Forth Worth: Harcourt Brace, 2nd edn, pp. 1–49.
Tanenhaus, M. K. (1988) 'Psycholinguistics: an overview', in F. K. Newmeyer (ed.) *Linguistics: the Cambridge Survey*, Cambridge: Cambridge University Press.

LANGUAGE, SPEECH AND COMMUNICATION

*Aitchison, J. (1998) *The Articulate Mammal*, London: Routledge, 4th edn, Chapter 2, pp. 23–46.
*Aitchison, J. (1996) *The Seeds of Speech: Language Origin and Evolution*, Cambridge: Cambridge University Press.
Bickerton, D. (1990) *Language and Species*, Chicago: University of Chicago Press.
Deacon, T. (1997) *The Symbolic Species*, London: Penguin, Part 1: Language.
*Dobrovolsky, M. (1997) 'Animal communication', in W. O'Grady, M. Dobrovolsky and F. Katamba (eds) *Contemporary Linguistics: An Introduction*, London: Longman, pp. 625–63.
Hurford, J. R., Studdert-Kennedy, M. and Knight, C. (eds) (1998) *Approaches to the Evolution of Language*, Cambridge: Cambridge University Press, papers by Aitchison, Knight, Dunbar, Locke.

*Lieberman, P. (1998) *Eve Spoke*, London: Picador.
Pearce, J. M. (1997) *Animal Learning and Cognition*, Hove: Psychology Press.

LANGUAGE AND THE BRAIN

*Aitchison, J. (1998) *The Articulate Mammal*, London: Routledge, 4th edn, Chapters 3–4, pp. 47–90.
Deacon, T. (1997) *The Symbolic Species*. London: Penguin, Part 2: Brain.
*Harris, M. and Coltheart, M. (1986) *Language Processing in Children and Adults*, London: Routledge, Chapter 9, pp. 230–52.
*Libben, G. (1997) 'Brain and language', in W. O'Grady, M. Dobrovolsky and F. Katamba (eds) *Contemporary Linguistics: An Introduction*, London: Longman, pp. 416–37.
*Obler, L. K. and Gjerlow, K. (1999) *Language and the Brain*, Cambridge: Cambridge University Press.

'KNOWING' A WORD

*Aitchison, J. (1994) *Words in the Mind*, London: Blackwell, 2nd edn.
*Altmann, G. (1997) *The Ascent of Babel*, Oxford: Oxford University Press, pp. 65–83.
Emmorey, K. D. and Fromkin, V. A. (1988) 'The mental lexicon', in F. K. Newmeyer (ed.) *Linguistics: the Cambridge Survey, Vol. III*, Cambridge: Cambridge University Press, pp. 124–49.
*Ungerer, F. and Schmid, H. J. (1996) *An Introduction to Cognitive Linguistics*, London: Longman, Chapters 1–2, pp. 1–113.

LEXICAL STORAGE AND LEXICAL ACCESS

*Aitchison, J. (1994) *Words in the Mind*, London: Blackwell, 2nd edn, Chapters 17–20, pp. 197–237.
Garnham, A. (1989) *Psycholinguistics: Central Topics*, London: Routledge, Chapter 3, pp. 42–68.
*Harris, M. and Coltheart, M. (1989) *Language Processing in Children and Adults*, London: Routledge, Chapter 6, pp. 135–71.
Reeves, L. M., Hirsh-Pasek, K. and Golinkoff, R. (1988) 'Words and meaning: from primitives to complex organization', in J. B. Gleason and N. B. Ratner (eds) *Psycholinguistics*, Forth Worth: Harcourt Brace, 2nd edn, pp. 1–49.

INFORMATION PROCESSING AND MEMORY

*Carroll, D. W. (1999) *Psychology of Language*, Pacific Grove: Brooks/Cole, 3rd edn, Chapter 3, pp. 45–63.

Gathercole, S. E. and Baddeley, A. (1993) *Working Memory and Language*, Hove: Erlbaum.

Jackendoff, R. (1987) *Consciousness and the Computational Mind*, Cambridge, MA: Bradford/MIT, Chapter 6, pp. 91–120.

Kellogg, R. T. (1995) *Cognitive Psychology*, London: Sage, Chapters 2–4, pp. 31–130.

Smyth, M. M., Morris, P. E., Levy, P. and Ellis, A. W. (1987) *Cognition in Action*. Hove: Erlbaum, Chapter 6, pp. 121–42.

WRITING PROCESS

Bereiter, C. and Scardamalia, M. (1987) *The Psychology of Written Composition*, Hillsdale, NJ: Erlbaum.

Garman, M. (1990) *Psycholinguistics*, Cambridge: Cambridge University Press, pp. 23–47, 99–108, 164–7, 230–6.

*Garton, A. and Pratt, C. (1989) *Learning to be Literate*, Oxford: Blackwell, Chapter 8, pp. 154–85.

Grabe, W. and Kaplan, R. B. (1996) *Theory and Practice of Writing*, Harlow: Longman, Chapter 5, pp. 113–46.

*Harris, M. and Coltheart, M. (1986) *Language Processing in Children and Adults*, London: Routledge, Introduction, pp. 3–25.

Kellogg, R. T. (1994) *The Psychology of Writing*, New York: Oxford University Press.

*Scardamalia, M. and Bereiter, C. (1987) 'Knowledge telling and knowledge transforming in written composition', in S. Rosenberg (ed.) *Advances in Applied Psycholinguistics, Vol. 2*, Cambridge, CUP.

Sharples, M. (1999) *How We Write: Writing as Creative Design*, London: Routledge, 1999.

READING PROCESS

*Ellis, A. W. (1993) *Reading, Writing and Dyslexia*, Hove: Psychology Press.

Goodman, K. S. 'Reading: a psycholinguistic guessing game', Journal of the Reading Specialist (6): 126–35.

*Harris, M. and Coltheart, M. (1986) *Language Processing in Children and Adults*, London: Routledge, Chapter 4, pp. 82–106.

Just, M. A. and Carpenter, P. A. (1987) *The Psychology of Reading and Language Comprehension*, Newton, MA: Allyn & Bacon.

Oakhill, J. and Beard, R. (eds) (1999) *Reading Development and the Teaching of Reading*, Oxford: Blackwell.

Oakhill, J. and Garnham, A. (1988) *Becoming a Skilled Reader*, Oxford: Blackwell.

*Paran, A. (1996) 'Reading in EFL: Fact and fiction', *ELT Journal* 50/1.

Stanovich, K. E. (1980) 'Toward an interactive-compensatory model of individual differences in the development of reading fluency', *Reading Research Quarterly* 16.

LISTENING PROCESS

*Cutler, A. (1989) 'Auditory lexical access: where do we start?', in W. Marslen-Wilson (ed.) *Lexical Representation and Process*, Cambridge, MA: MIT, pp. 342–56.

*Ellis, A. and Beattie, G. (1986) *The Psychology of Language and Communication*, Hove: Erlbaum, Chapter 12–13, pp. 211–37.

Flores d'Arcais, G. B. (1988) 'Language perception', in F. K. Newmeyer (ed.) *Linguistics: the Cambridge Survey, Vol. III*, Cambridge: Cambridge University Press, pp. 97–123.

Grosjean, F. and Gee, J. (1987) 'Prosodic structure and spoken word recognition', *Cognition* 25.

*Harley, T. A. (1995) *The Psychology of Language*, Hove: Taylor & Francis, pp. 41–66.

Miller, J. (1990) 'Speech perception', in D. Osherson and H. Lasnik (eds) *An Invitation to Cognitive Psychology: Vol. 1, Language*, Cambridge, MA: MIT.

Nygaard, L. C. and Pisoni, D. B. (1995) 'Speech perception: New directions in research and theory', in J. L. Miller and P. D. Eimas. *Speech, Language and Communication*, San Diego: Academic Press, pp. 63–96.

SPEAKING PROCESS

*Aitchison, J. (1988) *The Articulate Mammal*, London: Routledge, 4th edn, Chapter 11, pp. 237–59.

*Ellis, A. and Beattie, G. (1986) *The Psychology of Language and Communication*, Hove: Erlbaum, Chapters 7–8, pp. 115–50.

Fromkin, V. A. and Ratner, N. B. (1988) 'Speech production', in J. B. Gleason and N. B. Ratner (eds) *Psycholinguistics*, Forth Worth: Harcourt Brace, 2nd edn, pp. 309–46.

Garrett, M. (1988) 'Processes in language production', in F. K. Newmeyer (ed.) *Linguistics: the Cambridge Survey, Vol. III*, Cambridge: Cambridge University Press, pp. 69–96.

*Harris, M. and Coltheart, M. (1986) *Language Processing in Children and Adults*, London: Routledge, Chapter 8, pp. 206–29.

Whitney, P. (1998) *The Psychology of Language*, Boston, MA: Houghton Mifflin, pp. 273–84.

MEANING CONSTRUCTION

Cohen, G., Kiss, G. and Le Voi, M. (1993) *Memory: Current Issues*, Milton Keynes: Open University, 2nd edn, Part I, IIA.

*Ellis, A. and Beattie, G. (1986) *The Psychology of Language and Communication*, Hove: Erlbaum, Chapter 13: 237–51.

Greene, J. (1986) *Language Understanding: A Cognitive Approach, Part I*. Milton Keynes: Open University.

Greene, J. and Coulson, M. (1995) *Language Understanding: Current Issues*, Buckingham: Open University Press.

*Harley, T. A. (1995) *The Psychology of Language*, Hove: Taylor and Francis, Chapter 7, pp. 207–42.

Oakhill, J. and Garnham, A. (1988) *Becoming a Skilled Reader*, Oxford: Blackwell, Chapter 5, pp. 103–43.

SPECIAL CIRCUMSTANCES

*Bishop, D. V. M. (1997) *Uncommon Understanding*, Hove: Psychology Press.

Bishop, D. and Mogford, K. (eds) (1993) *Language Development in Exceptional Circumstances*, Hove: Psychology Press.

*Chiat, S. (2000) *Understanding Children with Language Problems*, Cambridge: Cambridge University Press.

Crystal, D. and Varley, R. (1998) *Introduction to Language Pathology*, London: Whurr, 4th edn.

*Ellis, A. W. (1993) *Reading, Writing and Dyslexia*, Hove: Psychology Press.

Strong, M. (ed.) (1988) *Language Learning and Deafness*, Cambridge: Cambridge University Press.

REFERENCES

Adams, M. J. (1990) *Beginning to Read: Thinking and Learning about Print*, Cambridge, MA: MIT Press.

Aitchison, J. and Straf, M. (1982) 'Lexical storage and retrieval: a developing skill', *Linguistics* 19: 751–95.

Aitchison, J. (1994) *Words in the Mind*, Oxford: Blackwell, 2nd edn.

Anderson, J. R. (1983) *The Architecture of Cognition*, Cambridge, MA: Harvard University Press.

Anderson, R. C. and Pichert, J. W. (1978) 'Recall of previously unrecallable information following a shift in perspective', *Journal of Verbal Learning and Verbal Behavior* 12: 1–12.

Armstrong, S. L., Gleitman, L. R. and Gleitman, H. (1983) 'What some concepts might not be', *Cognition* 13: 263–308.

Asch, S. E. and Nerlove, H. (1960) 'The development of double-function terms in children', in B. Kaplan and S. Wapner (eds) *Perspectives in Psychological Theory*. New York: International Universities Press.

Atkinson, R. C. and Shiffrin, R. M. (1968) 'Human memory: a proposed system and its control processes', in K. W. Spence and J. T. Spence (eds) *The Psychology of Learning and Motivation: Vol. 2*, New York: Academic Press, pp. 89–195.

Baddeley, A. D. (1986) *Working Memory*, Oxford: Oxford University Press.

Baddeley, A. (1990) *Human Memory*, Hove: Erlbaum.

Bar-Adon, A. and Leopold, W. F. (1971) *Child Language: A Book of Readings*, Englewood Cliffs, NJ: Prentice Hall.

Baddeley, A. D., Thomson, N. and Buchanan, M. (1975) 'Word length and the structure of short-term memory', *Journal of Verbal Learning and Verbal Behavior* 14: 575–89.

Bartlett, F. (1932) *Remembering*, Cambridge: Cambridge University Press.

Barton, S. and Sanford, A. J. (1993) 'A case-study of pragmatic anomaly detection: relevance driven cohesion patterns', *Memory and Cognition* 21: 477–87.

Bates, E. and MacWhinney, B. (1991) 'Cross-linguistic research in aphasia: an overview'. *Brain and Language* 41: 123–48.

Bates, E. and Wulfeck, B. (1989) 'Comparative aphasiology: a cross-linguistic approach to language breakdown', *Aphasiology* 3: 111–42.

Beattie, G. (1983) *Talk: an Analysis of Speech and Non-Verbal Behaviour in Conversation*, Milton Keynes: Open University Press.

Bereiter, C., Fine, J. and Gartshore, S. (1979) 'An exploratory study of microplanning in writing', paper presented at the American Educational Research Association, San Francisco.

Bereiter, C. and Scardamalia, M. (1987) *The Psychology of Written Composition*, Hillsdale, NJ: Erlbaum.

Bever, T. G. (1970) The cognitive basis for linguistic structures, in J. R. Hayes (ed.) *Cognition and the Development of Language*, New York: Wiley.

Bishop, D. V. M. (1982) 'Comprehension of spoken, written and signed sentences in childhood language disorders', *Journal of Child Psychology and Psychiatry* 23: 1–20.

Bishop, D. (1993) 'Language development in children with abnormal structure or function of the speech apparatus', in D. Bishop and K. Mogford (eds) *Language Development in Exceptional Circumstances*, Hove: Psychology Press, pp. 220–238.

Bishop, D. V. M. (1994) 'Grammatical errors in specific language impairment: competence or performance limitation?', *Applied Psycholinguistics* 15: 507–49.

Bishop, D. V. M. (1997) *Uncommon Understanding*, Hove: Psychology Press.

Bond, Z. S. and Garnes, S. (1980) 'Misrepresentations of fluent speech', in R. Cole (ed.) *Perception and Production of Fluent Speech*, Hillsdale, NJ: Erlbaum.

Boomer, D. S. and Laver, J. D. M. (1968) 'Slips of the tongue', reprinted in V. A. Fromkin (ed.) *Errors in Linguistic Performance: Slips of the Tongue, Ear, Pen and Hand*, New York: Academic Press.

Bowerman, M. (1978) 'Systematizing semantic knowledge: changes over time in the child's organization of meaning', *Child Development* 49: 977–87.

Bowerman, M. (1980) 'The structure and origin of semantic categories in the language learning child', in D. Foster and S. Brandes (eds) *Symbols as Sense: New Approaches to the Analysis of Meaning*, New York: Academic Press.

Bransford, J. D. and Johnson, M. K. (1973) 'Consideration of some problems of comprehension', in W. G. Chase (ed.) *Visual Information Processing*, New York: Academic Press.

Bransford, J. D., Barclay, J. R. and Franks, J. J. (1972) 'Sentence memory: a constructive vs interpretive approach', *Cognitive Psychology* 3: 193–209.

Britton, J. (1978) 'The composing processes and the function of writing', in C. R. Cooper and L. Odell (eds) *Research on Composing: Points of Departure*, Urnana, IL: National Council of Teachers of English, pp. 3–28.

Brown, G. and Yule, G.: *Discourse Analysis*, Cambridge: Cambridge University Pres, 1983.

Brown, J. S., McDonald, J. L., Brown, T. L. and Carr, T. H. (1988) 'Adapting to process demands in discourse production', *Journal of Experimental Psychology: Human Perception and Performance* 14: 45–59.

Brown, R. and McNeil, D. (1966) 'The "tip of the tongue" phenomenon', *Journal of Verbal Learning and Verbal Behavior* 5: 325–37.

Butterworth, B. and Goldman-Eisler, E. (1979) 'Recent studies on cognitive rhythm', in A. W. Siegman and S. Feldstein (eds) *Of Speech and Time: Temporal Speech Patterns in Interpersonal Contexts*, Hillsdale, NJ: Erlbaum, pp. 211–24.

Carey, S. (1978) 'The child as word learner', in M. Halle, J. Bresnan and G. A. Miller (eds) *Linguistic Theory and Psychological Reality*, Cambridge, MA: MIT Press.

Chomsky, N. (1965) *Aspects of the Theory of Syntax*, Cambridge, MA: MIT Press.

Chomsky, N. (1972) *Language and Mind* (enlarged edition), New York: Harcourt Brace Jovanovich.

Chomsky, N. (1980) 'Discussion', in Piattelli-Palmarini, M. (ed.) *Language and Learning. The Debate between Jean Piaget and Noam Chomsky*, London: Routledge and Kegan Paul, 73–83.

Clark, E. (1973) 'What's in a word? On the child's acquisition of semantics in his first language', in T. E. Moore (ed.) *Cognitive Development and the Acquisition of Language*, New York: Academic Press.

Cooper, W. E. (1976) 'Syntactic control of timing in speech production: a study of complement clauses', *Journal of Phonetics* 4: 151–71.

Coulmas, F. (1989) *The Writing Systems of the World*, Oxford: Blackwell.

Cowan, N. (1999) 'An embedded processes model of working memory', in A. Miyake and P. Shah, *Models of Working Memory*, Cambridge: Cambridge University Press, pp. 62–101.

Crystal, D. and Varley, R. (1998) *Introduction to Language Pathology*, London: Whurr, 4th edn.

Cunningham, A. E., Stanovich, K. E. and Wilson, M. R. (1990) 'Cognitive variation in adult college students differing in reading ability', in C. T. H. and B. A. Levy (eds) *Reading and its Development*, New York: Academic Press, pp. 81–128.

Cutler, A. (1980) 'Errors of stress and intonation', in V. A. Fromkin (ed.) *Errors in Linguistic Performance: Slips of the Tongue, Ear, Pen and Hand*, New York: Academic Press, pp. 67–80.

Cutler, A. (1983) 'Speakers' conceptions of the function of prosody', in A. Cutler and D. R. Ladd (eds) *Prosody: Models and Measurements*, Heidelberg: Springer.

Cutler, A. and Butterfield, S. (1992) 'Rhythmic cues to speech segmentation: evidence from juncture misperceptions', *Journal of Memory and Language* 31: 218–38.

Cutler, A. and Carter, D. M. (1987) 'The predominance of strong initial syllables in the English vocabulary', *Computer Speech and Language* 2: 133–42.

Cutler, A. and Norris, D. (1988) 'The role of strong syllables in segmentation for lexical access', *Journal of Experimental Psychology: Human Perception and Performance* 14: 113–21.

Dalton, P. and Hardcastle, W. J. (1989) *Disorders of Fluency*, London: Whurr, 2nd edn.

Deacon, T. (1997) *The Symbolic Species*, London: Penguin.

Della Sala, S. and Logie, R. H. (1993) 'When working memory does not work: the role of working memory in neuropsychology', in F. Boller and H. Spinnler (eds) *Handbook of Neuropsychology*, Vol. 8, Amsterdam: Elsevier.

Dingwall, W. O. (1998) 'The biological bases of human behavior', in J. B. Gleason and N. B. Ratner, *Psycholinguistics*, Fort Worth: Harcourt Brace, pp. 51–105.

Eimas, P. D., Siqueland, E. R., Jusczyk, P. W. and Vogorito, J. (1971) Speech perception in infants, *Science* 171: 303–06.

Ellis, A. and Beattie, G. (1986) *The Psychology of Language and Communication*, Hove: Erlbaum.

Ellis, N. C. and Hennelley, R. A. (1980) 'A bilingual word length effect: implications for intelligence testing and the relative ease of mental calculation in Welsh and English', *British Journal of Psychology* 71, 43–52.

Elman, J. L. and McClelland, J. L. (1986) 'The interactive activation model of speech perception', in N. Lass (ed.) *Language and Speech*, New York: Academic Press, pp. 337–74.

Epstein, W. (1961) 'The influence of syntactical structure on learning', *American Journal of Psychology* LXXIV: 80–5.

Erickson, T. A. and Mattson, M. E. (1981) 'From words to meaning: a semantic illusion', *Journal of Verbal Learning and Verbal Behavior* 20: 540–52.

Ericsson, K. A. and Delaney, P. F. (1998) 'Working memory and expert performance', in R. H. Logie and K. J. Gilhooly (eds) *Working Memory and Thinking*, Hove: Psychology Press.

Fay, D. (1980) 'Transformational errors', in V. Fromkin (ed.) *Errors in Linguistic Performance: Slips of the Tongue, Ear, Pen and Hand*, New York: Academic Press.

Fay, W. H. (1993) 'Infantile autism', in D. Bishop and K. Mogford (eds) *Language Development in Exceptional Circumstances*, Hove: Psychology Press, pp. 190–202.

Fodor, J. A., Bever, T. G. and Garrett, M. F. (1974) *The Psychology of Language: An Introduction to Psycholinguistics and Generative Grammar*, New York: McGraw Hill.

Forster, K. I. (1976) 'Accessing the mental lexicon', in R. J. Wales and E. Walker (eds) *New Approaches to Language Mechanisms*, Amsterdam: North Holland.

Fraser, J. (2001) 'A comparison of the writing of British deaf students and non-native hearing students', unpublished MA dissertation, Kings College London.

Fromkin, V. A. (1973) *Speech Errors as Linguistic Evidence*, The Hague: Mouton.

Fromkin, V. A. (ed.) (1980) *Errors in Linguistic Performance: Slips of the Tongue, Ear, Pen and Hand*, New York: Academic Press.

Ganong, W. F. (1980) 'Phonetic categorization in auditory word perception', *Journal of Experimental Psychology: Human Perception and Performance* 6: 110–25.

Garman, (1990) *Psycholinguistics*, Cambridge: Cambridge University Press.

Gathercole, S. E. and Baddeley, A. D. (1989) 'Evaluation of the role of phonological STM in the development of vocabulary in children: a longitudinal study', *Journal of Memory and Language* 28: 200–13.

Gathercole, S. E. and Baddeley, A. D. (1993) *Language and Working Memory*, Hove: Erlbaum.

Gerloff, P. (1987) 'Identifying the unit of analysis in translation: some uses of think-aloud protocol data', in C. Færch and G. Kasper, *Introspection in Second Language Research*, Clevedon: Multilingual Matters.

Goad, H. and Rebellati, C. (1994) 'Pluralization in familial language impairment' in Matthews, J. (ed.) *Linguistic Aspects of Familial Language Impairment*. Special issue of the McGill Working Papers in Linguistics 10. Montreal, Canada: McGill University.

Gollasch, F. V. (1980) *Readers' Perception in Detecting and Processing Embedded Errors in Meaningful Text* (UMI no. AAC 81-07445), Tucson, AZ: University of Arizona.

Goodall, J. (1972) *In the Shadow of Man*, London: George Weidenfeld and Nicolson.

Goodman, K. (1967) 'Reading: a psycholinguistic guessing game', *Journal of the Reading Specialist* 6: 126–35.

Goodman, K. S. (1993) *Phonics Phacts*, Portsmouth, NH: Heinemann.

Goodman, K. (1996) *On Reading*, Portsmouth, NH: Heinemann.

Goodman, K. S. and Burke, C. L. (1973) *Theoretically Based Studies of Patterns of Miscues in Oral Reading Performance*, Final Report OEG-0-9-320375-4269, Washington, DC: US Office of Education.

Gopnik, M. (1994) 'The perceptual processing hypothesis revisited', in J. Matthews (ed.) *Linguistic Aspects of Familial Language Impairment*, Special issue of the McGill Working Papers in Linguistics, Vol. 10, Montreal, Canada: McGill University.

Gough, P. B. (1983) 'Context, form, and interaction', in K. Rayner (ed.) *Eye Movements in Reading: Perceptual and Language Processes*, New York: Academic Press.

Gough, P. B., Alford, J. A., Jr and Holley-Wilcox, P. (1981) 'Words and contexts', in O. J. L. Tzeng and H. Singer (eds) *Perception of Print*, Hillsdale, NJ: Lawrence Erlbaum, pp. 85–102.

Graves, D. H. (1978) 'Research update: Handwriting is for writing', *Language Arts*, 55: 393–99.

Greenberg, J. (1963) *Universals of Language*, Cambridge, MA: MIT Technology Press.

Grosjean, F. and Gee, J. (1987) 'Prosodic structure and spoken word recognition', *Cognition* 25: 135–55.

Halle, M. and Stevens, K. N. (1962) 'Speech recognition: a model and a program for research', *IRE Transactions of Information Theory*, IT-8: 155–9.

Halliday, M. A. K. and Hasan, R. (1976) *Cohesion in English*, London: Longman.

Hammett, D. (1930) *The Maltese Falcon*, London: Cassell.

Harris, M. and Coltheart, M. (1986) *Language Processing in Children and Adults*, London: Routledge.

Haviland, S. E. and Clark, H. H. (1974) 'What's new? Acquiring new information as a process of comprehension', *Journal of Verbal Learning and Verbal Behavior* 13: 515–21.

Hayes, J. R. and Flower, L. S. (1980) 'Identifying the organization of writing processes', in L. W. Gregg and E. R. Steinberg (eds) *Cognitive Processes in Writing*, Hillsdale, NJ: Erlbaum, pp. 3–30.

Heaton, B. (1975) *Composition Through Pictures*, London: Longman.

Hirst, W. and Brill, G. A. (1980) 'Contextual aspects of pronoun assignment', *Journal of Verbal Learning and Verbal Behavior* 19: 168–75.

Hockett, C. F. (1963) 'The problem of universals in language', in J. H. Greenberg (ed.) *Universals of Language*, Cambridge, MA: MIT Press.

Hockett, C. F. (1973) 'Where the tongue slips, there slip I', in V. A. Fromkin (ed.) *Errors in Linguistic Performance: Slips of the Tongue, Ear, Pen and Hand*, New York: Academic Press, pp. 93–119.

Hotopf, W. N. (1980) 'Slips of the pen', in U. Frith (ed.) *Cognitive Processes in Spelling*, London: Academic Press, pp. 287–307.

Hotopf, W. N. (1983) 'Lexical slips of the pen and tongue: what they tell us about language production', in B. Butterworth (ed.) *Language Production, Vol. 2: Development, Writing and Other Language Processes*, London: Academic Press.

Hunter, I. (1985) 'Lengthy verbal recall', in A. W. Ellis (ed.) *Progress in the Psychology of Language*, Vol. 1, London: Erlbaum.

Inhelder, B. and Piaget, J. (1964) *The Early Growth of Logic in the Child*, London: Routledge and Kegan Paul.

Jarvella, R. J. (1971) 'Syntactic processing of connected speech', *Journal of Verbal Learning and Verbal Behavior* 10: 409–16.

Jenkins, J. J. (1970) 'The 1952 Minnesota word association norms', in L. Postnam and G. Keppel (eds) *Norms of Word Association*, New York: Academic.

Just, M. A. and Carpenter, P. A. (1987) *The Psychology of Reading and Language Comprehension*, Boston: Allyn and Bacon.

Katz, J. J. and Fodor, J. A. (1963) 'The structure of a semantic theory', *Language* 39: 170–210.

Keil, F. C. and Batterman, N. (1984) 'A characteristic-to-defining shift in the development of word meaning', *Journal of Verbal Learning and Verbal Behavior* 23: 221–36.

Kellogg, R. T. (1996) 'A model of working memory in writing', in C. M. Levy and S. Ransdell, *The Science of Writing*, Mahwah, NJ: Erlbaum.

Kuhl, P. K. and Miller, J. D. (1978) 'Speech perception by the chinchilla: identification functions for synthetic VOT stimuli', *Journal of the Acoustic Society of America* 63: 905–17.

Labov, W. (1973) 'The boundaries of words and their meanings', in C-J. N. Bailey and R. W. Shuy (eds) *New ways of Analyzing Variation in English*, Washington, DC: Georgetown University Press.

Laver, J. (1994) *Principles of Phonetics*, Cambridge: Cambridge University Press.

Leech, G., Rayson, P. and Wilson, A. (2001) *Word Frequencies in Written and Spoken English*, Harlow: Pearson.

Lenneberg, E. (1960) 'Language, evolution, and purposive behavior', in *Culture in History: Essays in Honor of Paul Radin,* New York: Columbia University Press.

Lenneberg, E. H. (1967) *The Biological Foundations of Language*, New York: Wiley.

Lenneberg, E., Nichols, I. A. and Rosenberger, E. R. (1962) 'Primitive stages of language development in mongolism', *Proceedings of the 42nd Annual Meeting for Research in Nervous and Mental Diseases.*

Leonard, L. (1989) 'Language learnability and specific language impairment in children', *Applied Psycholinguistics* 10: 179–202.

Leonard, L. B. and Eyer, J. A. (1996) 'Deficits of grammatical morphology in children with specific language impairment and their implications for notions of bootstrapping', in J. L. Morgan and K. Demuth (eds) *Signal to Syntax*, Mahwah, NJ: Erlbaum.

Leonard, L. B., Sabbadini, L., Leonard, J. S. and Volterra, V. (1987) 'Specific language impairment in children: a cross-linguistic study', *Brain and Language* 32: 233–52.

Leonard, L. B., Sabbadini, L., Volterra, V. and Leonard, J. S. (1988) 'Some influences on the grammar of English- and Italian-speaking children with specific language impairment', *Applied Psycholinguistics* 9: 39–57.

Levelt, W. J. M. (1983) 'Monitoring and self-repair in speech', *Cognition* 14: 41–104.

Levelt, W. J. M. (1989) *Speaking*, Cambridge, MA: MIT.

Levelt, W. J. M. and Cutler, A. (1983) 'Prosodic marking in speech repair', *Journal of Semantics* 2: 205–17.

Liberman, A. M., Cooper, F. S., Shankweiler, D. P. and Studdert-Kennedy, M. (1967) 'Perception of the speech code', *Psychological Review* 74: 431–461.

Light, L. L. and Capps, J. L. (1986) 'Comprehension of pronouns in young and older adults', *Developmental Psychology* 22: 580–5.

Linden, E. (1986) *Silent Partners. The Legacy of the Ape Language Experiments*, New York: Ballantine Books.

Logie, R. H. and Baddeley, A. D. (1987) 'Cognitive processes in counting', *Journal of Experimental Psychology* 13: 310–26.

Logie, R. H. and Gilhooly, K. J. (eds) (1998) *Working Memory and Thinking*, Hove: Psychology Press.

Logie, R. H. (1995) *Visuo-Spatial Working Memory*, Hove: Lawrence Erlbaum.

Logie, R. H., Gilhooly, K. J. and Wynn, V. (1994) 'Counting on working memory in mental arithmetic', *Memory and Cognition* 22, 395–410.

Logie, R. H., Wright, R. and Decker, S. (1992) 'Recognition memory performance and residential burglary', *Applied Cognitive Psychology* 6: 109–23.

Longman Dictionary of Contemporary English (1987) Harlow: Longman, 2nd edn.

MacKay, D. (1987) *The Organization of Perception and Action: A Theory for Language and Other Cognitive Skills*, New York: Springer.

Macnamara, J. (1982) *Names for Things*, Cambridge, MA: MIT Press.

Marslen-Wilson, W. (1987) 'Functional parallelism in spoken word recognition'.

Massaro, D. W. and Cohen, M. M. (1983) 'Evaluation and integration of visual and auditory information in speech perception', *Journal of Experimental Psychology: Human Perception and Performance* 9: 753–71.

McClelland, J., Rumelhart, D. and PDP Research Group (1986) *Parallel Distributed Processing: Explorations in the Microstructure of Cognition: Vol. 2*, Cambridge, MA: Bradford.

McCloskey, M., Harley, W. and Sokol, S. (1991) 'Models of arithmetic fact retrieval: an evaluation in light of findings from normal and brain damaged subjects', *Journal of Experimental Psychology: Learning, Memory, and Cognition* 17: 377–97.

McGurk, H. and MacDonald, J. (1976) 'Hearing lips and seeing voices', *Nature* 264: 746–48.

Menzel, E. W. (1978) 'Cognitive mapping in chimpanzees', in S. H. Hulse, H. Fowler and W. K. Honig (eds) *Cognitive Processes in Animal Behavior*, Hillsdale, NJ: Erlbaum, 375–422.

Merriman, W. E., Scott, P. D. and Marazita, J. (1993) 'An appearance-function shift in children's object naming', *Journal of Child Language* 20: 101–18.

Miles, T. R. (1993) *Dyslexia: the Pattern of Difficulties*, London: Whurr, 2nd edn.

Miller, G. A. (1956) 'The magic number seven, plus or minus two', *Psychological Review* 63: 81–93.

Miller, G. A. (1990) 'Linguists, psychologists and the cognitive sciences', *Language* 66: 317–22.

Miller, G. A. and Isard, S. (1963) 'Some perceptual consequences of linguistic rules', *Journal of Verbal Learning and Verbal Behaviour* II: 217–28.

Miyake, A. and Shah, P. (eds) (2000) *Models of Working Memory*, New York: Cambridge University Press.

Moberly, P. G. C. (1979) *Elementary Children's Understanding of Anaphoric Relationships in Connected Discourse*, Ann Arbor, MI: University Microfilms.

Monk, R. (1996) *Bertrand Russell: The Spirit of Solitude*, London: Jonathan Cape.

Morais, J., Cary, L., Alegria, J. and Bertelson, P. (1979) 'Does awareness of speech as a sequence of phones arise spontaneously?', *Cognition* 7: 323–31.

Morris, P. E., Tweedy, M. and Gruneberg, M. M. (1985) 'Interest, knowledge and the memorization of soccer scores', *British Journal of Psychology* 76: 415–25.

Morrow, D. G., Bower, G. H. and Greenspan, S. L. (1989) 'Updating situation models during narrative comprehension', *Journal of Memory and Language* 28: 292–312.

Morton, J. (1970) 'A functional model of human memory', in D. A. Norman (ed.) *Models of Human Memory*, New York: Academic Press.

Motley, M. T., Camden, C. T. and Baars, B. J. (1982) 'Covert formulation and editing of anomalies in speech production: evidence from experimentally elicited slips of the tongue', *Journal of Verbal Learning and Verbal Behavior* 21: 578–94.

Myers, J. L., Shinjo, M. and Duffy, S. A. (1987) 'Degree of causal relatedness and memory', *Journal of Memory and Language* 26: 453–65.

Nicolson, R. (1981) 'The relationship between memory span and processing speed', in M. Friedman, J. P. Das and N. O'Conner (eds) *Intelligence and Learning*, New York: Plenum Press.

Nooteboom, S. (1980) 'Speaking and unspeaking: detection and correction of phonological errors in spontaneous speech', in V. A. Fronkin (ed.) *Errors in Linguistic Performance*, New York: Academic Press.

Passingham, R. (1982) *The Human Primate*, San Francisco: W.H. Freeman.

Paulesu, E., Frith, C. D. and Frackowiak, R. S. J. (1993) 'The neural correlates of the verbal component of working memory', *Nature* 362: 342–45.

Perfetti, C. (1985) *Reading Ability*, New York: Oxford University Press.

Perfetti, C. and Roth, S. (1981) 'Some of the interactive processes in reading and their role in the reading skill', in A. M. Lesgold and C. Perfetti, *Interactive Processes in Reading*, Hillsdale, NJ: Erlbaum.

Pinker, S. and Bloom, P. (1990) 'Natural language and natural selection', *Behavioral and Brain Sciences* 13: 707–84.

Posner, M. I. and Raichle, M. E. (1994) *Images of Mind*, New York: Scientific American Library.

Premack, D. and Woodruff, G. (1978) 'Does the chimpanzee have a theory of mind?', *Behavioral and Brain Sciences* 4: 515–26.

Rasmussen, T. and Milner, B. (1977) 'Clinical and surgical studies of the cerebral speech areas in man', in K. J. Zulch, O. Creutzfeldt and G. C. Galbraith (eds) *Cerebral Localization*, pp. 238–57, New York: Springer-Verlag.

Rayner, K. and Pollatsek, A. (1989) *The Psychology of Reading*, Englewood Cliffs, NJ: Prentice Hall.

Rice, M. M. and Oetting, J. B. (1993) 'Morphological deficits of children with SLI: evaluation of number marking and agreement', *Journal of Speech and Hearing Research* 36: 1249–57.

Richards, M. M. (1979) 'Sorting out what's in a word from what's not: evaluating Clark's semantic features acquisition theory', *Journal of Experimental Child Psychology* 27: 1–47.

Rosch, E. (1975) 'Cognitive representations of semantic categories', *Journal of Experimental Psychology: General* 104: 192–233.

Rubenstein, H. L. Garfield and Millikan, J. A. (1970) 'Homographic entries in the internal lexicon', *Journal of Verbal Learning and Verbal Behavior* 9: 487–94.

Rumelhardt, D. E., McClelland, J. L. and the PDP Research Group (1986) *Parallel Distributed Processing: Vol. 1 Foundations*. Cambridge, MA: MIT Press.

Saariluoma, P. (1995) *Chess Players' Thinking*, London: Routledge.

Sanford, A. J. and Garrod, S. C. (1981) *Understanding Written Language*, Chichester: John Wiley.

Saussure, F. de (1966) *Course in General Linguistics*, translated by Wade Baskin, New York: McGraw-Hill Book Company.

Schank, R. C. and Abelson, R. (1977) *Scripts, Plans, Goals and Understanding*. Hillsdale, NJ: Erlbaum.

Schegloff, E. A. (1979) 'The relevance of repair to syntax-for-conversation', in T. Givón (ed.) *Syntax and Semantics*, Vol. 12, New York: Academic Press.

Schegloff, E. A., Jefferson, G. and Sacks, H. (1977) 'The preference for self-correction in the organization of repair in conversation', *Language* 2: 361–82.

Schwanenflugel, P. J. and Rey, M. (1986) 'Interlingual semantic facilitation: evidence for a common representational system in the bilingual lexicon', *Journal of Memory and Language* 25: 605–18.

Siegel, G. M. and Pick, H. L. (1976) 'Auditory feedback in the regulation of voice', *Journal of the Acoustical Society of America* 56: 1618–24.

Simon, J. (1973) *La langue écrite de l'enfant*, Paris: Presses Universitaires de France.

Skuse, D. H. (1993) 'Extreme deprivation in early childhood', in D. Bishop and K. Mogford (eds) *Language Development in Exceptional Circumstances*, Hove: Psychology Press, pp. 29–46.

Smith, F. *Understanding Reading*, Hillsdale, NJ: Erlbaum, 1988.

Smith, N. and Tsimpli, I. (1995) *The Mind of a Savant*, Oxford: Blackwell.

Spelke, E. S., Hirst, W. and Neisser, U. (1976) 'Skills of divided attention', *Cognition* 4: 215–30.

Stanovich, K. E. (1980) 'Toward an interactive-compensatory model of individual differences in the development of reading fluency', *Reading Research Quarterly* 16.

Stanovich, K. E. (1982) 'Individual differences in the cognitive process of reading II: Text-level processes', *Journal of Learning Disabilities* 15: 549–54.

Stigler, J. W., Lee, S. Y. and Stevenson, H. W. (1986) 'Digit memory in Chinese and English: evidence for a temporally limited store', *Cognition* 24: 1–20.

Swinney, D. A. (1979) 'Lexical access during sentence comprehension: (re)consideration of context effects', *Journal of Verbal Learning and Verbal Behavior* 18: 545–569.

Tallal, P. and Stark, R. E. (1981) 'Speech acoustic-cue discrimination abilities of normally developing and language-impaired children', *Journal of the Acoustical Society of America* 69: 568–74.

Tent, J. and Clark, J. E. (1980) 'An experimental investigation into the perception of slips of the tongue', *Journal of Phonetics* 8: 317–25.

Trivers, R. L. (1971) 'The evolution of reciprocal altruism', *Quarterly Review of Biology* 46: 35–57.

Tulving, E. (1972) 'Episodic and semantic memory', in E. Tulving and W. Denaldson (eds) *Organization of Memory*, New York: Academic Press.

Underwood, M. (1971) *Listen to This!* Oxford: Oxford University Press.

Vygotsky, L. S. (1962) *Thought and Language*, trans. E. Hanfmann and G. Vakar, Cambridge, MA: MIT Press.

Watkins, R. and Rice, M. (1991) 'Verb particle and preposition acquisition in language-impaired preschoolers', *Journal of Speech and Hearing Research* 34: 1130–1141.

Werner, H. and Kaplan, E. (1950) 'Developments of word meaning through verbal context', *Journal of Psychology* 29: 251–7.

White, T. G. (1982) 'Naming practices, typicality and underextension in child language', *Journal of Experimental Child Psychology* 33: 324–46.

Whiten, A. and Byrne, R. W. (1988) 'Tactical deception in primates', *Behavioral and Brain Sciences* 11: 233–73.

Wilson, E. O. (1972) 'Animal communication', *Scientific American* 227(3): 52–60.

GLOSSARY

Specialist terms are generally highlighted in bold when they first occur in the text. The figures below indicate the page on which these words first occur and subsequent important occurrences of the same term.